Tales of Bellerophon

On the banks
of the Shalimar

by

Tony Ashenden

Tales of Bellerophon

On the banks

of the Shalimar

First Published 2008

ISBN 978-1-4092-2106-7

The Author

Figure 1

Acknowledgments

Without the help of my immediate family, my wife Pam, my sons Clive and Richard and my daughter Clare-Louise, it is unlikely this book would have been completed. Whilst I was forever conscious of the need to make public the nature of these communications, their help and insistence overcame my aversion to self publicity, that allowed would have ensured this tome did not see the light of day until I had passed from this world.

I am indebted to Pam's talent as a psychic artist for the illustrations that appear in this book in which the eternal youthfulness of the communicators depicted is effectively represented. And she has my loving thanks   for encouraging and supporting me to remain strong and grounded during the traumatic period these communications were received without which the painstaking process of recall might never have been completed. To Steve Lashley whose technical support has been invaluable and whose psychic ability encourages me to believe that my life's work will have a future. Also special thanks are due my eldest son Clive whose own writing skills and constructive criticism enabled me to effectively add a personal dimension to this account and for his many hours of patient proof correcting.

Finally I would like to thank pupils past and present and key workers of the JCPF charity, who aware of my task demonstrated the kind of enthusiasm which strengthened my resolve to ensure the work was completed.

Preface

You would normally expect an author to be knowledgeable of the work that bears his name and where necessary provide notes of explanation on terms used and concepts referred. The nature of much of this work is such that I can only claim to have written it down. In the main I believe it to be self explanatory but there are terms used that deserve some prior description as they may have different meanings to different readers, not withstanding that some could be entirely ignorant of what is meant. There are three concepts in particular –that of the 'Astral', the 'Spirit' and of 'BodyMind' which would benefit you to know before reading this book.

Astral worlds

The word 'astral' is today most often associated with New Age Philosophy used to describe worlds, higher vibration form and space conceptions, that exist in concert with physical realities. The word was popularised by Theosophists in the 19th and 20th century in such works as 'Isis Unveiled' and 'The Secret Doctrines' describing the higher consciousness environment of Man and the Cosmos. It was also used by alchemists in the Middle Ages to describe the 'universal fluid' that permeated everything. Similar concepts are to be found in virtually all philosophical and religious systems from ancient Hindu teachings to Modern Spiritualism.

In this book whilst particular levels of existence are described such as the 'Grey Spheres' and the 'Realm of Compassionate Being' and it may be inferred there are others, the seven planes described by Theosophists, the Spirit planes of Spiritualism and the hierarchical order of other systems of astral consciousness are nowhere referred.

The astral worlds are often otherwise generically described as thought worlds. The nature of thought is such that it can traverse space and time instantly. From this we can infer it travels as fast as the speed of light and vibrates in frequencies that objective science is unable measure, however describing astral worlds as worlds of thought limits our understanding of them. Thought is an expression of the human energetic nature and the energies that comprise creation are significantly more than that.

Kama is the name given in ancient Hindu teachings as the God of Love and in its lowest definition means desire. Esoterically Kama is the name given the order and type of energy comprising the manifest worlds. All forms of life have bodies comprising Kama energies, self aware individual conceptions like man, amorphous states such as water and the elemental construction of universes, both seen and unseen. As a consequence the astral worlds are not only higher consciousness worlds of men but of all other forms of life. Our interaction with creation is entirely dependant upon the awareness we have developed of the nature we possess.

BodyMind

The term BodyMind referred several times in this book deserves explanation as it likely means different things to different people. I myself first used the term as coined to me by afterlife communicators to embrace the entirety of man's being –physical, emotional, mental, etheric and astral energies that comprise his soul. At every level the BodyMind is intelligent – it is not a machine or a slave to higher intelligence.

The term Body Mind began to appear in print from the 1970's and is mostly used by bodywork exponents who recognise interdependence of mind and body, though it must be said that most therapists using the term are concerned to engage the physiological and psychological relationship for the betterment of lifestyle and health generally. A study of yogic practise will show that the body has many levels of consciousness and is intelligent on its own account and cannot be accounted for, as some religious systems imply, simply as a shell in which we live.

Spirit

As you will have noticed I don't use the word Spirit in the definition of BodyMind –this attribute is mostly used in the present day to describe the realm of higher (non-physical) worlds without differentiating between individual, group or universal consciousness. Spiritualism uses the term to describe the afterlife. The root definition of Spirit is something completely different to the consciousness we possess in this world and in the hierarchy of worlds beyond. The bible alludes to this understanding being outside our ability to define in John (chapter. III, v. 8).

The wind bloweth where it listeth, and thou hearest the sound thereof, but canst not tell whence it cometh, and whither it goeth: so is every one that is born of the Spirit.

The English word "**spirit**" coming from the Latin *spiritus*, meaning "breath" which in turn was taken from the Greek word pneuma (πνευμα) refers only to the *expression* of Spirit. No one language extant can describe it – likely the nearest we have achieved is *nous* as described by the philosopher Anaxagoras of Clazomenae, (circa 500 BC), who stated that *nous* was the primordial Mind that arranged all other things in their Right Order, started them in motion, and continues to control them. Right order might otherwise be described as *nous* in motion.

Anaxagoras wrote:

All other things partake in a portion of everything, while nous is infinite and self-ruled, and is mixed with nothing, but is alone, itself by itself. For if it were not by itself, but were mixed with anything else, it would partake in all things if it were mixed with any; for in everything there is a portion of everything, as has been said by me in what goes before, and the things mixed with it would hinder it, so that it would have power over nothing in the same way that it has now being alone by itself. For it is the thinnest of all things and the purest, and it has all knowledge about everything and the greatest strength; and nous has power over all things, both greater and smaller, that have soul.

The *nous* principle advised by Anaxagoras is unlikely to have been invented by him but realised from more ancient sources. Both Plato and Aristotle accepted the divine order of this concept howbeit they interpreted it differently as did latterly the Neo-Platonist movement and the Eastern Christian Church.

Such definition I have shown you is sufficient to show that Spirit is not a place nor in any manner describable in form or time. The heavens commonly called are the Astral Kingdoms –worlds of form in which it may be said we arise in order to perfect. Perfection has no voice, no form and no consciousness we can relate too.

A cautionary note

Bellerophonic Letters are any species of communication that are prejudicial or dangerous to the bearer

As Bellerophon unwittingly carried the letter that was prejudicial to his life from Proteus to the King of Lycia so I in ignorance became the medium of communications that questioned the very nature of my existence. This book didn't begin as an idea on my part –in fact it didn't begin at all in the conventional sense, I simply reacted, instinctively you might say to understand what was happening to me.

After 40 years of psychic & spiritual development practise I was comfortable in the understanding that I had, as you would say, 'got the tea shirt' -How wrong can you be! To be confronted with revelation more 'real' than conscious existence that clearly shows you are not who you think you are, is to say the least, a troubling experience. The communications in this book are not only thought provoking they question the foundation of belief and knowledge –whatever your philosophy and most avant-garde view of science. It's my identity that lives the alternatives in the pages of this book; selves that have me struggle to retain compos mentis status quo.

You may have read books on mediumistic communication –this is not one of them. If you think you won't be comfortable with what you read, go no further –because once the Spirit is awoken you will never slumber. In the period beginning January ending October 2005 my consciousness is an endless stream of self revelation. Like the passage of a Tsunami, nothing in its wake is the same as before. And still it rumbles on affecting my outlook on life. I am certain only when I am being instrumental of the hierarchical mind, a chasm exists between that and my personality self –reason doesn't close the gap.

If on reading this book you savour the thought of being other selves, of opening your mind to this kind of journey –forget it. If the choice was mine it was made long before I knew my conscious self. My teacher once said, 'If you stay with me you will get the reputation of being the sorcerer's apprentice.' He was odd; maybe I am too, despite strenuous efforts to be 'normal'. There are things I have witnessed I cannot write about for I fear to speak of angels bliss. This book is written that it might humble the mighty and give hope to Simple Simon. Put aside your expectations and the security of your present knowledge and live with me the wonder of it all.

Tony A.....

Bellerophon slays the Chimera

Figure 2

Introduction: The Myth of Bellerophon

Bellerophon was said to be born to King Glaucus of Corinth some hundred years or more before the Trojan wars but other versions of the myth say he was the son of Poseidon, God of the Sea. Glaucus, a skilled equestrian taught Bellerophon –or as you may otherwise believe, his true father being Poseidon and the inventor of horses, he inherited the skill.

Longing for adventure he visited the neighbouring King Proteus of Tiryns (who, incidentally in God like being was the old man of the sea with prophetic powers –another son of Poseidon), who became insanely jealous of Bellerophon who he mistakenly thought was seducing his wife. Again according to other versions Bellerophon sought out Proteus to be cleared of the manslaughter of his brother Bellerus (hence as some believe his name is derived; meaning he who has killed Bellerus). In any event Proteus sought to cause his death. Feigning goodwill Proteus gave Bellerophon a sealed message for the King of Lycia –his father in law King Iobates.

On his arrival in Lycia Bellerophon learned of the Chimera, a monster with the head of a lion, tail of serpent and a goats head at its centre was ravaging the countryside destroying crops and killing the people. When Iobates read the letter Bellerophon had delivered, he found that Proteus requested Bellerophon be put to death (hence the term Bellerophonic letters). Though he wanted to please his son-in-law, he knew that an outright execution would risk war against the Corinthians. He slyly sent Bellerophon to slay the Chimera, sure that he would never return alive.

Bellerophon's sense of adventure and desire to alleviate the sufferings of the people caused him readily to accept the quest –but before setting out he sought the advice of Polyidus, the wisest man in Lycia. Impressed by the youth's courage, Polyidus told him of the legendary Pegasus and advised he spend a night in Athena's temple, and offer her gifts. In return, the goddess might help him obtain the horse.

Bellerophon took his advice, and Athena appeared to him that night in a dream. She gave him a golden bridle and instructions as to where to find the well from which the Pegasus drank. In the morning, Bellerophon awoke to find the golden bridle beside him and journeyed into the forest, locating the well of which Athena had spoken. When Pegasus arrived to drink he slipped the bridle onto its head.

Pegasus flew into the air, trying desperately to shake Bellerophon off. But Bellerophon was up to the challenge, skilled in the handling of fierce horses and astride Pegasus he set out to the ledge where the Chimera dwelt. As a number of brave warriors had already met with their demise not being able to get close enough to deliver a fatal blow, Bellerophon decided to fire darts tipped with lead. Out of reach of its dragon like fire the leaden darts melted in the mouths of the lion and goats' head bringing about its death.

Bellerophon and Pegasus returned to the palace carrying the heads of the frightful Chimera much to the surprise and dismay of King Iobates who now still intent on meeting his son-in-laws wishes despatched Bellerophon and Pegasus to subdue the Amazons. This they did and also vanquished other foes of the kingdom. Iobates now realised that the Gods favoured Bellerophon and sought no more to kill him but instead gave his willing daughter to Bellerophon as a bride.

For years the couple enjoyed happiness and when Iobates died, Bellerophon became ruler but the spirit of adventure within was still strong so he decided to ascend Mount Olympus to visit the gods. Zeus displeased with Bellerophon's arrogant attempt to scale Mount Olympus' heights, sent a gadfly to punish the mortal for daring to ascend to the home of gods.

The fly stung Pegasus, and so startled the horse that he suddenly reared, and Bellerophon was hurled off of his back. He plummeted to the ground. Athena spared his life by causing him to land on soft ground but he sustained crippling injuries. For the rest of his life Bellerophon travelled, lonely and crippled, in a vain search for Pegasus His resting place is not known.

"There are more things in heaven and earth,
Horatio, than are dreamt of in your
philosophy."

--From *Hamlet* (I, v, 166-167)

This book is dedicated to my earthly teacher
Len Burden 1929 – 2003
Whose phenomenal ability changed my life
To pupils past & present & yet to be
And
To my wife and children
Whose love and respect made this book possible

It is noble to serve

Contents

Illustrations

Chapter ONE:

On the Banks of the Shalimar

'There are many worlds of Spirit, or as you might otherwise name them - Astral kingdoms'.

'Can you give me that as a number?'

'As many as there are men and more'

We are lying on couches of reeds on the banks of the river Shalimar –it is not wide; should I throw a stone it would easily reach the opposite bank. Behind us and on the far bank barely six feet from the waters edge is a thick forest of trees. Brown and dark green illuminated in various places by light bursting colour, olive green, pale gold and silver in ever changing hues. I am aware of an interactive presence, a constant enquiring life force. Eyes in the trees, in the water and the sky, eyes that know my every thought, so much so I cannot think of place in the objective sense or determine time as night or day.

We came here to settle and talk after walking the bank side footpath an intimate journey through beds of multi coloured flowers hymned by the sound of water tumbling through stone breaking shallows. The sky is indistinct, embedded with stars and to gaze upon them is to feel the land and yourself moving upon a celestial carousel. The area in which we are settled is strong with light emanating from flowers, trees, reeds and other vegetation.

Likewise my Persian companion glows from an inner light. Bearded white and grey he wears a gown of royal blue laced in gold and white, a high necked undershirt around which are three strings of crystalline stones, some clear others opaque and veined in a rainbow of colours. A ruby stone on a silver crest and two lines of small seed pearls adorn the high front of a white turban. His name is Omar.

I am barely conscious of my self in the earthly sense, entirely at ease wearing a robe of green satin and shoeless. I am a young man, light in body; feminine in character. Between us there is a dish of dark grapes and a vessel not unlike a stylised teapot with a long curved spout containing a mellow yellow wine –the taste of which is like ambrosia.

'Is is true', I ask, 'That man is a hybrid creature and because of it has difficulty in knowing his identity?' Omar laughs, slowly nodding his head. He smiles awhile before answering.

'Very much so and the power that binds him is stronger than a thousand beings, yet he cannot be content like the vine or accept change harmoniously as the grape does when it is harvested and changed into wine. For all his power he has not the intelligence of peace to maintain harmony in transformation. He is governed by his objective understanding of form, space and time. His constant striving creates an ever-growing web of illusion that seeks to subjugate all forms of life he touches. There is no end to his restlessness.'

'I guess you must be talking about physical man –all this', I say, casting my hand about, 'can hardly be described as restless or for that matter you and me in this state'.

'Ah, I see we must talk more about the understanding of what you term physical'. And he takes from inside his robe a small scroll and unrolls it before me. 'You recognise these words?'

I do indeed –in my own scrawled hand is a poem I had composed:

"In secret place I dance the mystic rites of spring
Forswear the binding that illusions bring;

Slough the old skin, dissolve the marriage ring.
Here where no man made thing may live
I touch earth skin and seek my darkly distant self,
Press body to the boles of mighty oaks
Until I hear their drumbeat in my head.
Then dance until the trees are fiery red,
The sun has risen cold and fears have fled."

'What do you understand about the poem?'

'The secret place is here, in this world, and my dance is the dance of an Arapahoe Indian celebrating spring, that reminds him what he sees and otherwise senses is not the truth of things. The old skin is the earth born self that must die to renew itself else he will become its prisoner. The secret place is a place of power -only here can the inner man be known. In his dance my Indian friend invokes the source of his physical being's energies from the oaks, until the fear of death is overcome'

Omar leans toward me with a twinkle in his eyes, 'And of course you in your physical form understood that when you wrote it?'[1]

'Well, partially I did –it felt right but I've never expressed it like I do now.'

'That's what makes it poetry –you describe and make statements that arise from the conflict of the seen and unseen nature of your physical being, but you can't understand with your brain mind the source of inspiration. You write that the sun is cold –that is an expression of understanding in this world.'

'As you say it does in this world –I changed it on revision to 'gold' believing I was mistaken. I can also say now the dance described is an Arapahoe Indian dance. At the time of writing I couldn't express that influence –likely because the environment I believed to be England. Awareness of the Indians' culture would have seeded conflict in my mind and the poem would never have been written.

'Had you known of the elemental spirit influence that sought expression in your mind –again you would not have written it', Omar replied.

---

[1] This poem 'Rite of Spring' was composed in the 1970's

I shake my head in wonderment. 'Then it is true -the experience of physical life is largely unknown!'

From the bowl Omar picks up a bunch of grapes and holds them before me, 'Now without putting grapes into your mouth, tell me what they taste like'

I look at them, my awareness so complete I know it to be unnecessary to taste or eat them. 'They feel wonderfully cleansing, sweet but not over sweet and slightly drying on the palette'-

'-and that is because?'

'They were grown in a slightly chalky soil?'

'Excellent! Indeed they were –now do you see? Here and now in this life the seen and felt world has being just as your poem has, the nature of which is revealed when you harmonise with it. And more –just as the grape ceases to be grape when it's made into wine and wine ceases to be wine when it is drunk so also will everything change as it interacts. The form of the poem like the grape is determined by its life force. The form of everything is life force potential. Its interaction is the expression of manifest life.'

I look at him blankly 'I'm confused –inwardly I know you are right but I find I cannot express agreement.'

'You began this conversation by asking me how many worlds of Spirit there are. I prefer to call them astral kingdoms because they are created by the world of matter in conflict with the world of Spirit. Spirit is totally unlike matter; it is a force without form. Earthly worlds of this or of any other kind are governed by form. All intelligence is matter seeking to define itself and this it will do in two diverse ways, by making more forms, or by causing form to consolidate. In the former it expands dominion and multiplies differences, in the latter it arises as the essence of intelligence in which form becomes abstract and universal, ultimately able to release itself from the process of rebirth –thereafter free to ascend into Spirit.'

'Is this why Man is such a restless creature and finds no peace in his own company?'

'Indeed, not only in the incarnate earthly world but also in all other worlds of form –Man is a hybrid being and comes from many sources. No sooner he arrives at an understanding he can identify with, other influences within his psyche react and disseminate conclusions. The quest for knowledge is never ending.'

We sit in silence –if silence you can call it. The nature of everything about us appears to be communicating and constantly interacting. When I look at the river it becomes translucent. Images of place and people unknown appear and disappear within its flow interweaving like form and colour in kaleidoscope.

Omar turns toward me smiling –his energies so gentle and calm. I want to be here with him always, never to change. 'We are all subject to change my beloved –now you must return; else nothing of our conversation will be remembered. For this mission of remembering you have undertaken changes are taking place and having effect on your mental, emotional and physical being.

Before we speak again in this manner you will journey to other realms. Remember this, remember this –when confusion and doubt arise and the root of all your understanding is in question, my love will guide you. When all journeying is done and the task complete, together we will rest again on the banks of the Shalimar. Keep this knowledge in your heart always.'

I resist and feel a sense of grief within; my soul crying out and pleading to stay. He holds me, his arm drawing my head into his chest –I feel his warmth and heartbeat. I become calm and for one magical moment all questioning ceases and time no longer holds its scythe against my throat. I lean closer and draw upon his strength of being. In wondrous embrace I flow like a river into dreamless sleep.

**Ghiyath al-Din Abu'l-Fath Umar
ibn Ibrahim Al-Nisaburi al-Khayyami**
Figure 3

On the Banks of the Shalimar

Chapter TWO:
All Roads lead to Mecca

A garble of base notes jar and vibrate my body. I see strange shapes that surround my space so close I feel claustrophobic. I panic. Where am I? I recognise the form of my dog at my feet and panic subsides - the relief is palpable. Gradually the noise becomes language and the strange shapes I am observing become recognisable as furniture. Neither what I hear nor what I see means anything to me. The dog looks real and I stretch out a leg to touch her. Oh my God –I've got another leg moving inside the one I'm looking at!

I feel weird –I move my hands, my arms –now my head and generate the same response, I don't feel they belong to me. I think I'm sitting on a vibrator pad. It's coming back to me now –this is my living room but when was I last here? It feels like an age. I'm suddenly aware of my wife Pam –I can hear her moving around but she's not in this room.

The language sound I hear is making sense now –it's the local TV news for Southern England. With an effort I move about in my chair –the sensation of having an inner and outer body has gone, the vibration ceased. Arms and legs now feel very heavy and my attempts at moving are pathetic.

My memory is returning, I've had lunch, I exchanged a few words with Pam and was watching the One 'o'clock news before whatever happened - happened. I make a quick mental calculation recognising the local news is ending and come to the conclusion I've been 'somewhere else' for 10-15 minutes.

Who am I? My name is Tony. I'm 63 years old –father of three children and a Spiritualist medium, teacher and healer. I've had a successful career in business, own my house, have last years motor car and despite what you might think having read this far –have my feet on the ground. At least I did until a short while ago.

It's a cold January day 2005. With an effort I get up from the chair and still with this feeling of newness to my house (we've been here since 1986), I walk through the passage into my healing/study room. Even here I have the impression it's a place revisited after long absence but the feeling gets weaker as I walk about. My eyes wander aimlessly about the bookshelves looking for something to focus on and browse the poetry section. I thumb the volumes, Eliot, Yeats, Brooke and Thomas, all the time thinking –get your head straight boy, get your head straight!

I stop at the Rubáiyát of Omar Khayyám –and then it hits me. The event of my speaking with Omar on the banks of the Shalimar fills my mind in panoramic vision. Unsteadied by this dramatic visionary experience I sit down. I am consciousness expressing another dimension of reality! I experience a gamut of emotions that challenge my reason and belief. I am amazed, curious, delighted and fearful all at once.

You are probably thinking I've had a weird thought provoking dream and it's the product of an overactive imagination. As a medium and healer for over 40 years I'm no stranger to unusual events and have experienced many out of the body events and lucid dreams. I know the difference between lucid and subconscious dreaming and know that this experience is different again –*I am unable to be objective about it.*

It is not an out of body or lucid dreaming phenomenon of a kind I've previously known. This event is different –it's a four dimensional experience of an objective reality in which I happily accept my own difference of being, my surroundings and my companion. Remembering the self that I am in this event has me questioning who this person is. Out of Body experiences (OOBE's) have depths that are consciously difficult to express and are mostly short on dialogue and interactive relationships. Here and now I have clear remembrance of an extensive dialogue and awareness of how I was feeling.

A lucid dreamer is at the centre of their activity and may also be seen to control its development. In this event I am not the centre of event (whoever I am!). The event appears to be directed by Omar. In no way do I feel in control of what is happening and for reasons unknown I do feel I am the cause of it.

I cannot adequately describe who I was with Omar on the Banks of the Shalimar. My self-consciousness there is a tangible condition interacting intimately with a galaxy of immediate worlds. So different to consciousness here, which by comparison is insensitive, as you might describe the difference between wakefulness and anaesthesia. I do not think –I act. I do not listen to consider –I listen aware that I know as of now. The emphasis is always now –time, as we know it doesn't figure.

Plans of activity fall by the wayside. My wife Pam is a Spiritualist medium, healer and astrologer and normally I share with her such psychic events that occur with me –to hear her views and interpretation which over the years have been more than helpful, but I can't share this –not now. I have to make some kind of sense alone and find out how I consciously relate to it.

My companion in this experience was Ghiyath al-Din Abu'l-Fath Umar ibn Ibrahim Al-Nisaburi al-Khayyami, more commonly known to history as Omar Khayyam, mathematician and poet of 12th century Iran. We were first introduced, so to speak, forty years ago. Then in my early twenties I had been persuaded by a girl friend who for reason most likely selfish had fixed appointment with a local medium for me to receive guidance on my intention of leaving Portsmouth to seek my fortune in the theatre world of London. I was passionate about play writing and thought that one day I might act in and direct my own play.

I had never been to a medium before and my knowledge and awareness of psychic matters was just about zero. I was curious (what would be writer wouldn't be?). I acquiesced to the arrangement and duly arrived at the medium's council house one overcast autumn day accompanied by my girl friend Shirley. To hushed whispers I placed five shillings on the mantelpiece and waited.

A diminutive middle aged woman appeared, bobbed her head in my direction and sat down. My immediate impression was of a simple minded woman behaving in an affected manner (I later learnt that she was strongly influenced by an oriental communicator). I suppressed my smiles and sat patiently to await the outcome. And outcome there was –she literally blew my mind away.

Not only did I receive after life evidence of deceased relatives, of my maternal grandfather –a farmer and my paternal uncle, a chemist, who had never known me as he had died in 1939 –two years before I was born but she spoke about aspirations and events that I knew I hadn't shared with anyone. Stunningly she spoke of a ridiculous pantomime act that had recently preceded my writing periods. Even now it's embarrassing to recall the memory. I would sit at my one and only bed-sit table, stare at the typewriter and then proceed to play an imaginary piano! I can't remember how long this would last for but in the aftermath I would have the inspiration to write.

Pragmatist that I am I encouraged the condition. I was influenced by my uncle Spencer she said –who I knew from my parents was a gifted organist and pianist. As if all this had not been startling enough and being told, by the way, that I was not going to leave the area (I'm still here 40 years later), she calmly announced that I was a medium and described two people she could see who were my guides. One of them was Omar.

The other person was a fisherman from the time of Christ who she said was casting a net over me. As she spoke I felt as if my skull was splitting open and the world I knew supplemented by some other kind of reality. Moments later, the session at an end, my girl friend, looking not a little anxious, supported my trembling frame at the doorstep and steered me the short walk to a local pub where I quaffed in double quick time a pint of beer which had the effect of sobering me up.

I guess we all have experience of being 'taken down a peg or two' but this was like being thrown down a mountain. On that day my life radically changed and I came to regard Omar as my spiritual guide. I have not only felt his presence –I have seen him clairvoyantly and I have heard him clairaudiently many times.

In terms of time Omar (or Umar) is over 800 years old yet in this 'real' event he looks about 50 years old, his movements are graceful and a youthful vigour characterises speech. Conversation in this world necessarily means we must listen to hear what is being said and then respond. In this event I am aware of what Omar is saying *as he speaks a language unknown to me,* which can only mean that speech was manifesting at the same speed as thought.

Given my beginnings and since then a known and active relationship as a medium and healer, the event is not entirely unfamiliar –but I have never had this *kind* of experience, never before this *kind* of closeness –and such a long and sustained communication. What does all this mean and who the hell am I in this event?

11

In the many psychic events I've been party too in nearly four decades there have been numerous occasions when other mediums and clairvoyants have spoken of my youthful appearance in the dimly lit séance rooms. It's been observed in the bright light of public halls when I have demonstrated mediumship and healing. I have always accepted this as evidence of communicators working with me who have that form –every now and then a client will remark upon it. What middle-aged and elderly man is not pleased to hear such comments? I'm just as susceptible as other men to flattering remarks –but under psychic influence an overshadowing can occur –and in this state I'm unaware of what other people sense and often dismiss their observations out of hand.

OK. So I'm older than I look. I'm not the first person to describe myself younger in an altered state of consciousness. For many years I've been an active trance medium and in the aftermath of trance I feel younger and sexless (physically all I want to do is hide away somewhere). My astral self 'on the banks of the Shalimar' is a young man -but my dress is feminine and I feel like a woman.

In my teens and early twenties I did wonder for a while if I had homosexual leanings but a couple of experiences (undertaken when I was under the influence) soon clarified that I was avowedly heterosexual. The self of my astral experience besides not looking like me doesn't feel like the private self I know –yet I feel happy to be him in that reality; an awareness that's uplifting and exciting to observe –he makes my conscious self feel complicated and at best a worm like labourer. If these reactions are not reason enough to be 'disturbed', after exhaustive checking I find there is no such river as the Shalimar.

I'm like a dog in search of a buried bone –I keep looking. The word is likely Iranian meaning abode or place of love and gardens bearing that name were constructed by the Mughal emperor Jehangir in honour of his queen at Srinagar, Kashmir during the 17th century. A canal ran through the gardens – was the tree-bordered river I saw a canal? It didn't appear so to me and neither did the near and far banks look as if gardeners had landscaped them. Omar lived 300 years before this garden was created –why would he be 'resident' in Kashmir when he lived his life in what we know today as Uzbekistan?

Omar lived in ancient Iran –a country significantly larger than present day Iran and at the height of its influence included areas of Afghanistan. During the reign of Cyrus the Great, Uzbekistan was with Afghanistan a gateway into the Kashmir valley. In the 8th century Kashmir became the centre of a great kingdom, spanning much of North India and parts of

Central Asia under Lalitaditya Muktapida, who was builder of the Martand (sun) Temple, and founder of the Kashmir valley's irrigation canal system.

But then there's a feeling of timelessness to the reality I've experienced – is this scene lost to ancient Kashmir's recorded history and the 'Shalimar' feeds or runs from the great Lake of the goddess Sati, (also known as Durga), home to ferocious demons? Are these demons the djinn named in a poem I wrote some 30 years ago under the influence of my muse Omar and described as "commissionaires of dancing grass?[2]

My mind runs on looking for explanations. Omar was a Sufi –that is clear from his poetry and Islam came to Kashmir through traders, warriors and missionaries from the eighth to the twelfth centuries and it was thereafter to become a centre of Sufi faith, finding wide acceptance in the 14th Century through the Sufi saint Bulbul Shah. So was Kashmir Omar's spiritual home? Am I to think that the river and the untouched landscape was known by the warrior king Pravarsena II of the first century AD –was it not he who brought the name Shalimar to Kashmir?

'Is everything alright?

Pam walks into the room and automatically I shrug compliantly but my eyes, I think, are a giveaway.

'Why don't you take a break –you never give yourself time.'

And when I don't immediately answer, she says, 'What's the matter?' Pam perceptive as ever, has 'picked up' that something is 'out of the ordinary'. I'm naturally talkative anyway –the silence in the house must be deafening! The computer is idle, I'm not dashing about readying myself to be late somewhere, I'm not on the phone and for some hours I haven't shared the usual daily events. At the very least I'd have confided my usual complaint -the need of an eight-day week!

The best I can manage is– 'I'm meditating on an astral communication I've received.' True of course, albeit somewhat short on particulars.

She wants to know more –I mumble something about Omar and encouragement. God! I feel even more withdrawn now I can't even talk to my wife! Pam and I have been together over 30 years. Between us we have brought up three fantastic children –the family is really tight knit; our offspring's respectful and interested in what we both do. Moreover whilst

---

[2] The Poem 'Poetry of Djinn' was composed in the sixties and appears in the appendix

Pam and I first met in a pupil and teacher relationship, psychically she has been my helpmate and a source of independent psychic authority for the greater part of our time together. So it's a bit of an understatement to say I feel withdrawn! Strange as it may sound I feel if I speak about it whatever is in the process of happening it will stop.

Not only am I preoccupied with understanding the meaning of my experience with Omar —my world is beginning to vibrate differently. I see, hear and feel outward relationships normally but intermittently the objective world appears as a cloak hiding some other world reality. The phrase 'babe in the wood' repeatedly comes to mind as I struggle to adapt and relate to my day-to-day world. I am expressing consciousness aware of another space time continuum —I cannot see or mentally articulate the difference but I can feel its constant presence.

Will I feel like this tomorrow?

Chapter THREE:
Appointment in South Dakota

A fortnight passes and the 'promise' of more journeys hasn't materialised. I have mixed feelings -I'm a little disappointed but also relieved. The relieved part of me is wholly Capricorn, its getting order back into the daily round of chores and commitments not to mention the pleasure of simply feeling normal. I manage a small complementary health business, effectively run two healing charities, teach my skills to others and work as a psychic & spiritual healer. I have more to do than a full life can achieve. Right now I'm pleased with my days' effort and sit relaxed, aimlessly watching the passers by through the window of my healing/study room, smiling at the sunshine. It's sort of nice to be normal again. Then it happens –a feeling of inertness and my body becomes heavy –I am carefree and timeless and slip out of this time into another place.

The man before me smiles broadly. He sits, or rather sprawls in a rocking chair on a wooden floored veranda that looks out over hilly wooded country. I am standing beside him conscious of the wooden cabin behind me, of the sun bleached facia panels, window frame and a door flaking grey paint. My companion appears to be about 60, stocky and clean-shaven. His hair is thin and grey, short on top, longer at the sides and swept back untidily. He wears faded worn jeans, heavy shoes and a check top.

I know him well –his name is Don.

'As you don't fancy beer I've got you a soft drink'. The accent is American mid west and he speaks in a very relaxed manner. I am now sitting in a canvas chair –to the side a small folding table on which stands a long glass filled with something smoky looking. I hold it up.

'Is this your idea of a soft drink?'

'Aw com' on now, won't do you no harm –its medicinal!' Got to be one of his herbal recipes, it tastes earthy and flower sweet. 'Thanks Don, I see you have the best of the evening.' The sun is dipping low at tree level the landscape flaming red and silhouetted against the sky.

'It sure is and as good a time to talk as there can be.' He pauses for moment and then shoots out a question. 'That right you call yourself a mechanic?'

'I'm a fixer or at least that's what my pupils think –so the label seems appropriate'. Don stabs a finger at me. 'You don't remember our previous conversations, do you?'

Previous conversations? We've had them right enough -I look on Don as something of a teacher. Right now nothing comes to mind and curiously I don't feel fazed by the question. He doesn't wait for me to answer. 'I thought not –but it don't matter any, you fire away and we'll see what you can carry back'.

'To be honest Don, I don't know where to start I guess it'll have to begin with some reflections on you part'.

He reaches over to a table behind him and picks up a pad and pen, flips a page over and draws a circle. 'There, bit simple but does the job, that's good old mother earth, OK?'

'Mine?'

'Ours –stamp your foot –see solid stuff, take it from me its earth. Should know I've been resident here for some years and I'm growing taters out back and they are doing just fine'.

'Right –so this is earth and it's the end of the day, so where are we exactly?'

'Huh? I've definitely got the new you. This is South Dakota, 'bout 100 miles south west of Lake Traverse, Minnesota.'[3]

---

[3] The location described by Don appears to be in an area around the towns of Redfield and Faulkton, South Dakota.

Appointment in South Dakota

'You seem to be miles from anywhere. I can't see any roads or houses. Nothing seems to be moving here –just you and me in the middle of nowhere!'

'It's Indian country not far from Gettysburg.' Don chuckles at my remark, 'True in the sense that my nearest neighbour is some miles away. But don't believe it son –it's quiet like right now 'cos I've been expecting you. What you are is where you are –you can follow that. It's calm like so you can get a grip on things'. A howl fills the air coming from my right where the ground, rough and patchy with grass and stones inclines upward into a wooded area. Again the howl sounds out and ends in a moan. 'Wolf –get 'em here this time of the day and right on through the night when they get busy.'[4]

He taps me on the arm. 'Now you keep your focus here', he says softly, 'You'll be wandering off before you know it and we won't even get started'. I look at him quizzically. What is he about to say?

'You've been travelling before –right?' I nod. 'And what did you remember?' He goes on quickly, 'Bits of this and that and what your mind lets through, most of it don't make any sense –right? Am I right?'

'True –I guess'. My voice falters. Part of me wants to say not true, that everything is remembered and I can choose what to recall. For a moment I am conscious of myself being younger and something else besides. I feel like two people in the same body contending with one another.

'Now concentrate and we can make a bit of progress –Lord alone knows why you want to do this, best of my knowledge no one's ever tried before'. He thrust the pad against my chest. 'Circle –right? Let's start from here. You ain't got long so let's make the most of it'.

Don's face creases into a broad smile. His eyes are kind and gentle – suddenly I feel very warm toward him. I grasp his arm, 'OK –you're the boss, I'm listening'.

'What goes around, comes around', he says tracing the circle again with his finger, 'everything is connected with everything else. Now rest your palm on that chair arm and tell me what it feels like'.

---

[4] There is no evidence of wolves currently inhabiting this area of Dakota –likely they were last here in any numbers when buffalo roamed the plains, late nineteenth century. Given the nature of the communication i.e. this is not our physical reality, it cannot be assumed that the known history of this area directly relates to the event Don is describing.

'It's warm and feels as if it is moving within itself. '

'Right', says Don, 'Now kick that sandal off and tell me what that foot feels like on the ground'.

'It feels warm also and kind of moving just below the surface, like the chair arm felt under my hand'.

'Like it did, eh?' He stands up from the rocker and kneels down beside me placing one hand on my foot and the other on my hand that rests on the arm of the chair. 'Now can you feel the same vibration in both hand and foot at the same time?'

'Well, sort of –can feel this movement under the surface but it feels a bit more complex than…'

'Good'. He interjects releasing his hands and standing up. With a satisfying sigh he returns to his chair. As I put my sandal back on I find myself looking at it, first wondering when and where I had bought them and then admiring their strength and style. 'Concentrate on me, Peter'. His hand is on my shoulder straightening me up. 'Else you are going to disappear 'fore we get anywhere'.

'I'm sorry Don, I got distracted'. I feel a little more centred now he calls me Peter. 'Everything is connected to everything else. The knee bone is connected to the leg bone; the leg bone is connected to the anklebone – etcetera, etcetera! Your hand is connected to the chair arm and your foot is connected to the ground –the ground is connected to the wood, etcetera, etcetera! ' He leans forward and rummages in his jeans producing a corncob pipe, sticks it in his mouth and puffs away producing an aromatic smoke. I don't see him fill or light the pipe. [5]It just happens.

'Ok, I can follow that –everything is connected to everything else –so I guess everything is in a state of exchange'.

'Absolutely –but it ain't just a shared world is it? Two things in exchange don't just remain two things, now do they?'

'They intermingle?'

'Did you notice', he says pointing the pipe stem at me, 'the movement you felt was in you?' I think about it for a moment –he is right; he has to be right. I feel within myself. 'So what are you saying?'

---

[5] I myself have been smoking a pipe for some 30 years –what I find interesting is firstly I smoked corncob pipes but found they were hard to get hold of and whenever I smoke a pipe I feel a 'different' person. Does this communication give me answer?

'I'm saying you are not conscious of the chair arm or the ground you are only conscious of yourself'.

'But it can't be as simple as that', I expostulate, 'you for example appear quite independent to me and I'm conscious of you. The ground stays where it is whether I take notice of it or not –and that wolf; I didn't dream him up did I?'

'I'm enjoying this' Don says with relish, 'I didn't think it would be quite so interesting when it was first suggested but you've come prepared to be a real pain in the arse!' He shakes his head in disbelief, smiling at the thought. For a while he just puffs at his pipe. I watch and savour the smell. He continues.

'Everything is in a state of exchange –right? We agree that. We also agreed whatever you felt was in *you*, which makes sense, don't it? Whatever you interact with is an experience you feel. If you ain't connecting, say with that white sports car you admired recently, it ain't gonna register-'

With a jolt I realise he is referring to the Supra I saw parked on double yellow lines in the town. 'Well, it did register; otherwise I wouldn't be able to recall it now would I?'

'Sure. And you are recalling it 'cos I've prompted your memory. There am a lot of things you notice but they don't live for long 'cos you don't need them. Look, I'm present but what do you know about me –more to the point what do you need to know of me?'

This understanding is getting away from me –he's making it out to be black and white. With an effort I focus my attention on Don but our history refuses to coalesce in my mind. I'm thinking I will get to understand the point he is making one statement at a time. 'The ground is real right?' I say flatly.

'It's at least as real as you are', he says with a mischievous grin. 'Everything is connected to everything else but because it's you that knows that, everything is relative. You know as much about these other independent states, like me and the wolf for example, as you want to know – and even then wanting don't necessarily make it happen. Exchange has to take place and the moment it does you alter as does the person, animal, earth and whatever you interact with.'

My power of concentration is returning. 'I follow', I respond, but I'm still determined to get into the independence issue, so I try again. 'I'm conscious of the world about me in a limited way, but that doesn't mean the world beside myself doesn't have a dependence of its own. The earth, sky, your house here, that wolf we keep mentioning and Gettysburg in the distance, and you of course, are all independent of me –are they not?

'Of course, but what I'm trying to get you to grasp is the fundamental nature of life can only be realised within you. In the physical world the vibration of life's energies are slow and you will feel separate from it, cos on the inside you ain't slow at all. The earthly intellect develops its understanding in that state of separation. It's like your understanding has gaps in it –here in this life things are more joined up, so to speak, and that makes us who live here, and I don't just mean people, more conscious of who and what we are.'

I am silent for a while, beginning to feel vulnerable, unsure and out of place. 'This is the easy bit, he says with a grin, 'writing it down is going to be a lot harder -'

Suddenly I hear a female voice cut in, 'you confused him Don, what did I tell you!' Her voice is high pitched and shaking with laughter. 'No I ain't, no I ain't –but he's had enough, I can see that'. And he laughs–they both laugh. I swing round looking into the house but can't see anyone.

Don

Figure 4

Chapter Four:
Questions of Identity

I'm at it again –where am I? No panic this time, instead I'm viewing a memory aged about ten, sitting in the hall of my step grandmother's house. I can hear my father talking to her –grown up talk I should imagine since I've been parked some distance from them with a book. The sun is streaming in through the windows and I can hear the loud ticking of a clock beside me.

As I remember this childhood experience, feeling timeless and unconscious of the meaning of age, the present world begins to take over – the bright sun and the passers by are still there. I look at the clock on my desk –it shows 9.35 p.m. It's not working –it hasn't worked for sometime. I look at my wristwatch –surely only minutes have passed? As I realise this my childhood remembrance is interrupted and a semblance of control asserts itself.

I move in the chair and it triggers recall of my astral journey. I'm initially stupefied by the experience that fast plays into my consciousness. The experience becomes mentally audible and when I simply allow myself to look other sensory impressions are received. I find the subject of my discussion with Don fascinating but at the same time find myself arguing against it.

This won't do. I get out of the chair walk about, fiddle with papers, pat the dog and sit back down again. Again I view the memory and immediately begin to question -who is Don? I've never met him before, not psychically, not here on terra firma. Peter –am I Peter? Who is Peter? What was I doing in Dakota of all places? I've never been to America –good as it must be I have no desire to go.

No. No. Don't question –write!

I'm putting words down to express the 'movie' –and bit by bit recalling the dialogue. Don is right, remembering in one state is one thing, remembering in the physical world what I experience in another state is hard. The event is here in my brain panoramically teasing me to focus on the detail. I'm not writing in any order –just reacting anxiously.

My wife Pam looks in. 'Are you writing?'

She's probably thinking I've begun work on the healing book I've talked of doing. Pam is familiar with my mental concentrations that can run into hours when I focus on poetry composition. What she is really saying is do I want a cup of tea?

I'm still not ready to talk about this. 'Oh, it's another psychic communication. I'm just trying to get some words down –I'll tell you about it when I can make some sense of it. And yes I would like some tea please'

She smiles at my assumption –I've never been known to refuse an offer of tea, I even anticipate the question! Make sense? –Come to think of it my earliest memories didn't make sense either. Frequently I'd have nightmares, waking terrified as if I was falling from a great height. Just remembering makes the stomach nervously tic. My elder brother never seemed to have this kind of problem –but then he was always more grounded than me. I admired his practical nature –to me he was the clever one and still is.

I was a dreamer; even the physical reality of war didn't touch me. My family lived in Kent outside of Maidstone. The airways above were euphemistically called 'bomb alley.' I remember occasions of sheltering under the kitchen table, the angry sounds of aircraft overhead, playing with toy cars with my elder brother and watching my mother's legs moving to and fro in the kitchen. If she was fazed by these events she didn't show it to us kids. On occasions the activity overhead got to be really intensive and to the sound of sirens we would all evacuate the house and go to the dugout at the bottom of the garden.

I clearly remember one such event and wanting to be helpful in the Anderson shelter I took the teapot outside to empty it –and stood there gazing up at spitfires, hurricanes and Messerschmitt's dog fighting in the grey skies. My observing didn't last long; I was dragged back under cover – protesting of course.

Perhaps the dream like quality of life then –one step removed from physical reality is still with me. As I grew up interacting as needs must, learning the ways of the world my dream like nature internalised –but unlike many who lose touch with it forever I remained conscious of a difference between the inner and outer world of my consciousness.

I've learnt the hard way that it's neither a refuge nor a panacea to right wrongs. A sailor's world is unforgiving; the world of business is no more understanding. I am as a result unconsciously secretive –a defence I believe that has preserved my dream like child nature. Psychic work since my early twenties has given expression to this sensitivity. Maybe in life's school I've got the 'forces within and without' reasonably right and maybe that's why I'm able to do what I do.

I had the sense of being detached throughout my youth. No matter what I did, on my own or with others I always had the sense of watching myself and others whilst being 'involved'. Games were uninteresting –maybe because they were too physical; I much preferred to read, particularly books about sea adventures. And make believe was a serious business.

The girl next door used to play the servant to my eastern potentate much to the amusement of my mother and the consternation of hers. I'd lie languidly on a couch of old car cushions next to the dividing fence playing the role for all it was worth and she would make drinks in her plastic tea set and pass them to my outstretched demanding hand. This game ended when she insisted I eat a pigeon pie. I'm sure her mother put her up to it –but I was not to be mocked and haughtily removed my 'court' and refused to play the game anymore.

I'm trying to make sense of what is happening to me right now –at an age when it should come easy! My darling wife would love to know more as would psychic friends and associates. How can I, an experienced medium and teacher, tell them about this? How am I able to explain the event is mind blowing because it doesn't fit with anything I've previously experienced – and, more the point, how do I tell them that I know the man Don yet have no memory of our history? And how is Peter both known and a 'stranger' to myself?

Has my past finally caught up with me? Are all these 'selves' me?

Chapter Five:
Communing with Nature and Wolves

If I'm having an identity crisis – all the more the reason for keeping this 'business' to myself, at least until I am ready either to confess I've lost the plot, or when (if *when* it ever will be) I make sense of what is happening.

Fortunately for me my mediumistic and healing skills still function. This is helpful as I can really focus my mind on what I do best. I'm in demand and busy days take over. Once again I stop thinking about questions I can't answer –when the journeys do come to mind I'm more detached and less emotional. I mull over the 'circle philosophy' that Don talked about and have to admit that from his standpoint it makes sense.

I'm walking my dog on the familiar 'bone yard run'.[6] It's a welcome exercise. I've a busy day of healing consultations ahead and need to clear my mind as it will all start to happen when I get back home. Creature of habit that she is I follow on after without needing to lead her. We now need to cross a busy road and given her road sense is zero I hold the leash tight and wait for a break in the traffic. I gaze left at the florists thinking how fresh and clean the flowers are displayed in the troughs outside –an idea forming to buy some for my wife when suddenly everything changes. And I mean everything.

---

[6] Cemetery

I'm standing on a rise between trees and bushes looking down into undergrowth; Don is standing at my side.

He beckons me to stoop down and examine something. I can see a dark impression surrounded by leaves and squatting down I see it's a hole and peer inside. 'I can see its muzzle, it's a young one!'

'Yup, she's got three cubs'

'She's in there Don –I want to see her!' I feel really excited.

'Nope –she's up there on the rise, watching us'.

Don doesn't turn round but I look up to where cedars overshadow the hill –search but see nothing. At Don's suggestion we walk up the hill to its crest and into a clearing where trees have been felled and the smell of sawdust and sap is strong. 'Lets rest up here a while', says Don fishing in his pocket and bringing out his corn cob pipe.

'You got a thing about wolves and foxes, ain't yer? I nod. 'You disappointed you didn't see her?'

'I guess so', I look at him quizzically, 'what are you telling me?'

'You rely too much on your eyes –or to put it another way if you'd allow it, you'd see out the back of your head'.

'Psychically you mean?'

'Well, yes and no, you're thinking like a physical man. Even when he's got the gift, he'll only see out of the side –you know what I mean?'

'Yes I do. I sometimes think I might see what's behind but it's either centre or side I get the picture'. He continues, 'and when you get to move your head toward the side you mostly lose it, don't you now! He sounds amused. Clenching the pipe stem in his teeth he leans down and rakes the soil with his hands, picking up loose stones and casting them to one side.

'What you doing?' I am curious. For a moment he ignores my question and continues to rake the area with his fingers until the round patch is about a foot in diameter.

'I'm gonna learn you something. Now, you sit here and I'll move along'. I settle myself in front of the raked patch of brown earth.

'A circle right? I feel triumphant as I think this exercise is a continuation of our last conversation. 'More so than not I guess, but that ain't the point. Now you look at that and tell me what you see'.

It takes a few moments for me to consciously put away the images of cubs. At Don's urging I stroke the earth with my fingers and that helps focus my mind upon the patch. For a while it just remains brown and then a shadow settles over it and the brown becomes dark grey, deeper still until it is black. Again suddenly it changes to milky white and –'I can see her! It's her isn't it? God she's beautiful!'

There she is facing me, jaws slightly open, saliva glistening on her mouth the white ruff accentuating the dark eyes. The brown earth is a portal through which I can see the wolf standing on a bank flanked by trees.

'Well, she ain't there, he says bluntly, 'you just think she is'.

The portal dissolves and I am looking at brown earth again. I felt a bit foolish as if I've been wrong footed. 'OK, you're the boss, what's this I've been seeing then, 'a mirage?'

'Hell no, that's the wolf I said was behind us back down there on the path, what you seen is what I perceived at that time'.

'But you didn't look back –did you?'

'No I didn't. I use my other senses, what you call the feeling, smelling, touching and hearing senses. Now you try it'.

'How?'

'Simple enough put your hands on the earth and feel it. Now listen to that feeling'.

I do as he instructs and feel the moistness of earth soft and yielding at the tips of my fingers and a movement that feels vaguely like a damp wind. I remember that moment outside his house feeling the arm of the chair. 'It's like you showed me with the chair –right?'

'Sure it is –now stay with it. Don't ask yourself what you're doing, just pick up on what happens and follow it'.

The firm softness dissolves into a feather like touch –the earth feels liquid and gaseous and encompasses my hands. The sound I perceive that began like an intermittent heartbeat is now rhythmical, not constant like a drumbeat but of character varying in pitch and pattern, giving the impression of purpose and action. Now I sense tree roots and a buzzing and humming sound coming from within them.

I follow this difference of being and now feel as if I'm standing at the foot of a tree –the space around me populated with more trees, bushes and ferns. I smell the sweetness of briar wood. Taste the acidity of earth. And I hear a multitude of sounds, not confusing, muted or cacophonous, but distinct. I feel the rasp of wind on bark, creaking sounds of grass, of ferns, tree boughs and bushes. I sense individuality of mind in everything, even the tree is a character overshadowing me with open and accommodating feelings. I am aware of the sky and the stars. I'm seeing but no longer interested in seeing for seeing sake; it is like being born again, aware a hundred times more so.

All is individual and distinctly 'simple minded' quite unlike the complex nature of human beings that reflect inner conflict. Everything here has an interactive relationship that is direct and purposeful. The tree I stand before has roots that spread away into the distance and there are changes taking place within and above the earth, alterations in feeling and character. Amongst this teeming myriad of being I cannot sense conflict –the time honoured battle of physical life preserving itself against the finality of death.

No. What I am experiencing is the positive acceptance of change of everything conscious of being in a state of change. My own form is permeating and being permeated by this earth like world. I can move but moving is like expanding, and as I move I absorb into myself character of the earth, vegetation, bush and sapling trees; the wind is cold but not chilling, elemental but not impersonal. A creature with red eyes and a rat like face crosses in front of me, foraging for food. I hear it digging, its jaws masticating. Momentarily it pauses aware of me but shows no fear, instead unconcernedly continues its hunt.

I'm aware of other eyes watching, suddenly appearing and disappearing. I move on, gliding now rather than walking, half in the earth and half out of it. She is coming toward me; I sense her shape, the sureness of her feet and feel a mind of ancient awareness. It is the she wolf.

I stop moving and my immediate world pauses within me. She halts and I see her standing a little way off, enquiring eyes surveying my presence. When two human beings meet they interact as they want, taking and receiving to satisfy, probing to see how far they can go –what more can be given or taken, but the she wolf appears to be idly curious, not demanding and not the least protective of herself.

She seems to be querying –what do I want with her?

I impart without words what joy it is to receive the contact of her kind, thanking for help given to manifest my healing powers, thoughts of hope for a closer more united world of animals and men. She looks into me searchingly as if to discover a path on which she might have purpose to share. Her curiosity seemingly satisfied, she turns and walks away, but her presence is still with me, as if to say 'when our needs coincide I will be with you'.

Once again I'm aware of trees, undergrowth and watching eyes. One tree in particular has my attention –the bole seems to pulsate and stretch until it shows the form of a man. Tanned dark by the elements, dressed in dark leathers, tight trousers and open jacket the man has a necklace of bones and feathers about his neck. He is lightly built with long dark hair that drapes his shoulders. He is strangely familiar to me but I can't say how I know of him.

He looks at me as if to say. 'What now?' In a kind of reflex action I think of Don and immediately I'm brushing my hands and standing up. Don sits there as he had been before my experience, still smoking his pipe. 'What you make of that then?' He looks amused and satisfied.

I'm lost for words and sit down, feeling the environment and savouring the sense of its completeness for some while. Then I speak of the wolf and how I marvel at her sense of being. 'She is an old soul,' I remark, 'how is that possible?'

'Ah, yes –quite a surprise now ain't it? In all his thinking of self, Man don't consider the incarnation of animals for themselves –it's a salutary lesson, not only are there many paths to God, there are many Gods'.

I want to question that but think better of it. We sit together in silence for a while, drinking in the awareness of the woods, listening to birds and undergrowth sounds.

'Well son, now you know.'

'Do I?' I half say this to myself, watching Don clean his pipe with grass stalks. 'Who was the man I saw, looked Indian to me'.

'You recognised him?' Don makes the question sound like a statement. 'I did and I didn't, if you understand me. He was very familiar, but then I don't know why as I can't remember how or when I've known him'.

'All part of your education, young Peter. Course you know him – difficulty you're having is the knowing of yourself. What did we agree? Everything can be expressed in the circle. Contact goes both ways –life is exchange. Now you are beginning to use your senses in a balanced way the self can be appreciated as many not one.'

He's rising to his feet now and stuffing the pipe in his pocket.

'It's about time we were getting you back, remembering is difficult enough and you got problems to deal with'.

'Problems –what problems?'

'Now don't go worrying', he says reassuringly, 'it'll turn out alright'. I turn to follow him. 'You haven't answered my question', I remind him.

'All part of your education, let's be moving'. There's a note of finality in his voice. I say nothing and follow his stocky figure. Every now and then I am sure his form changes to the slim Indian I saw in the tree.

The noise of traffic is deafening –I'm frightened out of my wits. My dog Kya is looking at me with a pained expression on her face –I am holding the leash too tight for her comfort and just maybe she is questioning *my* road sense.

How long have I been like this -seconds, minutes?[7] I can't tell and I cross the road like I'm walking on glass. The sound of everything is very harsh and Kya is pulling hard, impatient to enter the cemetery. Appropriate I am thinking –I'm a dead man surrounded by graves, stepping on the live grass, walking under live trees unchallenged by these receivers of rites.

Hellfire. I'm not sure I can do this!

---

[7] In retrospect I would say it was less than a minute –for two reasons, one; My dog is not respectful of roads and would have agitated to move after a minute and secondly; I was not aware of anyone looking at me curiously as I might expect them to do if I'd been standing statue like for any length of time.

Chapter SIX:
Out of Balance

Did I live this experience in real time? The question hangs in the air as I struggle to re-establish objective consciousness. My feet are on the ground, I am breathing in the cold air and my eyes register the cemetery road, its forking paths, trees and tombstones but nothing feels real. I don't feel connected to my surroundings. As Kya pauses to savour smells I do some stretching exercises. I practice focussing my senses on objects and sounds, and gradually my physical responses improve and my senses relate to space, time and light. Mentally however I am still overwhelmed by the present nature of the journey experienced. Walking home I am fragile as if walking a tightrope between this and another present state. Is this possible? Can I be in two present states at one time?

And the nature of this communication –I have no comparison in the conscious world. Nothing 'normal' and nothing psychic comes near to this total sense of involvement. Just remembering makes me feel disabled –half blind, half deaf and the highest order of my feelings crude attempts at expression.

I focus on the healing work I am about to do –this will give me a way to channel the energies and 'ground' my conscious nature. The healing work goes well and I have satisfied and grateful patients –and yes I now feel more grounded. Relaxation should be the next thing on the agenda but my amazed mind will have none of it. I write a few notes in an effort to still my restlessness.

Until now I've accepted these events as 'one off' astral memories believing them to be experiences of another existence unrelated to my present timeline of life but my experience with Don, communing with nature and the wolf cannot be explained away like that.

The message from my recall I can't avoid is that these four dimensional 'journeys' are connected and the last two appear to be in 'real time'. Not only does the dialogue in my last experience relate to the previous, I as 'Peter' am conscious of connecting events. The question now overriding all others is –who's directing affairs? It's patently not me –is it Peter, or is Peter directed by others; by Don, or by Omar, or whomever? These unanswered questions are troubling and as I dwell on them I start to feel mentally fragile again.

With an effort I put all this to one side –there are domestic matters to deal with. Pam and I are expecting a visit from a solar heating representative. He arrives and talks up a very positive picture of benefits. We are both very green minded and the initial information suggests this is affordable. Any way you like to say it, this guy is good –so good in fact we can't wait to sign up and pay deposit. Full of enthusiasm I tell one of my sons about it later and he sounds dubious –so late at night I go back to look over the figures that we've been given and lo and behold there's a hole in my understanding of Grand Canyon dimensions! I hastily make a few calculations and realise this deal is completely unaffordable.

I've allowed myself to be duped! We are not talking peanuts here; I've given credit card authorisation to the tune of thousands of pounds.

So this is the problem that Don alluded to.

I spend a nervous and angry twenty four hours trying to get the money back –the rep that came to us is up country (how convenient!) and his manager is unavailable. Daily I wait for their response. So much for statutory rights –I even think of driving to Bournemouth to beard them in their 'den'. In desperation I lay my problem at the door of the credit card company –now all I can do is wait recovery of the money.

Truth is I'm angrier with myself than with the solar heating business. For 18 years I worked for a large international computer company as an administrator and business analyst, handling budgets of millions of pounds. How could I be so stupid?

'Because something is happening here, but you don't know what it is, do you, Mister Jones? –so goes Bob Dylan's 'Ballad of a Thin Man'. I have to say it's fitting right now. This Peter fella is so much more with it than I am –perhaps

we could change places? However this change in consciousness pans out my psychic beginnings clearly has something to do with the present phenomenon.

After having my mind blown by the diminutive Mrs Hickey I took her advice and sought out the medium Len Burden. In my late teens I had travelled extensively with the Royal Navy visiting 37 countries and at that time in my life I reckoned myself immune to the "slings and arrows of outrageous fortune" –but that 'reading' turned my life upside down. You are a medium she said –really? Whatever that was I had to find out about it. The following day after an uneasy night I was knocking on the door of a semi detached house sporting a stencilled wall plaque written -St Joseph's. A middle aged woman opened the door. 'No, Mr Burden isn't available.'

'When will he be?'

'Tomorrow –come back tomorrow.'

And so I did and met the man who was to have a major influence on my adult life. Some kind of psychic chemistry was evident between us from the beginning. I felt very much at ease in his company whereas many thought him a somewhat scary character. We enjoyed a rare combination –able to be friends, pupil and teacher without conflict.

I always called him 'the kid' –to call a person that, who is 13 years older, doesn't sound appropriate, does it? He doesn't take offence, my apologies are accepted. I've never understood why --maybe the name has other connotations. Jokingly those of us who were 'members of his inner circle' described him as 'three parts ether' for he was psychically very gifted.

Len's powers of clairvoyance were startling and accurate. I would overhear asides from recipients at his public meetings exclaim 'how on earth does he know that?' I couldn't have had a better teacher, his example was always something to reach for and his healing powers were phenomenal. Clients would seek him out from far and wide.

Beyond all this Len was a deep trance medium, the practise of which contributed to his failing health in latter years. Deep trance is a rarity amongst psychics. Most trance mediums are overshadowed by afterlife communicators; their mediumistic personalities supplanted in varying degrees causing them to either partially or completely lose consciousness. Deep trance works differently –the medium's personality is withdrawn and experiences an out of body awareness as the communicator takes over the physical state. Any disruption of atmosphere during these trance states can be injurious to the medium. It is not surprising therefore that his main guide

Out of Balance

Joseph Carey, a black American from 19th century Louisiana always 'masterminded' the entry and exit of other communicators. Joey as you might expect was zealously protective of Len during his trance states which was evident from the control he exercised over 'afterlife visitors'. His personality and approach to sitters in séances was completely different to Len who was a highly nervous individual. The joy of talking with Joey was so relaxing and interesting we would lose all sense of time.

Almost overnight my psychic powers emerged and I experienced phenomenon of all kinds –Astral communications, telepathic connections with my teacher, clairvoyance, clairaudience and artistic inspirations, painting and sculpture but mostly poetry. Shortly after our meeting at St Joseph's, a difference of opinion between himself and the married couple that ran the church resulted in Len having to vacate his rented room in that house. My bed-sit was a hell hole so we clubbed our finances together and rented a large flat in Southsea.

It was my good fortune to have him close at hand, as a period of intensive learning began, much of which was governed by astral communications. Regularly three or four times a week an hour or so before planned sleep time I would feel as if my insides were being drawn out. It was quite comical, I'd stagger around the flat like one pole axed and stubbornly try to watch television until Len insisted I lie down. No sooner had I done so I literally felt drawn out of my body into some gigantic hole. The following morning I'd wobble to work on my bike still suffering the effects of being 'absent' during my sleep state, this phenomenon lasted for a little over one year.

With Len's help I recalled partially the consciousness of my astral events. A theme emerged; I was aware of being a woman, tall and strong like I think Amazons must be. Her name was Atlanta but beyond that I didn't know anything about her. Len told me she was a Queen of Atlantis –he even drew a picture of her and encouraged me to talk of the experience I could remember. I spoke of a city built on a plain amid a complex of canals –large buildings of stone and brick. In her form I experienced a consciousness of doing that I found impossible to express when awake. Occasionally my recall was vividly pictorial and as Atlanta I am in communion with others, in large assemblies and being accorded great respect.

I appear to be a teacher in most events –I discussed such detail as I could describe with Len who in turn would explain the purpose and meaning of them. Being able to talk was mentally and emotionally relieving –so much so the memories recalled would disappear soon after.

These events were different to my present astral journeys –there was always the feeling on recall of viewing a past event. As a consequence I tended to think of the experiences as a kind of referred clairvoyance. Over time it became evident that I was 'descending', so to speak, into lower levels of astral consciousness. My astral character changed and became male –a personality I could only assume was me. Remembrance of places and events then began to feature people of our own time.

As this cycle of activity drew to a close my trance ability manifested. Late one afternoon Len complained of a headache and asked me to give him healing –at this stage in my development I had never practised. By his direction I placed my hands about his head and suddenly found myself the other side of the room close to the ceiling watching myself. On reflection I realise he had 'set me up' knowing full well what the outcome would be.

This experience brought my dream nature down to earth with a bump. The grown up me started to impose conditions of acceptance that had the effect of barring my psychic access. Consciously I would seek confirmation of who communicated and what was intended by the trance. Clairvoyantly instead of just letting it out I'd question to satisfy myself of its meaning before expression.

The trance ability stopped manifesting, my clairvoyant and ESP ability dried up and I stopped dreaming. Len was a hard teacher; whilst assuring me my psychic gifts have not deserted me he nonetheless insists I try to exercise them. 12 months of undiluted misery follow during which time my efforts bear no resemblance to my initial development experiences. In the weekly development groups I was a complete duffer.

'My mind is a blank', I'd say. Len was unphased –'there's no such thing as a blank mind'. When Len is in trance I appeal for understanding from his guide Joey. He assures me it will happen, that this is just a period of adjustment. The only psychic impressions that freely flow are those from my pen, mostly poetry and I happily accepted this as inspiration familiar.

Then one day I became so dispirited with my mediumistic training I said to myself –'that's it, in the next development group, say the first thing that comes to mind. If it's a load of rubbish, which I expect then I'll stop all this nonsense -get back to ordinary life and focus my creative mind on writing.'

I was astounded. Everybody said they could accept what I gave them - messages ranging from advice on material matters to proof of survival. It took all of my control, ably encouraged by threat of 'excommunication' from Len, to stop myself going into trance. As my psychic ability was rediscovered I inherited another problem. I was totally mindless about my ability and nervous as hell to practise outside of my teacher's presence. With Len's urging I agreed to demonstrate in a local Spiritualist church. No. I won't let my name be used, because I'm demonstrating in trance. I began teaching –that too in trance. I set up a healing group and practised healing and mostly I found that manageable without letting the unconscious take control.

Why am I telling you all this?

My unconscious dream nature seems to have guided the early phases of my psychic development. Gradually with Len's help I got control of myself and my feet stayed on terra firma when I insisted they should be. My control was speeded by the need to earn decent money and falling in love with one of my pupils. Falling in love came first of course –my wife to be, Pam, was more than happy to live on fresh air which only made me more determined to get the material world in perspective. Oh to be a physical man!

Right now I appear to have returned to those early days of doubting my psychic ability –I can think of some who on reading the communications described here would give their eye teeth to experience them. I have to admit that identity questions to one side the experience of entering into the natural world and communing with a wolf inwardly warms me. When I am psychically aware I detect on occasions the presence of wolves and I regard them as important influences helping to establish links with afterlife communicators and as part of the energy chain that provides power in my healing work.

My darling wife is doing her best to pour oil on troubled waters and 48 hours after my 'stupid mistake' her wise counsel is beginning to take effect. I retire to bed and thankfully stop worrying –sheer exhaustion, I guess. Sleep comes quickly –too quickly you might say since some time during the small hours….. I wake in an entirely different place.

Chapter SEVEN:
Something more than a Teacher of Dancing

I'm standing inside the double doors of a hall, aware that it's a flat roofed single storey brick building. I can hear dance music and a hubbub of conversation of within. I queue behind a middle aged man and woman getting tickets. They appear to be a couple for as they approach the small foyer table the man signs for them both. An elderly man extracts tickets from a cloth bag. No money changes hands. It's my turn and I sign in, writing my name, Peter Renaud.

I playfully tap the man's jowl. 'I take it you are well', I say smilingly. He looks up, his eyes rheumy, 'Course', he replies, but his age worn face belies a pessimism that prompts me to say, 'you certainly don't look any worse than last we talked. Take heart Lionel, life gets better.'

Next I'm aware of being in the hall itself walking amongst the people - some sitting at tables and chairs bordering the dance floor, others in the centre dancing to a quick step tune. At the far side on a raised stage is a dance band; players of double base, violin, guitar, clarinet, piano and drums pump out the music. Everybody in the hall is dressed in 20th century fashions. From the ceiling hang old-fashioned single bulb lights under white conical shades. I make a beeline to a row of wall seats and sit down in a round-seated cane chair, feeling it buckle and sway as I settle.

Something more than a Teacher of Dancing

'You won't like the music here'. The voice comes from a dark haired woman in her late thirties early forties sitting to my left. She looks a bit frumpy; a decorative clasp broach crosses the ruff braid of her white blouse, the dark red jacket and skirt is formal and her shoulder length hair is pinned back.

Sounding tense she says, 'It's a bit dated, don't you think?'

'Oh, I don't know, I find it quite relaxing.'

In fact I don't think it's dated at all and smile inwardly. Nervously she dabs her nose with a balled up handkerchief. 'I don't know anyone here', she says abruptly.

'Relax, it's alright, there's nothing to worry about'.

Now, apparently without any conversation, I am dancing with the woman, moving her manfully about the floor. I'm conscious of my skill and of her feeling awkward, for she looks to see what my feet are doing and tries to keep me at arms length. We don't speak but I feel I'm reassuring her mentally and emotionally. The music changes amid cheers to the Paso Doble. 'Now', I say, 'think Spain!'

Suddenly she seems to accept me and her brown eyes lighten and shine with confidence. She straightens up, looses her hair and tosses back her head. The change is miraculous and she begins to look quite alluring. I poise myself like a bull fighter and step the dance with precision and force. The more I stamp my feet and entice her toward me the more she weaves to avoid my control. An animal power possesses me outpouring inexhaustible energy. Now she is dancing with passion bringing her arms high above her head, smiling at me with half closed eyes. The frumpy person has entirely disappeared; she is now lithe and young the dress transformed to a swirl of bright red satin and black lace. The music climaxes in a clash of cymbals and we finish with a flourish.

I'm aware now of sitting relaxed and self assured having drunk some kind of cocktail; a cherry stick rests on the rim of the glass. My dance partner of a moment ago is not present, instead before me at the table is a thin man sporting a chequered bow tie clipped to the collar of a pale checked shirt. Not the best of combinations I note. He is clearly ill at ease and reacts defensively to the thronging crowd of revellers talking and laughing about us. I glimpse the woman I have danced with still wearing that red satin dress and looking sensuous, talking animatedly with a man costumed not unlike a Mexican.

'Are you sure this is the right place?' the man anxiously inquires of me.

'Just be yourself', I exclaim, '-just go with the flow'.

'I am being myself', he says defensively, 'I've really no idea what I'm doing here. It doesn't feel right.'

I don't reply and he leans across the table and eyes me intensely. 'I don't know what I'm doing here', he reiterates. It sounds like a final statement.

'Do you like dancing? He doesn't answer me, instead looks around slowly taking in all he sees -then looks at me questionably. 'Do I know you?'

'Yes, way back when you were younger but you probably don't remember -it doesn't matter, you're here now. Have you seen your wife?'

'No. She's not here'. He stands up and looks anxiously around. I can't help notice his scrawny neck and untidy iron-grey hair. Turning he questions me again. 'I don't remember you -when was it I knew you?'

'I taught you dancing -many years ago.' His eyes are lustreless and look painful. 'I'm sure I'd remember something like that -anyway you are a bit on the young side.'

I laugh, 'most people get to look younger here. It doesn't matter you don't remember; I'm just trying to be helpful right now.' Compared to the vitality expressed by other people in the hall he is noticeably old. His haggard looks and sallow skin reflect an inner pain. He remains standing looking anxiously in all directions, fingers alternatively clutching at his trousers and smoothing imaginary creases. 'How can I expect to find her here -she's dead'.

It sounds as if he's repeated this statement many times before with the same result. His eyes brim with tears and I touch his elbow and gently sit him down. 'I'll find her for you', I say confidently.

He doesn't reply but sits there bent in resignation. I wend my way through the chattering throng, passing dancers, small groups talking and some singly moving about oblivious to all but themselves. The music is in waltz time now to the tune 'I'm forever blowing bubbles'. I am conscious of moving like a panther, silent and purposeful. I feel insulated from unnecessary contact my senses tuned to a space beyond sight of my immediate environment.

The lady in the red dress is dancing with the Mexican man. Their waltz looks more a Samba in slow time. I interrupt, swaying to the music; the

Mexican man lets go of her arms and begins to dance away from her as if holding an invisible partner, apparently oblivious of my interruption.

'This is much better', she says flashing me a smile. 'Are you going to introduce yourself?'

She speaks as if we have never exchanged words before -this is the same lady I talked with earlier who had changed before me from a middle aged frumpy woman to an alluring athletic female in her early thirties. Not a little Latin in manner her movements are magnetic and for a moment I sense her coming on to me.

'Not necessary ', I say, 'he's here'. She stops moving and looks at me wide-eyed and incredulous. 'He's here!' she says breathlessly grasping my wrists with both hands. 'A bit lost', I say softly, 'he can't find you. Think about him now, it'll help.'

Immediately she begins to look older, just the eyes at first, then the face gently relaxes filling out a little until she appears more like the woman I initially spoke with, but the youthful charm of a few moments prior is still present.

'Now close your eyes for a moment and call his name'. She looks at me unsure of the right thing to do and then complies. The noisy hubbub and the moving mass of people fade into the background as we both tune into the man I had previously been talking with.

'Are you there Di? Di?' I hear the man I befriended calling out but he's unseen, hidden by people milling about. Firmly I press her hand 'call him again -keep calling him.'

Her eyes close in concentration and I notice her dress has changed back to the twin set dark red costume. She wears the white blouse and sports the same broach.

'Di you there -Is that you?' Sounding suppressed with controlled emotion he appears from out the dancing throng and sees us standing together. Unsteadily he approaches, arms outstretched to embrace her.

'Alan' she gasps. 'I've been waiting for you -you do look well!'

And so he does. Gone is the disconsolate look, the stiff pale faced figure. They eagerly hug one another -his face a wrinkle of smiles. I watch in pleasure as they hug and kiss one another. The surrounding scene, the movement, chatter and music fades to a whisper. As of now they are the centre of the world.

I have accomplished what I came to do. I smile my goodbyes and turn to leave but Alan reaches out and catches my arm. 'I really don't remember who you are but something in here,' he taps his head, 'is telling me I do know -strange isn't it?'

'Call me Peter.'

Thanks anyway -thanks a million'.

I feel gentle more like a woman than a man as I respond. 'When you've had a nice long chat and begin to notice other people, look out for the Mexican man'.

'Oh, I liked him -you must meet him', exclaims Diane to Alan.

'He will help you fill in the gaps Alan'. I say.

'It doesn't feel like there are any', responds Alan, looking flushed and excited. 'You will see what I mean -he will help'. And with that I turn on my heel and walk out of the hall into the foyer now deserted except Lionel who sits reading 'The Stage' newspaper. I go up to him, peer over the paper and ruffle his hair.

'Careful now, I don't have much', he grumbles.

'Have you met him?' I say, pointing to a photograph of Ivor Novello in the paper.

'Not really -no can't say I have. I would like too', he adds wistfully. 'You can and you will Lionel, you will.' I assure and put my hand gently on his shoulder.

'What makes you think that then?'

'Chorus boys are not forgotten.'

'I was young -one of many -I wasn't noticed -hey! How come you know that?'

'In the same way you can tell the difference between a visitor and a resident.' He looks at me as if he's trying to work it out and then a smile lightens his face.

'You mean them that are dead and don't know it and them that are dreaming?'

'Something like that.'

'But there's more to it?' Lionel has the look of a younger person as he speaks.

'Some', I say and thinking it unwise to continue I change the subject. 'It's doing well in there tonight -keep up the good work.'

'Well good I suppose', he says grudgingly, 'I get a lotta smiles when they come out -'

'And some invites too?'

He grins. 'You're one for knowing ain't yer?'

'Lucky guess, I reckon.'

'Guess my foot -the last time you came here you said my missus would pull through her operation, and she did. You're one of them clairvoyants aren't yer?'

In response I do a soft shoe shuffle ending with my arms spread, 'How's that?'

'I knew it', he says triumphantly, 'I knew it.'

The half of it, but it'll do I'm thinking. I wave goodbye and step out into the street. The sound of music and conversation, faint but distinct, lingers in the air as I walk away from the hall. The stillness feels like a Christmas night in the city, every house warm and contented. I look up into the night sky and think to myself -those stars are very close.

I'm staggering to the loo. My dog is stretched out on the landing and we collide. I know I've been somewhere -I go downstairs and stand on the patio looking up at the stars. I'm somewhere between sleep and the place I have just visited.

A silent picture of my astral journey burns in my brain. I accept it all without argument and wend my way back into bed. It's 4.25 a.m. The darkness of the bedroom is tangible. I reach out and touch Pam.

She stirs but remains asleep. I stare out into the dark half expecting it to possess me. The silence is deafening.

What should I tell her Peter?

Chapter EIGHT:
An Indian with hazel eyes

For someone who has had a mind bending experience in the deep of the night I feel remarkably normal as I tuck into breakfast. I plan out the day and suppress thoughts of questioning my astral journey. I still can't talk about what is happening to me but expect Pam to be understanding when I finally feel I am able. I need answers. I guess I'm getting used to having two minds at work. Later in the day I find some quiet time and recall the previous night's event. It's weird -it's like watching a film.

I can recognise the dance teacher 'personality' as part of myself, though I have to admit I never was as good as that at the Paso Doble! I try a few steps in the privacy of my healing room and feel so wooden I laugh at myself. Then there's that man I was helping to reunite with his wife -I remember him! He was a widower who came to the dance club I worked at. This was before my fateful meeting with the medium, Mrs Hickey.

Alan came to learn ballroom dancing with his daughter as partner. They invited me to their house once and remember him being handy with hifi and stereo equipment -he'd set up speakers all over the house and proudly demonstrated the sound effects of a train that appeared to go from one room into another. There were three young children as I remember in addition to the eldest, the daughter with whom he danced. It was clear to me then she had taken on the mother role. As daughter and father's dancing skills developed they competed in amateur contests held at the club. I thought him possessive and didn't much like him.

An Indian with hazel eyes

Some years later long after I had left the dance scene I was shocked to hear he had been jailed for incest -given his age then he could be dead now, but I have no way of knowing.

I continue to be fascinated by my Peter self who has now revealed a surname. The name, or rather the sound of the name, does mean something to me. Whilst I was trying to write plays in my early twenties I 'invented' a pseudonym -Peter Renault. With this name I planned to try out my 'works' and only reveal my real name when publishers said yes. I didn't get that far - I never finished anything I started. Renaud and Renault have very similar pronunciations. Does this mean that Peter was 'alive and well' 30 odd years ago?

Given what I know of Alan's moral behaviour and the oppressive control he exercised over his daughter during dance events I doubt I would have been as helpful as Peter.

Peter is definitely his 'own man' despite me feeling part of him in some way. It's clear from the conversation with Lionel; Peter had visited the hall before and was there on this occasion expressly to bring about a meeting between Alan and Diane. He exudes a confidence I cannot claim for myself. I also read into the journey that Peter is restraining himself -deliberately avoiding some subjects; in short, limiting his involvement. The building in which this event takes place is unknown to me –yet further evidence that Peter is Peter, not me.

I'm still puzzling over my recall of this experience later in the day. I help out with the chores and when Pam leaves the house to go shopping I decide to tidy my healing/study room. I put on some music and get to work. I'm absorbed in what I'm doing when a pulsing vibration starts in my right ear. The sound grows louder and I feel myself internalising and losing reason and the purpose of what I am doing.

I'm out in the open air standing about six feet from an open fire. To my side is a felled tree trunk, dark and shorn of bark, the shiny surface cracked and dried. A man in leathers sits cross-legged the other side of the log fire.

Above the firelight I'm aware of a night sky speckled with stars. The man motions me sit down. I smell cooked meat and a sweetness I can't define from the warmth and smoke, yet there are no utensils or foods in sight. The man, I believe to be a Native American Indian, gazes at me through the firelight. His eyes are bright and penetrating -they are also hazel which doesn't fit my understanding of his race. I feel my dress rather than see it -leather trousers and waistcoat similar to the figure before me. Don comes to mind and immediately I feel this is the Indian I saw when communicating with the wolf.

'Are you well? He asks. His voice is light but serious and reflects an intense awareness of my situation.

'I think so', but I immediately feel dubious of my statement.

'You think too much', he says easily, as if it's a matter of fact. His lips open into a smile revealing teeth more bronze than white. 'You can't stay long so why don't you tell me what's on your mind?'

I get the impression of an economy in thinking from the way he speaks - as if dialogue mental or otherwise is a last resort. He speaks English with a slight American accent.

'Can you tell me your name? I feel it's only right I should address you by your name'. At once I feel foolish for saying it. I'm sure I know him, but something in me is prompting me to check it. He gives me a knowing smile; 'Of course, I understand -you need a name'. He pokes the fire with a stick until the flames brighten our atmosphere. 'What name comes to your mind?'

He's playing a game with me. Alright, since it's not important to him I'll say the first thing that comes in my head.

'Wolf', I say, 'a wolf alone -Lone Wolf.'

He inclines his head. 'I am honoured. Now ask your questions while the fire still burns'. There is so much I want to know about the here and now.

Why's and wherefores crowd my head but instead I speak about the dance hall event. He listens intently; head cocked to one side and nods every now and then in understanding of the events I describe. 'How did I get to be in that place?' I conclude.

'Similar events are in your memory. You did not act as a stranger but as one familiar. There are no accidents in Manitou's kingdom. All events have a before and after -be they here or in the physical world.' He lifts a staff that rests across his thighs and points it toward me. I feel a gentle tap on my ribs even though the pointed stick has not extended across the fire. 'In this world you are not the person you are in earthly memory -your body being is more vital -you would say younger. The body is a living temple of thought -a present state of being: here you express differently and the body and mind evolves accordingly. This is true for all life.'

'I was not aware of knowing the woman Diane -and yet I didn't feel as if I was talking to a stranger. How come that I knew of her?'

'The woman is the man Alan's wife -you made contact with her when you met him, though she was on my side of life'.

'I see', I say doubtfully, 'that was many earth years past. Surely she should have evolved more so. I have the impression of person who didn't know where she was or what she was doing!'

'We must return to the teaching of the circle. Think of it like a wheel of fortune -that which goes up must also come down'. He pauses for a moment, lifts and swings the staff back and forth like a metronome. 'If you set out on a journey and realise during your travel you've left something behind you need -what then would you do?' I am grinning to myself. It seems like a constant occurrence in my life, having to turn back for something I've forgotten. 'I would return for it, of course'.

'Ah, of course, of course', he says repeating my words with emphasis, 'but you cannot always do that, can you? Events may dictate otherwise.'

'Well, that's true too', I reply wondering what he is getting at.

'Everything is affected by everything else. Human relationships by the very nature of their being cannot evolve entirely within the physical world. When a soul sheds the physical skin it becomes more aware of its hybrid nature; of its separateness. Seeking to harmonise, the arisen self discovers that some parts of its purpose are within states it cannot enter. What then does the person do? Their souls' needs give birth to other relationships - agreements able to progress awareness beyond the limits of earthly incarnation.'

In my minds eye I am seeing life like some gigantic web stretching outward from myself to infinity, but the essential question still remains, so I ask again, 'Why given this awareness should she appear unversed in the way of this world?'

'Because, Silver Wing, that part of being in need stays as it is until change moves it'

I feel a sudden inward glow of self-realisation as he evokes the name Silver Wing -the dance hall memory vanishes and I become aware of another dimension of self.'

'You came here seeking the man Don as the man Peter and what you find is Lone Wolf and Silver Wing. Peter will remain as himself until he is resolved, likewise Silver Wing. You are both bound to the man Tony who is also bound to souls here and beings in other dimensions. In the physical world the incarnate soul externalises that which is within and internalises that which is without and calls this awareness truth. It is not so in this world. Here all being is without; all understanding of that being is without.

The woman you helped unite with her husband is as she appears, a person in search and unsure of herself -yet even so she is at another level evolving and no longer in need of the physical embrace to demonstrate love to her husband.' He pauses for a moment and again points the staff at me. 'Like you she is many things besides'.

Lone Wolf lays the staff back across his thighs and sits impassively crossed legged awaiting my response. I am aware that in earthly life remembering is an exercise of validation and we customise our memories to serve the purpose of the present world. Here nothing is hidden or can be forgotten and I wonder how needs and their apparent contradictions can be resolved.

'Surely the woman Diane is aware of her husband's sexual relationship with their daughter -would that not create a gulf between them? How can she still love him?'

Lone Wolf is swinging the staff again and as it moves back and forth I see it as a straightened serpent. 'Love is not a moral force, though you might think so given the teachings of your world. Love is a harmonising force. What appears as a contradiction is a separate awareness. In this world nothing is hid.'

I am losing motivation to ask questions -I think I understand what Lone Wolf is saying but can no longer articulate thoughts in response. 'There are many worlds of Spirit -are there not?' Lone Wolf is smiling across the fire's dying embers. I smile back as he evokes in me the memory of speaking with my beloved Omar on the banks of the Shalimar. Lone Wolf stands and motions me to do the same.

He holds the staff above his head, and extends his free hand toward me across the fire bed. 'Remember, what comes around, goes around and nothing is what it appears to be. Sight alone is not your guide. Be guarding of yourself as you journey'.

I hear the staff whirl and feel myself dissolving and leaving this place.

Lone Wolf
Figure 5

Chapter NINE:
Feelings

What exactly am I doing? It's a few moments before the beige coloured shapes before my eyes are recognised as folder files, a while later unlocking my legs I rise feeling remarkably light, trip the light fantastic to the kitchen and make myself tea. I'm remembering something but as daft as it sounds I'm not yet consciously aware of anything in particular. It's not until one of my cats plaintively meows for food I recall sitting on a log looking at a person lit from within etched against a black background I realise I've had another psychic experience but right now the detail of this doesn't show and I'm not angling to find out.

I talk nonsense to the animals; remember my housekeeping tasks and return to sort the files I had started. Idly I glance at the clock, surprised to see that time (unusually) is on my side. I check my watch -I check another clock; they all show the same time. I could swear I started this job or sorting files around 10.30 a.m. making tea and feeding the cat took about 15 minutes. I survey the untidy formation of files on the floor and note those I've dealt with and assess it must have taken me at least 20 minutes to get this far -now it's barely two minutes past eleven. I know I've been somewhere -I know its taken time. I add it all up and make allowances -and it still doesn't compute!

The time issue triggers into consciousness my meeting with Lone Wolf and I write down what I remember in feverish haste fearing to lose it. I now have detailed awareness of an event that chronologically I cannot explain. The insight is making me nervous and jumpy, shrinking my attentiveness of the objective world. Once again I am questioning who I am in these astral events.

Silver Wing is a name I know. My teacher Len advised me of this many years ago. This is your name in the afterlife, he said -there you are female. In the first part of this event Lone Wolf addressed me as Peter -yet he was talking to me -Tony. When he called me Silver Wing I shifted consciousness and lost what little objectivity I appeared to have. What am I to make of all this?

And is Lone Wolf the communicator I've known of for many years? Yes - I feel sure of that now. Visions I've had of the man known simply as 'Wolf' have never been clear, so I can't compare with my astral journey. But instinctively I know he's the same person.

Yes -I must trust my instincts. Feelings not visions have determined my choices and caused major changes in my life. As a boy I could never explain to my parents why I was so obsessed with nautical matters. Most of the books I wanted to read were seafaring stories and I only truly 'switched on' to a subject or event if it was water related. 'He's a dreamer' everybody said and perhaps that's why my school reports would always end 'could do better if he tried', or 'capable of better things.'

Dreams get shattered by the real world, don't they? At thirteen my parents paid for me to join the training ship 'Arethusa'. I reckon my Mum and Dad thought of it as a kill or cure remedy to wake me up to the real world. Many of the kids on that ship had come from the Shaftesbury Homes charity and were orphans or juvenile delinquents. The fact that my parents paid cut no ice with the ships officers, we were all boys to be educated and disciplined -there were no special cases.

Someone 'up there' was looking out for me -shortly after arriving I was sitting at one of the mess tables immersed in a book (I had been an addicted reader since the age of five) when a male voice clear and concise, said, 'you must put the book away now and join the others.'

I accepted the authority of this voice and began to objectively realise the world about me. Even as I took my first tentative steps to develop my conscious personality, special things began to happen. In those two years onboard the 'Arethusa' in the river Medway the officer who taught English, a Mr Wightman an enthusiast of ships heraldry, persuaded me I had writing talent, which resulted in my first publication -an article in the Nautical

Magazine about life on board that training ship. The chaplain Reverend Sims-Williams, a short barrel of a man with a withered right arm, got me interested in Christianity.[8] He was also a wizard one handed wood carver of statues and models and fired my interest in woodwork and model making. I think he took care of me in ways I didn't understand at the time. Many years later, my sea career a distant memory, he appeared to me as an after life communicator!

Another event during my time aboard the training ship 'Arethusa' left its mark. I was learning to swim when a couple of my mess mates decided it would be a good idea to drag me under. They kept doing this until I was swallowing water wholesale and sinking. I remember the fateful calm that overtook my panic. Fortunately for me the physical training officer was nearby and he hoisted me out and pumped me dry. In some strange way the experience helped me learn to swim -my fear had been overcome.

Years later during my psychic development period a memory was revealed to me of a previous life that ended by drowning on HMS Hood on 24th May 1941, seven months prior to the day I was born; reason enough for me to understand why the sea figured so strongly in my early life. It was a feeling that crystallised into the decision that changed my career plan at the last moment from entering the Merchant Navy as a trainee deck officer to joining the Royal Navy as an ordinary seaman. My parents, understandably, were shocked and disappointed.

My feelings had been a true guide throughout my life -why shouldn't I trust them now? Yes I am confused about my identity -and no I don't know where all this is taking me, but my feelings are telling me to press on.

If I hadn't joined the Royal Navy, perhaps I would never have known Portsmouth, never met my teacher -never met Pam. I would not have met the chaplain of HMS Belfast who introduced me to the classics and gave me an education that stimulated my writing interests, or met the marine who held me spellbound reciting from memory 'The Ballad of Reading Gaol'.

You see, if I'd developed logically as it seems most do, I'd have weighed my options. As a 15 year old I could have gone into the Merchant Navy - easily the better career bet given my training background. I had graduated from the 'Arethusa' with honours. In the Royal Navy I was short listed as a special duties officer candidate. What more could I want, the Navy a secure

---

[8] This culminated in my being confirmed by the Bishop of Rochester in 1956.

career and everybody in the family proud of my achievements? No. My feelings decided otherwise.

In the afternoon and evening that followed the experience with Lone Wolf I became progressively unwell and by evening time succumbed to the flu. I thought - 'I'm unwell because my body clock is confused by these inter-dimensional experiences I'm having.' The money is still with the solar heating 'devils' and I'm worrying that the credit card company are not going to act. Pam is serene and confident, 'the money will come back.' she says. And I try to believe her; after all she is a very good medium.

Trouble is I have a horror of debt and no matter how well I reason I remain anxious. We stay up late watching a TV film -I don't take much of it in. I'm contemplating the possibility of a second mortgage.

Chapter TEN:
The Grey Spheres

I fret myself to sleep expecting mega subconscious horrors to surface and wake me -but they don't. A necessary visit to the loo does. Its 3 o'clock in the morning and am I'm trying to get back to sleep but my nose is bunged up, so I sit up and gaze into the darkness. My head is throbbing, is that why the darkness seems to pulsating? My thinking is slow -not surprising given my flu symptoms. When the pulsations begin to bang on my head I get nervous and close my eyes in an effort to shut them out -then miraculously my brain feels clear and the darkness disappears.

These are the grey spheres I'm thinking as I walk, my shoes scuffing the dry ground. Earth or sand I'm not sure because a film of grey haze obscures the colour of the surface I stand on. The atmosphere is thick with heat -and there is so much whiteness I'm unable to assess the size of the space I am in. I don't feel oppressed by the heat; inwardly I feel strangely cold, as if my body temperature is on permanent low.

I can hear voices ahead of my position -sounds of English but I can't make out what is being said. I'm on a road flanked by drainage culverts and ahead a wavy shape is solidifying into an armoured truck. It's about ten metres in front and the voices I heard must belong to the two men I see in combat dress standing close to the vehicle. Surely they must see me? They keep looking around the back and then the front of the truck -their movements are anxious as if expecting something to happen.

'Where the fuck are they?' The taller of the two, a black skinned man addresses his white companion. They appear somewhat overdressed in ammunition belts and holstered pistols and are holding automatic rifles. The white skinned soldier is small and sallow faced. 'Must 'ave gone -Jesus that shell was close, my head's still zinging!' They both continue to scan their surroundings but don't register my presence.

'Hell man, get down, down', shouts the dark skinned man and they both crouch in front of the truck and then drop to the prone firing position, weapons pointing away to the left of me. I hear a whooshing sound and instinctively crouch. There's a flash and a grinding thump directly on their position. I can feel a rush of warm air banging into me. I look up as it passes and see dust spiralling where the truck and the men would be. Slowly it clears away and I see the men motionless on the ground their bodies twisted, arms and legs akimbo. 'My God -they are dead! I think, and the scene is making me feel physically sick. Then I hear their muffled sounds of surprise and pain.

Mentally I remain calm and direct my thoughts to dismiss the physical feeling which threatens to overwhelm me. It's not my condition I say to myself and I won't accept it. Immediately the sick and nervous feelings disburse and a sense of well being returns. I view the scene before me. The vehicle is badly damaged; the front almost blown away and the driving cab area a mangle of metal and fabric.

For a moment all is still, nothing moves -it looks like a picture slightly out of focus. I notice small specks of dusk hanging in the air, remnants of fabric and plastic pointing upward. The 'picture' wavers and definition alternatively fades and regains clarity. The scene looks confusing as if two pictures before and after are mingled together.

The truck door swings open, bent and buckled, it makes no sound and surprisingly a man steps out apparently unharmed. He removes his helmet and gloves and tosses them to one side. Oddly the greyness that permeates everything is turning a shade lighter on his form. He stops for moment in the shadow of the vehicle as if sensing something is changed, and begins to loosely stride in my direction; now he runs. As he approaches I call out.

'Hey, soldier!'

He appears not to hear or notice me and passes by his eyes straining ahead as if they are guiding him forward to an important landmark. He yells: 'I'm American. I'm coming'

My attention is now focussing on the black man I hear say 'OK' -in response to what I don't know but he does look after the man who passed me by. Getting to his feet, self consciously straightening his jacket, he picks up his gun and stares down at what appears to be a dark bundle spread out on the ground. The Caucasian man also rises and he too leaves a ghostly image of himself in the prone position. Fishing through his pockets he finds a pack of cigarettes -puts one in his mouth but doesn't attempt to light it, instead stares into the shadow and feels his torso, every now and then pressing the flesh as if to confirm that it's there.

The black man shakes his head in a bemused kind of way; the dark bundle on the ground is disappearing. He calls out -'Wayne?'

The sallow faced man ignoring the black soldiers' call peers inside the mangled remains of the cab. 'Brett? Harry? Where the fuck are you?'

I feel like going over to them but inwardly I know it's not sensible and hold back. The sallow faced man is speaking again. 'I'm sitting me down, OK? OK.'

There's a hint of confusion in his statement then he and the other man suddenly become aware of each other. The black soldier says, 'Wayne 'where the fuck did you go to?'

'Nowhere man, nowhere -where the fuck did you go and where's Harry? Jesus I feel strange.'

'You and me both, I feel weird. Man do I feel weird!'

'Brett, tell me I'm not dreaming -we took a hit right?'

'The hell we did -anti tank mortar if you ask me'.

'There ain't a scratch on you'

'Nor you man!'

'Harry's gone -just gone man. He's not in the cab. I think we're dead Brett -that's what I think'.

'Don't be a fucking idiot -wouldn't be here would we?'

'I sure as hell don't feel normal - I can't describe it and I don't seem to care, I ain't got that sickly feeling anymore. I feel good.'

Wayne has a spaced-out look about him and Brett is shaking his head in disbelief. 'This ain't heaven, can't be, just smells of me and the desert.'

'Don't go moving off -right? Wayne says anxiously, 'not until we know where we are -right?'

'I'm going nowhere I'm fucked. I feel as if I've been hit by a truck!' Brett sits down breathing deeply like a man exhausted by strenuous effort. Wayne stubs out the unlit cigarette and yawning flops down beside him. 'Someone'll come'. He leans his head on Brett's' shoulder.

Both men appear to be asleep and I move tentatively toward them. It's an effort to walk, the inward cold is intensifying and my body feels like a suit of heavy material. Closing on this scene of carnage I see the truck cab is a mangled mess -nobody inside. I stand close to the soldiers and call their names. Nothing -no reaction, I lean over and touch the black man's shoulder and my hand goes through it -like the body is liquid. Again I call his name and this time he stirs and mumbles like a man disturbed from a dream.

'Hey man -what's with you man?' but he says no more. His companion Wayne noises incoherently when I attempt to touch him. I'm aware of their doubles now, lying on the ground like dusty holograms; clothes in shreds, great gaping wounds in their torsos; legs and arms grotesquely angled at the moment of death. Intermittently I hear the rasping sound of their breath and deep dull sounds like muffled explosions. I smell urine and sweat and taste a strange sweetness on my tongue.

Feeling ineffective I step away from the scene, turn and see three men and a woman approaching dressed in army fatigues with Red Cross armbands. The woman addresses me in a foreign language. She is white as are her companions, possibly Europeans. I ask if she speaks English but she shakes her head and speaks further in the language I don't understand but mentally I think she is telling me to stand aside and leave the men to them.

I watch as the Red Cross men lift the sleeping forms of Brett and Wayne onto stretchers. They stir as they are moved and respond to the rescuers' efforts to have them drink from bottles they carry.

'We get you out of here -OK?

One of the rescuers is speaking accented English. There is a muttered response from the soldiers but they remain in the prone position as the stretchers are lifted and the party starts to walk away. As they do a figure appears from behind the vehicle, turbaned and bearded carrying a rifle. He sees the group and races ahead of them to turn pointing the gun. He speaks violently in passionate tones, another language I don't understand.

The stretcher party carries on as if they are unaware of his presence - again the turbaned man yells -this time I can feel the fright in his voice. He points the gun -jigs it back and forth with a bewildered look on his face, clearly he is trying to fire it but nothing is happening. He is now jabbering incoherently to them. The woman says something to him and inclines her head toward the others.

The turbaned man throws down his rifle sinks to his knees lifting clasped hands skyward and praying noisily. Another man then appears similarly dressed sporting ammunition bandoliers, stops by the man, lifts him up and embraces him. Arm in arm they follow the stretcher party talking endlessly a stream of foreign language.

The ground and atmosphere begins to waver about the scene I am watching -the stretcher party appears to be moving in another space -it is like I am witnessing a mirage. I hear a male voice calling, 'come back Peter. Come back'.

I'm conscious and anxious about my body as I think it's swollen. For a while I keep touching my left side until I'm satisfied it feels normal. I know I've had an out of body experience and am telling myself that the dark that is darker than night will soon go away and I'll be fully awake. Instinctively I reach out for a tissue handkerchief, encounter the bedside lamp and recoil from its touch. It feels alive. I'm awake now - the darkness external.

As I snuffle into the tissue I'm relieved that my head is not hurting and I don't feel as if I've a temperature. I contemplate the events I have just witnessed sitting there in the warmth of my bed feeling favoured and fortunate -the misery of flu is nothing compared to what I have seen.

And the voice that called me back. Who was that?

Chapter ELEVEN:
In Danger of Disappearing

I wake feeling confident the flu bug has done its worst but after a couple of hours on my feet I feel awful. Beware a sick man -especially a healer; the worst of all patients. I confess to not being very spiritual right now -bad tempered would be a better description as I struggle to do all the right relaxing things and let the flu bug do its worst and leave. I'm in the complementary health business and a healer to boot -so getting the bug smacks of failure. Morosely I ring round and cancel patients' appointments and try to follow Pam's advice to, 'put your feet up and watch some TV'.

Rightly or wrongly I'm nursing my feeling that body & mind are disordered as a result of astral journeying. Resting I review again the astral events that have occurred to determine if their sequence and content can provide a progressive understanding. The first event evoked realisation within me that self is not only a multiplicity of faces it's a world of distinctly different beings and whilst questions inevitably arise as to who these persons are I feel a yearning to experience again that total sense of belonging I experienced.

In Danger of Disappearing

That sense of belonging also featured in my meetings with Don and Lone Wolf and evoked understanding of prior relationships. Unlike Omar and Lone Wolf my knowing Don cannot be explained by my knowing him mediumistically. It's clear that I'm being educated but not so obvious is the impression I have that Peter is also being taught something -not the 'circle philosophy', not communing with nature but something else that won't gel into an understanding in my mind

The dance hall event was different -I as Peter mentored the event and I felt he was an 'educator'. On recall it's clear that Peter's character is distinctly different to mine.

The 'Grey Spheres' experience is something else again -here I believe it to be me 'doing my own thing' and not being very effective it would appear. The voice that called Peter back replays in present consciousness and I feel guilty of treading 'where angels fear to go'. I can't even answer the basic question of why I was in such a place. What other levels of me are there I'm unaware of?

In the early hours of the following morning, patiently awaiting the return of sleep, I slip into another dimension. Unexpected as it is, this time I see it coming. I've been to the loo and am now sitting up in bed, wide awake, trying to blow my nose quietly so as not to wake Pam. My ears sing as they can often do when sinuses are full of mucus -but the sound changes to a deep hollow booming that vibrates throughout my body. I have a sickly feeling as if I'm falling -instinctively I try to balance with my arms but they won't move. I experience a whooshing sound and lose consciousness.

I recognise immediately I'm at Don's place standing on the veranda where we last talked. He is not there. The time of day feels like early morning, the countryside hazy and everything beautifully quiet. I feel young; my arms are smooth, virtually hairless and brown from sun. Dressed in jeans, sweatshirt and wearing sandals I'm comfortable with myself and the atmosphere is pleasantly warm.

I gently knock on the cabin door and getting no answer open it and call his name. Still no answer so I venture in. A short wood panelled passage leads directly to what looks like a kitchen area. Immediately inside the front door is a small table on which an oil lamp and a small framed photograph of a young woman wearing a stylish hat, dressed in 1930's style clothing stand. Also on the table is a clasp knife, a piece of wood partially cut in the shape of a curved dagger and shavings, some of which litter the wooden floor. I walk

61

over a tatty looking floor mat down the passage; on either side open doors show a bedroom and a living room area with easy chairs and a table.

In the kitchen, a window looks out over a garden area sloping away from the house, unfenced from the natural surrounding landscape. Either side of the garden are wide swathes of dark turned earth sprouting green leaf vegetables that form the garden borders. A shallow trench runs directly from the window to what appears to be a soak away. Growing from its edges are the broad leaves of rhubarb plants. I look at the sink and notice it has no taps. I'm curious, where does the water come from? I'm pondering this when I hear Don call out.

'I'm out here'

For a moment I'm unsure where he is calling from -he calls again.

'I'm out here on the porch young fella'.

Silently I pad back through the house feeling a bit like an intruder, wondering why I hadn't heard him arrive. 'Hi Don, hope you don't mind. I called but you weren't here so I went inside, thought you might be having a kip.'

Don is sitting in a rocker chair and beckons me with a lazy swing of an arm to sit in the canvas backed chair next to him. He grins broadly, aware of my embarrassment. 'Whad'd'yah reckon then?' he says, still grinning.

'Reckon about what? I only went out back to find you.'

'An' if I hadn't 'ave called yer, what was you going to do?'

'See where you got your water from'.

'Don't get any running water up here -got a well out back, dug it myself'. I'm thinking did he have help? Where did the tools come from, how did he get food, who is the lady in the photograph, who made the house?

'Now you keep your mind on what you came for -else you am going to disappear, and me too I reckon, as it is it takes some arranging to have you here -and get answers to your questions', he adds meaningfully. Don is reading my thoughts.

'You could say I made this cabin, yeah that'll be right, dug the well, set up the garden. That'd be in the 70's and 80's I reckon. Now I know you want to question that, and so on and so forth, but if you go down that road I ain't going to help much -'cos you just going to disappear and I can't be chasing after'.

As I listen I feel myself stabilising and realise that questioning is making me insensitive to what is actually happening -but nonetheless I must ask about something's.

In Danger of Disappearing

'Can I just ask about disappearing -what do you mean disappear?'

'I'll tell you a bit about that', Don hunches his shoulders and looks at me quizzically. 'You are identifying everything you see as if it's on the same level -like its all solid. Fact is nothing is -not even in the physical world. In this life what you focus on affects your consciousness, not just the thoughts in your head, but everything -body and soul. If you're not careful you end up running around like a headless chicken, just reacting'.

He pauses and then says, as if to himself. 'That's mighty apt, even if I say so.' I'm not so sure that it is, but I say nothing. More soberly, he continues, eyeing me all the time, 'I can see, as you call it, what's here, but I don't focus on it unless I got a purpose to do so-'

'But surely', I interject, 'you've got to eat. You're solid', I say poking his arm with my fingers, the chair's solid, the earth's solid, the cabin's solid - everything is solid, so you must need to eat, right?'

'Wrong. Sure I can eat if I want to, like I can smoke', he says producing his corn cob pipe from his pocket, 'but I don't need to. What you reckon as solid isn't so to me, I can see, I can feel but it's not solid', he pauses as if aware his words are not as clear as intended. 'It is so for you right now 'cos you're thinking with the mind of a physical man'.

I am beginning to feel unsettled again; it doesn't come over as an explanation to me. 'Relax, relax your mind Peter'.

He holds me firmly by the shoulder then loosens his grip and pats me gently. 'So you need to know about the physical world, eh? Once am enough I'm thinking. This is how it works. Objective consciousness has its root in physical creation, so everything seen, felt, heard, touched and tasted has its own separate life. That means the experience of life is made up of separate states that are only partially aware of one another. The sun in that world cannot be felt and understood like it is in this. It has being -of course. Its action is necessary to manifest life and affects cycles of birth and death in every living thing. Its power is related to mass and its function affects all physical creation in the solar system. Just imagine for the moment what effect that would have if you were not made of the same stuff?'

'I don't know -what would be the effect?'

'Well, to start with your BodyMind wouldn't relate 'cos it would be functioning in a different mass relationship. It would move into realities that respond harmoniously, the senses developing a different kind of consciousness. That's what happens when the physical BodyMind completes its cycle and life is realised here. We have the sun up here', he says jerking a thumb skyward, 'it looks the same but it ain't the same and it has different effects -to start with it don't generate heat.'

'But we get changes of temperature here, don't we? We get seasons and we get life being born -so what's different?'

'Sure we do and all what you see here has a physical correlate but it doesn't function in the same way. Physical man describes this world as a world of thought -but that don't describe it really. We are having thoughts right now and affecting everything we are aware of. Life doesn't die here - not like it does in the physical world.'

Die -you mean change consciousness?'

'I do -but it's more than that. Look Peter, we can't go any further with this at present -you understand don't you? Your present consciousness is a hybrid struggling to harmonise the earthly mind with this world and that's throwing up all kinds of unanswerable questions. You are in the process of change. Can you remember being conscious without the need to ask questions 'cos the answers were always there?'

I want to say yes but think that the answer is no. 'I guess you do, but right now you have a problem remembering -right?' I nod acquiescently but as I respond inwardly I'm acknowledging there is more than one of me.

'Now you concentrate on what you came to ask the best you can -else a part of you is gonna wake up with a sore head!'

I realise that Don is trying to help and I have to control my thoughts. With an effort of concentration I describe what happened in the desert scene of my last remembering. 'The grey spheres eh? Mighty confusing world that -not to be recommended! So what you want to know?'

'I felt like… like…' I falter trying to find the right words.

'Like you didn't matter?' he ventures.

'Well, yes -I tried to be useful but all I could do was watch.'

'To be useful there you need to be something of a specialist -yes,' he says after a pause, 'and have a particular need to be doing stuff like that.'

'But how could I feel so useless! Given the teaching I've received I should at least have been helpful!'

'I suggest had you been there like you are here, you'd have been more helpful -"

'Why couldn't I be like I am here then?'

'Now hold on young Peter, hold on', he says placing a reassuring hand on my forearm, 'you're trying to run before you can walk'. He takes a deep breath and lapses into silence.

He's trying to calm my mind I'm thinking -. 'OK, OK, I'm listening, I'm sorry'.

'You ain't sorry -you're just frustrated with yourself'. He grins and slaps my arm real hard. 'You felt that -right?'

I grin back -I sure did!

'I said you might have been helpful, but I doubt you would have entered into that state had you been aware of it from here. We need to go back to the beginning, else all this journeying will be so much nonsense -it won't hang together and you'll end up with more questions than you can count and answers that don't solve anything.

'Are we back to the circle teaching again?' I say doubtfully. 'That's right', he says slowly, 'how did you get here -with me?

'I wanted to know that, the last time we talked but-'

'But -you couldn't stay and besides how much can you understand in a session? No, this has to be done in small measures, else what you are trying to do will never be realised. Let's start with you -here and now at this level of existence you are Peter Renaud. You don't have a physical body; in fact you've never had one. You were born in this astral state though you were intended for the physical plane. Your earth mother is French Canadian and still lives in the physical world.

'But I'm not aware of that -this is news to me!' I exclaim.

'You are aware I can assure you but not as I tell it to you now -you won't recall much in your present state because in 1962, earth plane time, as the young unworldly Peter you met with the astral mind of the man Tony and a union was forged'.

'Around the time I began to sign my writing efforts with the name Peter Renault -a pseudonym to hide my own name. Yes?' Don nods in agreement.

'I did that because I thought having a name for dramatic works would allow me other names if I wanted them for poetry and other kinds of writing.'

'Quite -you must understand as Peter you've never had physical existence -your development from a babe to a young man has been in this life. You were destined to meet the man Tony and since then you have been closely associated with his earthly world. He needed awareness of the lower astral worlds to help develop mediumistic powers and you wanted understanding of the incarnate mind. The relationship began in this way - complimentary to each other.'

I'm aware that Don is saying as little as possible, but as he speaks it begins to dawn on me that he is more than a friend. 'And you knew me from before that meeting?'

'Let's just say I've been keeping a fatherly eye on your progress.'

'And?'

'That's the least of it, but that's all I'm saying right now', he says this with an air of finality but then seems to regret having spoken in such a manner and his face creases up into a smile. 'Having said that, the Peter I know is more athletic and doesn't age like Tony in the physical world!'

'So here and now I'm Peter -is that it?' I feel strangely excited by what he was saying.

'A bit of both -life is getting to be problematic for you -has been for a while, but more so now because your earth related self is beginning to wake up on its own account, making demands'.

'What demands?'

'Let's just say -thirst for knowledge, and leave it like that'.

'Oh', I say feeling disappointed by his refusal to say more.

'We'll get to it' he says reassuringly, '-in time as you would say, for the moment you must concentrate on the purpose that brought our meeting about. Suffice to say I am your friend and mentor. Growing pains, that's what you got!' He laughs uproariously repeatedly slapping the arm of his chair.

'Oh, I see, I'm a bit of a problem then?'

Don dissolves into more laughter, his face crinkling up with the effort, tears coming to his eyes. I feel laughter myself, like a small boy experiencing the amusement of others, without knowing what the joke is. Digging in his pocket he pulls out a handkerchief and dabs his eyes.

'Ah, dear me, dear oh dear me, if I go on like this I'll be taking on your condition and then where will I be?' The thought of that seems to sober him up and he continues.

'Thoughts in the physical world are more likely to be intentions than actions -the incarnate Man dreams more than doing. In this world thought is action and changes take place in the twinkling of an eye. If we don't control thoughts we don't control actions upon us. If our purpose is unknown or unclear we are prey to like conditions in other beings -we can idly indulge memory, get caught up in others events. Without direction the Self becomes clouded and identity confused.

I've taught you all this before, but must teach it you again so you can refer to it objectively in the physical world. Your destiny is changing the order of your psyche. You need to understand the same things but differently. In your old self you were never amazed or querulous and you understood without the need of analyses. And you never pushed your luck!'

'But Don -how can I possibly be both those people at the same time!'

'It's back to the circle again -what I tell you has a before and after according to the reasoning mind, but in reality -just call it my reality for the moment, everything is present.'

I'm saying 'Right', but I do not really understand what Don is telling me.

'As events unfurl in your physical mind more will be understood -so long as you are connected to the earthbound body questioning will never cease. It's part of the condition -you must expect it. 'In the grey spheres you are only part of what you are now -there the instinct of physical survival is still a powerful force. It limits your awareness as it limits those who have just died but there are some who have trained themselves to express in those spheres, to help them that are lost and in need of a guide'.

He lapses into silence again and I can feel the warmth of his being as he stands framed in the light -I sense harmony and order within him and in comparison I feel insubstantial and unbalanced. 'You will help me, won't you Don?' I say anxiously. He turns slowly, his eyes smiling.

'I will surely be in trouble if I don't. Off with you -I do believe you could wear me out Peter Pan!' He is laughing again, shaking his head and lifting that handkerchief to his eyes -and that is the last thing I remember.

My head is buzzing with recollection but my body won't have it; I feel well but too tired to think. I lay there barely conscious of Pam by my side and unsure of what world I inhabit. My dog sleeps outside our bedroom door and is noisily licking her hindquarters –it's a long time before I can make sense of the sounds. Eventually I call out and silence her.

Chapter TWELVE:
Shapes and Snakes

Where do I go from here?

My mind is in turmoil –half excited, half fearful. In the wake of Don's revelations I can no longer think of Peter in a detached manner –he is part of me as I am part of him. It's beginning to dawn on me that the supreme self control I've always had over matters psychic is the product of two selves.

It's also clear now my youthful self that manifests during periods of psychic expression, so often remarked on by others, is more Peter than me. It was easy to dismiss these observations as a younger man –my ego then was happy to accept such 'compliments'. Now older, care lined and less interested in personal acceptance I understand better that such observations don't result from tricks of light. These 'youthful impressions' are caused by psychically generated energies overshadowing my conscious form. The ability to 'switch in and switch out' of psychic expression is not so much a result of long training as the product of two selves.

Silver Wing –am I to think of her as another self in me? As a medium actively working to provide services for others, there are other astral world communicators I'm aware of who help and guide my efforts –are they as separate and different as I think I know them, or are they like Peter and Silver Wing, incarnations of a soul being of which I am part?

Shapes and Snakes

And this sense of detachment I've grown used to in many years of psychic practise –knowing it's my feminine mind that makes easy communion with peoples' finer sensibilities? Is that some kind of mix of mentalities, of Peter and Silver Wing? When I close down after working psychically I feel 'removed' from what I have done. The memory of it disappears almost immediately making it impossible to field questions from my recipients. The need to disappear into an environment that is not associated with the psychic self will take me off fishing, model making or simply doing manual tasks as 'man about the house'. If I don't take a break from psychic expression my sense of identity blurs and I begin to criticise all that I do. Are these breaks a necessity that arises from being different selves –my body being an instrument for them all?

How have I come to be such a person?

I was brought up in a very material down to earth environment; my mother, a farmer's daughter escaped servitude (that's how she describes it) when she married my father, a carpenter and builder, earthy and practical to his fingertips. Neither my mother nor father showed any interest in psychic matters –although it must be said that my mum has a natural attunement with nature, being an amazing green fingered magician. My elder brother has had a career as a flight engineer and my younger brother as a civil servant. Both have their feet in the solid earth. Memories of my grandparents don't suggest they were overtly psychic; my paternal grandfather was a builder and a religious man and his wife an invalid.

My mother's father who I liked immensely would recite to me a poem about the virtue of money after which he would laugh until the tears rolled down his cheeks. A country man to his fingertips, on understanding I wanted to be a sailor he suggested I should start as an admiral and work my way down! No. Hereditary influence and key relationships in my young life provide no clues as to my nature. By the time I was 14 however, it was clear to me I was the 'black sheep' of the family.

After my Navy days were cut short and I saw my P45 for the first time, what did I do? I did labouring, painting and decorating jobs and then completely out of family character –became a professional dance instructor. I showed no inclination in my youth for such fancies, but as they say necessity is the mother of all invention. There I was in a strange city without friends so I enrolled in classes at a local dance school –at the very least I'd meet other people and who knows maybe get a girl friend?

Imagine my surprise when I discovered I was good at it! A little over a year later I gained a professional qualification as an Associate of the

International Dance Masters Association (AIDMA) and began teaching in a local dance club. It was a lifestyle that suited my character; openly gregarious I enthused over my job and the social life that went with it, and when I wasn't working I became inwardly contemplative, bashing away on my typewriter aiming to be a playwright.

I would get the most amazing dialogues, pure Shakespearean that would chatter away in my skull whilst I was steering a dance hopeful about the floor and teaching steps at the same time. Needless to say I didn't write them down, after all it was not what I intended – I aimed to write in the modern idiom. The questioning analytical adult had yet to be born –else I might have behaved differently. To start with I'd question why I was thinking in the Shakespearean idiom when I hadn't read his plays for years –besides it had happened before in my navy days and I just put it down to an overactive imagination.

Was I being psychic? It never entered my head to think so; anymore than when as a naval rating I watched blips travel across the radar screens when others more proficient than I said there were none. Even after I had been packed off to Haslar Hospital for further examination I still didn't register anything unusual –it was an eye problem. I was you might say beginning 'to smell a rat' on being discharged medically unfit for duty, but there's a whole lot of difference between knowing and sensing something you can't explain. In the flush of youth I was not looking back, not for one second.

Nobody can describe me as an idle person; those who know me recognise I'm a workaholic. I always have a to-do list as long as your arm and don't understand the 9-5 mentality. As an analyst in the computer industry I would arrive home, change my clothes and commence 'work' of a different kind. Right now the usual motivating forces are not having effect.

Work of any kind is difficult –reactions to journeying are making me introspective. How does it all fit together? It's like being read selective chapters from a book; interesting but frustrating. What about the missing bits?

I've decided I must have a break from these communications – if only to steady up, but also in hope that in their absence I will be able to accept more easily what has occurred. I've asked my communicators, including Omar, to help me achieve this.

For a while I successfully focus my energies on teaching, healing, charity and business work –I even manage to have more of a home life! After a couple of days of this, late at night ensconced in my sofa chair watching TV with half closed eyes I drop my guard and allow myself to think of the dual nature within.

Suddenly I'm there (wherever there is), in a world of shadows lit by strange lights and moving luminous snakes of energy. It's like looking through darkened glass at shapes connected by conduits of light. Nothing is clear-cut –it's white and smoky yet arrestingly three dimensional, here and there energy glows in colour, concentrated in lines and irregular shapes.

After a moment I feel less amazed and am able to acknowledge my surroundings. I'm walking, kind of gliding, half in and half out of a dark mass sucking at my body as I move. Forms like misshapen human beings – squat, with tendrils of light moving about them partially appear out of a dark cloud like base of energy to which I'm connected. This dark mass lightens from a deep black to light luminous grey at eye level and I make out shapes of buildings, forms familiar from the world I know in day-to-day consciousness.

'I hear a familiar voice, 'this way Guv'.

I turn to see a youngish man garishly dressed in check trousers and jacket. His hair is oily black, stylish and long giving him a spiv-like appearance. I recognise him as one of my communicators.

'Is that you Georgie?'

'It's me Guv –stick with me Guv, I'll see you're alright.'

As we speak I am lifted up from the dark mass and the grey surroundings are lighter and softer now –more like dove grey. I'm relaxed and inwardly warmed by Georgie's presence. A sense of expectancy is fulfilled –this event is 'arranged'.

He cocks his head inviting me to follow and moves off as if treading a firm but invisible ground beneath. I move in much the same way –except he seems to be doing this more quickly and more ably than I am. He turns, 'see the light area Guv?'

I can, the grey atmosphere ahead is lighter and tinged blue –it opens up around Georgie as he moves ahead.

'Catch up then'.

I focus on his position and find I get close quickly –as I move I'm conscious of the immediate atmosphere exuding vitality and the amorphous shapes and snakes of energies encompass our position. From out of this a rounded structure of greyish material, like a huge dish, forms ahead

71

surrounded and permeated by coloured lines and dark blobs. The energies about this dish shape are silvery grey, brighter in some places than others.

'What is it?'

'It's a fountain Guv, that silvery stuff is water –see the dark grey colours around the edges? That's stone. Now look more closely –see them other shapes?'

As we move close the entire edifice appears translucent making it difficult to determine what is separate from what. Dark shapes veined in silvery light threads move about; some grouping together others singular. These forms clearly occupy the space I'm looking at but they are on the move all the time and I find it impossible to form a relationship with the phenomenon as these shapes dissipate, grow and shrink in arbitrary sequences –every now and then a shape will blaze with small balls of light that glow as they move within the shape.

I'm nonplussed. 'What's this then Georgie?'

'That's yer fountain with people round it –now come in a bit closer'. He points to a moving trajectory of small balls of light darting here and there – then again points to others that are stationary and holds a hand up to them. He grins at me, 'them are pigeons'.

I move closer to the structure and feel as if I'm joining myself to the activity about it. Forms seem to pass through me –they are mostly indistinct and grey like but some brighter than others give the impression of being people. As I acknowledge this to myself I begin to hear muffled unintelligible base sounds of human voices. I can see faded features of people's heads and bodies. Some images shimmer as they move.

'Is this real Georgie?'

'Oh, its real enough Guv –keep watching'. He sounds very matter of fact, standing there beside me, hands in pockets now with an apparent air of disinterest in proceedings.

'Just watch yer'self Guv, don't get hooked in to any of that chat'.

How's that possible I wonder –the sounds are unintelligible. Every now and then the muffled voices become a little more distinct and I'm able to distinguish male and female voices. George's own voice is clear and resonates easily with an unmistakable cockney accent but all around it sounds like a badly tuned radio station – I'm picking up sounds of music, and thumping sounds that might be moving machinery of some kind. The atmosphere is beginning to feel oppressive and I try to concentrate on the conversational noise.

'I 'ave to prepare me self to come here', Georgie says, 'it's a bit like doing porridge'.

'Where is here exactly –can you say?

'Trafalgar Square Guv'

'Wow! What time of day is it?'

'Gawd –afternoon'ish –it don't matter much does it Guv?'

He's making sense –it looks neither like night or day. I'm finding it an effort to put thoughts together. 'I guess I'm trying to understand if its real time – I mean time as it is in the physical world'.

'It can't be can it Guv? You're in my world now, vibes are different 'ent they? I'm slowing up so to speak to get here – so are you as it 'appens, so we pick up on it. For what it's worth this in your same day cycle, 'cos at the moment your uvvah self is fast asleep'.

Georgie sounds confident –obviously he knows what he's talking about. 'So my other self is sleeping now -right?'

'Sort of.'

I'm intrigued, 'Sort of what?'

'One self is sleeping –the other is here. Look at yer'self –yer missus wouldn't recognise you!'

I'm dressed in a light green coverall cling fitting costume –I feel tall and slim. My hands look distinctly feminine. I'm not surprised, I fact I feel quite comfortable and begin to laugh at my questioning self.

'Yer body's a bit different ennit?' Georgie says laughing with me. Been changing see – can you remember getting into a spot of bovver Guv and me 'elping you out?'

Instantly I do remember – one of my earliest astral experiences. At a time when they included walking through walls and finding myself standing aimlessly in the road outside of my flat. On the occasion he is referring to I was surrounded by figures in black and struggling to regain my earthly consciousness, feeling very scared of a man bearing down on me, a very tall man in strange dress. A paralysis prevented me running away, then Georgie appeared and in language too ripe to mention here warned the visitor to back off. This was many years ago. Although I had been made aware of Georgie by my teacher Len, that astral experience was the first of its kind.

'You were trying to get around then using your brain mind – in real time, as you call it. In that state yer influence on situations in this world am limited. You can get yourself into 'ot water like that. I pulled you out so you didn't do yer 'self a mischief'.

'Mischief?'

'Damage Guv –damage to the astral body and mess you up as a medium; it's sorted now. You and Peter 'ave got it taped'

He lifts his arm and points around, 'see what yer done now with all them questions – it's all changed ennit?'

The silvery energy has turned decidedly smoky; the translucent nature of the scene had vanished. I feel uncomfortable and look at Georgie feeling somewhat guilty.

'No 'arm done Guv, our little chat 'as taken us away, that's all. 'Ere see, you can't have it both ways, like you can't think at one level and do at another. Anyways I was about to take you on to something more interesting'. He straightens his necktie and smoothes his jacket.

'Tidy does it for where we're going', he says grinning cheekily, 'and you'll do as yer are. Keep yer eye on me now –don't want to drift off do yer? ' I suppress the desire to question and keep his form in my vision as I realise we are moving, the atmosphere brightening between us.

A Gothic like doorway appears ahead, above which are arched windows, soft powdery grey in appearance. Tiny swirls of colour illuminate the frames and like the fountain structure seems to grow out of a dark mass. We glide in through the window area and on doing so the atmosphere becomes light and dreamy. Images of people in statuesque pose and painted pictures depicting men and women, singly, in groups and historical scenes appear through a grey blue mist opaquely. Forms like I'd seen at the fountain move about; tubular extensions of white and coloured light seemingly attached to them. It feels like a museum or church.

I whisper to Georgie, 'Are we in a church?'

'Sort of Guv, sort of –you just hang on and listen about, the language that some of these nobs come out with ain't churchlike'.

The grey bluish atmosphere appears to be getting more dense – yet bright and full of vitality. I seem to have lost my sense of movement, as indistinct forms I take to be human are congregated in front of us.

Georgie is very close and speaks quietly into my left ear. 'Now just listen Guv, don't try so hard, jes listen'.

It's a humming noise I hear, an irregular pattern comprising dull lumpy and high-pitched sounds. As I continue to listen the sounds become words I recognise as English. It's an animated conversation, sounding alternatively defensive, analytical, and enthusiastic. The conversation bandies to and fro but I'm not able to make out sentences or understand the sense of what is being said.

'Keep listening Guv,' Georgie urges.

Gradually it's becoming clearer, I hear a woman saying "It would be better, much more workable with the amendment that George is tabling but it's still a dog's dinner". Other voices, male this time, chorus in approval – again I hear the woman's voice. It's strident and a little hard, "-Have to accept it's the best we're going to get. If we hold out then they'll bring in the guillotine and we won't even get that –we can't hope to overturn it"

"Have a drink Gwen!"

"It'll stand up –its work well done!"

There are long rumbling sounds and nothing further heard makes any sense. I turn to Georgie. 'Don't tell me this is parliament!'

'You bet it is –it's the so-called tea rooms – now follow me, got a bit more to show you'

We move into what looks like an enclosed energy space; opaqueness suggests the walls of a building with a high roof. Dark and light greyish shades show structural forms within. It feels like a church. A sense of being in the past is overwhelming and I'm vaguely aware of countless ghost-like forms wherever I look. The roof looks more like a grey featureless sky and the atmosphere impersonal. Underfoot its firm, yet the walls and structures within the building are below and above our position. I am beginning to feel disorientated.

'Focus here Guv, where it's lighter.'

Georgie points to an area that looks like a complex of patterned energies, showing up as such because of lightness in the grey white energy behind it. I focus on it and see a filigree sculpted wooden structure taking shape.

'Whatever this place is it lacks warmth Georgie.'

'Cos yer in a place of stone an' the natural energies 'ave strong roots in the earth; people of the physical world 'ere play second fiddle'.

The area I am focussing on is beginning to show strong light in places and it feels like I'm looking at a building within a building. An array of lightly coloured tubes some being quite thick and rounded, loop and bend; others are like the tendrils of roots, squiggling about in the structure.

'What am I supposed to be looking at?'

'Keep looking an' leave off the questions Guv – you'll know soon enough'. As I watch this array of light and form I become connected with the movements I am observing. I sense intelligence at work but I can't make any sense of it. I'm losing awareness of my surroundings, light emitting from the swirl of tubes and tendrils is becoming intense – until suddenly all forms merge and I see through the mass. I am looking down into the nave of a church. A ceremony is taking place and I immediately recognise it as a coronation. Everything is in colour and clear.

On a throne and surrounded by a host of clergy is a man who I know immediately as Prince William of Orange. Seated on the throne next to him is his wife Mary. They both wear coronation crowns and before them are a large congregation of people sumptuously dressed, many in ermine like robes. I can see someone kneeling before William and hear the solemn tones of an oath being sworn. Stirring music fills the air. My vision is now panoramic as I gaze at the internal architecture of Westminster Abbey. Then as quickly as it came it vanishes and the indistinct greyish surroundings of before return.

'Better than yer TV ain't it?'

'Incredible!' I feel quite excited. 'And I knew it was the Prince of Orange Georgie –how would I know that?'

'You pick it up. This place is full of events like that an' others besides – some not so nice'. Then as an afterthought he added, 'an' I can even show you where he had his pocket picked'. He laughs. 'He was the smart one!'[9]

'How does it all happen, Georgie?'

He shrugs his shoulders. 'They're impressions, recordings like. Your physical world creates 'em all the time.' He adds, 'even our chat is being recorded.'

'So even in this world activities get recorded?'

'They do 'ere at this level'. He stops and looks at me meaningfully, 'Look Guv, I can see what yer gettin' at but we can't deal with that 'ere, not the right place, see? Besides your pumpkin coach is going to disappear, its time you returned'. I feel disappointment. 'I'm just getting into this.'

---

[9] Curious of this comment I did some research. A rumour started after the coronation that the Prince had his pocket picked on his way from Whitehall to Westminster since it became apparent in the ceremony neither he nor the Queen had the necessary token gold pieces on their persons. As I recall George's comment, his tone suggests that it was the Prince who was the clever one –maybe he had no intention of bringing gold or knowing he would be pressed on by the crowds had coins of less value to disperse.

'I know Guv –but there are some things you can't have both ways. – Come on, stay close and I'll take you on a bit before you return.'

Again the atmosphere changes, the impression of history fades as we glide forward in a cocoon of light that appears to be a large pulsating tube. Banging and whooshing sounds assail my consciousness. Instinctively I put my hands over my ears.

'This noise is confusing Georgie.'

'Jes focus on yer sense of smell and it'll fade out,' Georgie advises. Far from showing signs of discomfort he appears unfazed by the noise.

For a while I struggle to work with this sense and then suddenly it's happening and sounds fade. I smell vegetables and flowers and see objects that look like tables with food produce upon them.

Balls of light are dancing everywhere. Long snake like luminous rods wriggle and twist and turn all over the place. The light show is fascinating. I glimpse people moving about the scene and sense a busy and lively environment. No one takes notice of the lights.

Every now and then a face and part of a person's body comes into focus. I appear to be looking at them through gauze. A hum of conversation is apparent which makes me feel relaxed and happy. Gradually the light show fades and the forms of people develop, colour of dress and place becomes clearer – it's like a scene from the fifties.

'This feels like a market place Georgie.'

'Well, it is – it's Covent Garden, that's what it is.'

We are moving over this scene and the fascia of a building comes into focus. As we get to it the wall of brick changes colour and becomes a dark grey mist.

'Careful Guv, things can change quickly like.'

I am very relaxed and curious to move forward.

'I'm fine, come on let's explore.'

Enthused with a childish sense of adventure I glide forward with Georgie following behind –his presence reassuring me. It's a dwelling and feels familiar. I see a drop leaf table and dining chairs, and a sideboard on top of which are photos in frames and a glass dish filled with fruit. I hear clearly the sound of a woman calling, her voice sharp and edged with concern.

"Sandra, Ester come on when I call yer – make it snappy". She bangs a pot or pan and I feel its metallic ring pass through my body. The scurry of feet and two diminutive forms sweep past shouting, "coming Mum, coming". –They sound breathless and excited.

"Git them coats on – come on sharpish now, can yer hear it?"

I listen for what she refers too and make out a wailing noise that grows in volume and sounds like a banshee. It's a siren. I hear a door bang as mother and children leave the house. I move into a passage and pass out of the building through a doorway. I'm through the door before I realise I haven't attempted to open it.

The scene is quite amazing, everything looks physical; I'm looking out on a street of terraced houses – it's either early evening in faded light or its overcast, I can't tell which, but the doors and windows and the pavement are very clear. A skipping rope with wooden handles lies on the step of the house close by. I see pigeons picking their way through the gutters. A yellow painted barrow half laden with vegetables is parked across the street. There's not a person in sight but from somewhere I hear people talking, laughing and the sound of feet on pavement.

I look up and down the street again and can see no one. The siren has stopped wailing and I can hear deep rending sounds somewhere ahead of me and the sky lights up and goes dark again. The ground trembles with a shock wave and I become aware of myself and suddenly feel claustrophobic.

'Seen enough Guv?' I can hear Georgie but can't see him. I'm feeling vulnerable and alone. 'I guess so Georgie, I guess so – where are you?

'Remember them smells from the market?'

'Well, sort of.'

'Well, sort of concentrate on them Guv – how about some peaches, apples and tangerines, eh? Make you feel hungry?'

I'm beginning to feel the taste – particularly the oranges. I can sense Georgie is beside me and hear the noise of people talking loudly.

'Recognise where you are then?'

I'm not in the street anymore – it's more like a square. I make out the forms of carts loaded with produce and people milling to a fro, but it's different from the market place we passed through. I notice a van with its doors open and crates of oranges inside and a young lad lifting them out.

'Where am I now Georgie?'

'Same place – different time – same place, that is, before you buzzed off down memory lane. More my time this is. Now it's 'bout time you got back – so grab 'old of me 'and'. Obediently, I reach out and grasp his hand. He pulls and I feel as if my arm is stretching and I'm getting lighter. His voice sounds tinny.

'Old London can be seen again if you want – it's my patch see'. I can't see him as I'm absorbed by the sound of air rushing past me.

'Time flies, don't it?'

And with that remark everything goes black. I have in mind Georgie's impish grin and realise that the sounds I'm listening to are coming from the television.

Georgie Barker

Figure 6

Shapes and Snakes

Chapter THIRTEEN:
Shifting Sands

It takes an age to orientate -Pam has nodded off and I glance at the TV and realise that the film she has been watching is ending. Loudly I tell her I agree that the film was good. She wakes up with a jolt complaining of missing the finish, not at all convinced I saw it either. 'You've been snoring for ages!'

Ages? I don't think so, but what am I to say? Yet again I'm not prepared to talk about my astral experience; I need time to assimilate what has happened. Its way past midnight now and my dog is anxious to get out for her bedtime walk. Leaving Pam half asleep on the sofa I fit Kya with her collar and leave the house.

Walking the silent streets in the February cold air I recall much of what took place. The event had me in new territory -in more senses than one. Peter and I in some dual sense are there and if I'm not mistaken the 'relationship' seems less fraught. I question and recall earthly memory without that unsettled feeling I've had in the Don communications. Making contact with Georgie makes me feel good.

I first knew of him as a communicator who occasionally spoke through my teacher Len when he was in trance. He's quite a character and the séance room rocked with laughter when he was present. In later years, when Len was no longer practising trance, Georgie would occasionally speak through me in psychic development groups. When speaking with my pupils he would always refer to me as the 'Guv'.

Shifting Sands

I can understand why it was London, (Georgie is a Cockney) but I'd never psychically experienced conditions like that before. It felt like I was between worlds, in some kind of celestial recording studio. The event amazes me the more I think of it.

I recall Don's words half questioning my purpose and other communications that hint at a plan of some sort - What plan? I ask myself. I don't get an answer and I don't see a pattern in my journeys to date. As I walk the empty streets appraising the cold star bright sky I am reminded that the starlight and the stars are separated by aeons of time. Appearances are deceptive -yet Georgie confirmed to me that the event was in real time. I'm unsettled. Having got an answer to my question I now question my question - what in God's name is real time?

My dog is doing better than I am - she has no ambition to exceed her territory, the 'what' of things don't concern unless they directly affected her well being. Shouldn't I try to live like that? Sensible or not, I know that I can't, I have to satisfy the need to know why these journeys are taking place.

A new day dawns and I breathe a great sigh of relief and Pam is all smiles - the credit card company says my account will be credited the money I've been trying to get back - and with interest too! So I'm light of step leading Kya on her morning walk. We head for the 'bone yard' and duly arrive without incident (I take special care now crossing the road by the florist!). Today Kya has a penchant for drinking from flowerpots on graves. Not a good idea! Such pots I see are either muddy or green with algae. As I walk between the rows of graves I come across a standpipe, a stone bowl at its foot. Just the job I think and two fills later Kya is no longer looking for flowerpots to drink from.

The following day I make a beeline for the standpipe taking care to avoid another run around the flowerpots. I can't find it. The next day I walk up and down the criss-crossing paths still searching for the elusive standpipe. I'm incredulous, how can I not find it? I give up the search and start the walk back home. Kya pulls at the lead wanting to take a circuitous route back]. 'C'mon sweetheart I've things to do' - I admonish, but I let her have her way because I'm a softie where animals are concerned.

And there is the missing standpipe large as life. I look around - how many times have I done this trip? It's here sure enough. I look at the gravestones nearby and recognise I've passed by them before in my search and I'm damn sure my head has not been in the clouds.

On the walk back home I'm thinking about this -has a time slip occurred? Is it possible for me to be absent from the physical world in some way, yet in all appearance be present? Can I be in two places at the same time? My analytical mind begins to work. Back in the summer of last year I began an experiment; I started to smoke cannabis resin. My purpose was to discover if my trance ability, now only manifesting sporadically, might be restrained by some kind of subconscious blockage. I came to this view, as mentally in the aftermath of trance I had begun to feel unduly sensitive and questioning of the expression. If the trance was light and I had awareness during transmission, I would feel dissatisfied, thinking I was suppressing it. After sessions in deeper trance I would be saying to myself -'thank God that's done with', and despite the blandishments of my pupils would set my mind against allowing it to happen again. I had done trance work for over thirty years -I asked myself was I losing the ability or was I unconsciously interfering?

I turned to one of my pupils who I knew smoked hash from time to time and who had a shaman guide. She agreed to help and having never smoked before I needed guidance on preparing and smoking a joint. After a few puffs I could feel my body inwardly vibrating and my physical character changing. As this developed an oriental communicator known to me as Chan physically and mentally began to control my expression. He advised my pupil of the time period of cannabis influence and spoke of energy changes. These were effortless expressions and in their aftermath I felt balanced and calm. Over a period of six weeks I smoked in session with my pupil three times -I would smoke about half a joint on each occasion and the effects I have described were similar in every session.

My trance work continued and the after effects that had been concerning me disappeared. I concluded from this that somehow smoking hash had released a subconscious blockage. As I had no interest in cannabis as a pleasure drug and it had served its purpose, I stopped the smoking sessions.

Some weeks later whilst driving home from a Sussex based group I was teaching I had switched on a favourite radio programme, treated myself to a bar of chocolate and settled back into the driving seat to enjoy the music. My mind was completely calm and had suffered no ill effects after manifesting trance that evening in Midhurst. The A272 road is narrow in places and without street lighting until it passes through Rogate on the way to Petersfield. It was dark and whenever the oncoming traffic passed I switched to full beam to ensure I could see clearly the road ahead and react to sightings of foxes, rabbits and badgers.

Shifting Sands

I looked out at one point on my journey and was suddenly aware of not knowing where I was -I thought nothing of it because as all drivers know you can in the familiarity of driving become oblivious of passing landscape. I drove on no longer paying any attention to the music until I became aware of familiar landmarks on the passing roadside. With a jolt I realised that I was well past the village of Rogate with its shining street lamps, tall church steeple and picturesque pub -I was nearly at the intersection between Petersfield and Liss. I thought hard but the harder I thought the more it made no sense. Somehow I had passed through Rogate and several miles thereafter without the slightest awareness of it.

How long had I been on 'auto pilot?' I made a quick calculation - it was near on 8 minutes! The village of Rogate and miles thereafter simply had not existed. I toyed with the idea of getting the map out to check distance. Given my usual attention to the road for fear of running down animals I could only conclude that something had happened to my relationship with the constant of time and space.

Other time problems occurred thereafter - as I pride myself on being an organiser it comes as a shock when something you remind yourself about one minute, totally disappears from consciousness only to reappear later after the event. At first I thought this was absent mindedness and redoubled my efforts to ensure 'my reminders' stayed in place -but still they would disappear and I would get a strange feeling on remembering as if the intended action belonged to someone else. How could this be an effect from smoking cannabis? These time out problems occurred many weeks after stopping smoking.

Pam, sensitive as ever, knew that something was changing and sat me down to describe the transit of Uranus across my ascendant that was occurring at that time - this she said represented a time of significant change. I couldn't help but agree but was unable to articulate why. I was becoming increasingly interested in elemental energies as these nature spirit forces had manifested during the smoking sessions, the room temperature noticeably changing. This revived in me the interest that had previously surfaced when conducting psychic outward-bound courses in the New Forest some years previous. It was here that the communicator I knew then simply as 'Wolf' manifested in trance sessions.

Three months passed thereafter and no further 'unbalancing' effects occurred before the start of these journeying events with Omar on the banks of the Shalimar.

Did some kind of mind shift occur as a result of my smoking experiment, or was it simply coincidental to changes taking place in my psyche - preparing me for the journeys that began in January 2005? Are my recent journeys and 'time out' conditions before and since expressions of my changing consciousness? I feel as if I'm standing on shifting sands -the stability we take for granted at the root of our consciousness no longer guaranteed.

Chapter FOURTEEN:
The Greatest of all Adventures

Almost a week passes and nothing unusual occurs during my dog walking visits to the bone yard. I'm very relaxed and dutifully take Kya to the standpipe and stone bowl to drink before turning for home. At the time I remind myself that I haven't yet reorganised the charity's library as I promised I would in the Christmas period. Unaccountably my mind begins to drift and whilst fully conscious of the world about me I have vision of being in another place. I am in a spacious room panelled with library shelves, high walled with tall windows through which sunlight streams onto carpet and furniture.

I'm sitting in a round backed chair - other chairs and small tables suggest this is a public reading room. I am alone. There's a large heavy looking door to my right and one much like it to my left. I sit looking out the windows conscious of a well maintained garden, listening to the sounds of nature; flower stems stretching and turning in a wind breezing through the herbaceous borders and the faint sounds of occasional birds. The door to my right opens and a tall distinguished gentleman with grey hair and spectacles enters. His dress is 19th century and I immediately recognise him as one of my communicators, Edward Everett.[10]

---

[10] Edward Everett, scholar, statesman, and one of America's most brilliant orators was born in Dorchester Massachusetts 11th April 1794. A graduate of Harvard he was appointed to the chair of Greek and later became its president. He was a member of congress, governor of Massachusetts and an ambassador to England, Secretary of State succeeding Daniel Webster, a

He carries a tray, two glasses and a flagon of water, which he sets down on the table before me. I am immediately struck by the familiarity I feel - this is not the first meeting of its kind. He in turn showing no surprise at my being here pulls up a chair and sits down.

'A glass of water perhaps?'

I nod assent and he speaks pleasantly about the surroundings as he half fills two glasses. 'It really is a charming room and raises one's spirits instantly on entering -do you find it so?'

'I do', I agree, 'but must confess I'm a little disorientated, more concerned with who I am than where I am, if you see what I mean.'

'Well, of course you will be -let me say immediately that you are as near as you can be to your physical mind state. This place was chosen deliberately to put you at ease in harmony with your selves. I think it provides the perfect backdrop to our discussions'.

'Then you are fully aware of what I'm brooding about?' I'm saying this lightly, almost too embarrassed to mention it.

'Completely understandable, I doubt however the physical world would understand your dilemma. Doctors of the mind would no doubt attempt to. I was expecting your request'

'Expecting?'

'You are not alone in your endeavours I assure you. May I call you Peter? We must be careful not to invoke your earthly mind more than we must'

'Well, of course', I say warily, 'and I may call you Edward?'

'Indeed, though as you know I will answer to Pegasus readily enough', he says laughingly.

It is interesting and reassuring to experience his humour. In all earthly communications Edward is received as a serious minded man of lofty ideals; a Greek scholar, orator, politician and churchman. I've long since known the Pegasus symbol is his chosen means of representing himself on occasions.

United States senator and a nominee for President. Before the outbreak of the American Civil ware he made strenuous efforts to prevent a rupture between North and South. He gave the oratorical address at Gettysburg, though history remembers Abraham Lincolns' short address that followed his. He died in 1865.

Seeing him so relaxed makes me realise how limited my earthly communication links are.

'Now feel free to ask any question you care to, don't let the idea of time govern how you satisfy your need to understand. Of course, time and its apparent limitation are part of your concern, so let us proceed, in the way you feel best'.

Now faced directly with the opportunity to ask all the questions 'under the sun' I am pensive and find it difficult to bring questions to mind. No doubt aware of my struggle he gestures -rest your thoughts; rises and walks across to the bookcase, selects a volume and returns. 'Spinoza's ethics', he proclaims holding it up for my inspection.[11]

'I'm not familiar with that', I say suddenly reminded that Edward's background would have included philosophical studies.

'No, but what he has to say here', he says thumbing the pages, 'will give us a place to start, and help you with your questioning. Ah, here we are - allow me to quote, "The order and connection of ideas is the same as the order and connection of things" He looks up at me with a questioning look.

'I take that to mean events and their causes cannot be separated?'

'Indeed, but it means more than that. Everything is connected to everything else and in a space time relationship connections are sequentially understood. A comes before B etc, and you cannot possibly come to Z without making the necessary 25 previous steps. The problem you are wrestling with is trying to sequentially relate your remembrance of this state with the awareness of your physical mind.' He put careful stress on the word 'remembrance'.

'Yes, yes that's exactly it -here they sort of make sense but on remembrance they just keep throwing up questions my memory seems not able to answer'.

'Here your consciousness is of a different order, but I must add', he said carefully, 'that 'here' has many variables -many more than your earth life being. Spinoza was right when he said that the order and connection of ideas and things are the same. Impulse and effect are one and the same. In this world your relationship with event is known by the impulse whereas in the physical world it is known by the effect. It is different because vibration

---

[11] I should say here that prior to this communication I'd never read anything of Spinoza's philosophy.

rates in the physical world separate impulse from effect to such an extent, that what is viewed cannot be immediately known'.

'But if I have idea and express that -surely it is immediately known?'

'You would think so, wouldn't you? But it's not so my dear -the idea as an impulse is itself an interpretation, an effect. The vibrational rate of your physical being determines that. As I have indicated there are many variables in my world -indeed there are many in the physical world but not nearly so many as here. These variables are vibrational rates of consciousness and that means remembrances you have are necessarily effects of different orders.'

'You are aware of my remembrances?'

'I am'. He smiles, hinting at the enjoyment of a private joke.

'Can you help me out here', I say weakly, 'I'm getting a bit lost'.

'Of course', he rejoins, assuming once again a serious mask, 'your remembrances so far are of three types. Meetings seeking explanation as with Don, Lone Wolf, Omar and now myself, guided experiences as with young Georgie Barker and solitary experiences in which you are apparently your own guide. The guided experiences are controlled environments set in place with the agreement of your higher self and they are all, of a type, different vibrational states.

The questions that arise from these experiences indirectly stimulate other remembrances. Amongst those remembered will be the solitary experiences. These explanations are helpful but I believe there's randomness, an arbitrary release into my consciousness of astral experience - and say as much to Edward.

'Ah', he said, his eyes lighting up, 'yes and no is the answer I'm afraid. Consider the life principle as it is registered in Matter - is there not randomness in this process? Yet one can see design arising from it. Don't be perturbed -there is a design, though I confess it is not fully apparent to me'.

This answer shocks me as I suddenly realise I'm assuming he know all the answers to my questions.

'So you don't have all the answers?'

He laughs. 'My dear Peter, no one has all the answers -not in the physical world as you know it, not here in this world either. All men arise in this world with that assumption - thereby hangs a tale!'

I'm beginning to warm to his candour. Leaning forward I grasp the glass of water and dip my finger into it. 'A watery tale perhaps?'

'Excellent my dear!' He says slapping his thigh enthusiastically.

The Greatest of all Adventures

'Indeed it is a watery tale'. He pauses for moment as if savouring the phrase. 'Men are mainly water based creatures on arising in this world. The mental and emotional body that is built from the physical root of consciousness is largely unconscious of the impulses that create it, a void that instinctively Man fills with the assumption that on arising, into heaven as he would say, all will be explained'.

'And it isn't you say?'

'Far from it my dear -re-education is the order of the day on arising'.

'Everything?' I'm sounding incredulous.

'Well, yes, but I can see that the answer is going to leave you with a headache on remembering, so let me explain it thus. When a snake sloughs its skin a new skin has already grown -you agree?'

I nod eager for the explanation.

'The old skin and the new skin whilst they appear to be of the same nature clearly can't be exactly the same as they are separated. The new skin grows, at first thin and only partially constituted until it performs all the functions of the old skin'.

'But then it is the same as the old skin', I interject.

'It looks the same or similar shall we say -but no, it is not exactly the same. The functions are the same but the snake is more alive and able because of the change. The inner vitality of the creature gradually confers itself to the new skin. Human beings on arising must undergo such a change -nature demands it'.

Fascinated by his explanation I urge him to tell me more.

'On arising the shedding of the physical form an immediate vitality is apparent, youthful feelings are generated and the outer image of a risen person will often reflect this change. Consciousness however is still restricted -strong memories are attracted to the sources that constituted them in the physical world and the change of vibratory existence produces perspectives different from those that brought such memories into being. At the same time the present order of the new world will attract and change outlook, and so the process of re-education begins.'

Edward stops speaking (even though I am willing him not too) and slowly drinks from the glass before him. These explanations are satisfying but it whets my appetite still further. I stand and walk across to the bookcases. Titles of all kinds are present, many old volumes on philosophy and the sciences, biographies, novels and -I notice with surprise modern works, in particular I notice the books of Carlos Castaneda, having read them all with great interest.

Taking out one called the 'Inward Reality' I return to Edward and hold it up to his view. 'This is a surprise; I expected only to find old books'.

'Ah, yes a most perceptive fellow. He's a very good example of opposites attracting'.

I wait for further comment but as none is forthcoming, I say 'You know about this -the strange worlds he writes about?'

'I am aware', he smiles and adds, 'but you haven't read that one.'

'Oh, I've read all his books'

'Not this one you haven't. It was not written in the physical world.'

I look again -is he right the title sounds familiar?

'As you have been taught there are many worlds of Spirit, but ultimately there is only one. In your quest you will discover many -men are part of creation, there are many parts. What is it that Don has been teaching you?'

I thought for a moment, recalling experience. 'What goes around comes around?'

He put his arm about my shoulder and we walk back to the bookcase where he takes the book from my hands and places back to where I'd taken it. Quickly I scan Castaneda's works —there are more than I expect to see. I manage to read the title of one I don't know - it's called 'In a World of Open-Headed Men'. If Edward notices he doesn't say.

'This library was begun by Benjamin Franklin; he in turn drew on sources that time determines are before him. Even now as we stand here seemingly alone, others are using this space -not only men. Some are governed by space and time, they who have yet to change the earthly balance of elements within. Others not so governed, to whom this library intelligence are manifest roads of discovery, embark upon causal journeys; and still more, others who are beings having crossed over from conception unlike our own, add by communing with this library a human measure to their existence. In its own way this library is a circle -just as you and I are. There is no beginning and no end. The oneness that all creation seeks is the ultimate circle -the balance that cannot be disturbed.'

He is now leading me across the library to the other door. I stop and restrain him from opening the door looking him full in the face.

'Yet this striving Edward is the greatest of all adventures!'

He laughs and squeezes my shoulder. 'And who could disagree with that?'

The Greatest of all Adventures

'Oh', I say pessimistically, 'there are bound to be some'.

He pushes the large heavy door and as it soundlessly glides open a dark and cold cloud envelops me and at once I feel very small and moved as if taken up by a large hand, claimed back by something or someone who had governance over my being.

Edward Everett

Figure 7

Chapter FIFTEEN:
A Cyclops Tormented

I hurry home anxious to record the detail I remember. My poor dog! She has never been so harried in her life; I disallow the usual stops to harvest smells in my rush home. I rush into the corner shop for the daily paper and the Cambodian lady (pretty as a picture she is) who usually expects a bright breezy hello asks if I'm well. 'Never felt better' I say. She doesn't look convinced and I sweep out before she can reply –must get to my computer and write this down!

Edward's explanations don't flow from my touch type fingers; some phrases I write directly, others elude exact remembering and I compromise with sentences that state what I think he was saying. After a couple of hours work my efforts look like a crossword puzzle half completed. I have to leave it, other matters are pressing. Finance is a worry again, though thankfully not because I've been conned.

My complementary health business is losing money. We can ill afford that and as I can't think how I can improve cash flow and write without my writing being the casualty, I scour living expenses to see what I can cut out.

That evening I return to my communication puzzle and satisfactorily complete it. I look out at the night sky aware of how much my internal sense of time has concertinaed whilst the external physical world has marched relentlessly on and I can hear Edward's voice distant and clear in my head. 'This is why you are here my dear.'

Am I remembering some words of his from the journey just experienced or is he speaking to me now? I simply don't know.

A Cyclops Tormented

I sit back after reviewing my first draft, happy with my efforts yet strangely disturbed. Although I feel I've been taken forward by Edward's explanations, this event is clearly showing I've the ability to relate other astral experiences whilst I'm in process of living another and it's giving me a panoramic sense of involvement. And more –reception of these journey experiences and my subsequent recovery from them is changing. I'm not able to explain why and I don't feel any more in control than I did at the beginning. I feel peculiarly sensitive to the randomness of event –who knows what next might come? This last event is different from the others –I remember and live it, so to speak, simultaneously.

Perhaps the meeting with Edward is clarifying my involvement –that quote from Spinoza referring the order of ideas and things expresses continuity. Am I seeking to express the inexpressible; the relationship of my physical life with 'other selves' resident in unseen worlds? It certainly appears as if I have a key, an ability of some kind, that can unlock the memory of relationships in other states –but it all feels rather odd as I feel I am the least able of all my 'selves'. Maybe I'm being educated on how to use the key? Am I entering into a maze of self-beings with the express purpose of centring myself in a quest to 'unearth' identity itself?

Providing evidence of life after death may be the prime purpose of some mediumistic minds but it's not mine. It's not that I have never provided it –I have, but proof is a very personal thing. Circumstantial evidence may be the touchstone for some whilst others argue the incontrovertible evidence of cross correspondence in their search for objective evidence.

Everything is connected to everything else –that's the underlying message in all my journeys and I'm adopting this premise to guide my analysis. Something that Don says about the connecting of man's limbs crystallises for me what I'm seeking to understand –the links that connect the so-called time related self and eternal being.

As I sit in contemplation my cat fixes me with a questioning look –is it possible I ask myself, can it be done? I am inclined to believe she is more one than I am and her presence passive though it is, challenges the conventional view of man as superior to the animal. Somehow I must glean from what is occurring, understanding that gives men reason to alter their way of being. I am chastened by the thought that my cat doesn't need to know and we who do stumble in the pain of our need; a Cyclops tormented. Our lordship is questionable –very questionable indeed.

Days pass and I tinker with phrases, scratching like a hen for the seed in the dust. It helps and I'm now feeling satisfied I've recorded the most of my conversation with Edward. At long last I feel able to talk about these communications and have long chats with Pam who is fascinated by what I tell her. Yes I agree I am thinking there's a book here –early days but nonetheless a start. Talking about it helps enormously and my mind quietens –I'm looking out at life no longer introspective like a guardian of secrets. I get re-connected and personal and business life gets to be busy again. I feel much more like my old self as the wintry days unfurl and strong winds buffet the house.

Today I elect to clean up the garden. The icy north winds of late are doing their worst in northerly climes and for a change it's pleasant to be outside. I'm clearing away the dead leaves, cutting back the dried stems of plants to make way for a spring renewal. Relaxed and untroubled by material events I am enjoying the closeness of nature. The smell of rosemary is particularly inviting and I linger about the bush sifting the earth for rubbish to dispose when I get the impression of a poem.

"Two buzzards soar high above the hillside

Momentary beings; lords of the sky"

The memory from which my inspiration springs stems from visits I've been making to an elderly couple I know who live on the Sussex Hampshire downs border. I've known them both for some years as healers and members of the Joseph Carey Psychic Foundation charity that I lead. Suffering from liver, gut and cardiac complaints Gwen has asked me for healing treatments. Both Gwen and her husband Philip are animal lovers and avid bird watchers.

The garden of the nineteenth century gamekeeper's house they live in slopes to a valley overlooking the downs and is a veritable paradise of living things. The outhouse is stacked with corn and nuts and every day Philip replenishes the nut cages and spreads corn and bread on the grass. From their living room window one can sit to observe pheasants, blue tits, yellow hammers, wood pigeons and chaffinch and see the garden deserted of birds in a twinkle of the eye as the sparrow hawk descends. Into this cosmopolitan sanctuary come squirrels, rabbit's badgers and foxes. A few days previous they had pointed out two circling buzzards and informed me of their recent observations, giving details of two pairs inhabiting that area.

I'm letting my poetic impression idle in mind and true to the craft seek to change, mix and match word and meaning, to fully express the idea. I'm trying to view the meaning of this couplet through the eyes of the birds. As I concentrate I slip into a kind of haze where no one form dominates

98

awareness. I'm still scrabbling about pulling dead leaves out from under the rosemary bush but a kind of formless space borders my environment.

I'm aware of movement now, a cluster of inexplicable images constantly changing. Is it my feeling sense promoting a kind of vision? Seeing objectively usually gives awareness of what, by depth and boundaries –in my vision the images appear from nowhere like a liquid alternatively taking shape and disappearing. The shapes I see vary in size and time of appearance from blips to long views of snaking colours –colour of intense red, yellow and blue mix to an endless succession of different browns and greens. The mixes continue to vary. Interspersed by white out views I get to feel as if I'm moving. The textures of some images are smooth and matt; others are luminous and glassy looking.

I am aware of some images moving independently –sometimes in straight lines, at other times bending into curves and circles. I am moving, rising up and looking down upon the images. The forms I look at are globular and out of focus but they move and I have the impression of travelling.

I'm intelligent in travel and am able to take particular notice of some images that appear in clusters and swim about in a kind of fluid. Every now and then I sense I am 'standing still' and observing colours and shapes moving independently against this fluid background. As I do the 'landscape' stabilises and looks like a living map. Rivulets of liquid border the coloured globular forms I see giving impression of depth and contour. This is an aerial view of territory.

Something else is happening –what I see is a view of history, yet it is of course present before me. I have the sense of viewing living things –these 'things' are pulsating life forms that are not individual or truly separate but parts of a pattern that live in a momentary world. I feel part of a regulated state and unaware of my individuality.

Now it's changing –a mix of long drawn out sounds interrupted by short tic like noises vibrate my being as I view –I'm not thinking, I am the noise – some kind of music. The images in the landscape suddenly loom large and I feel as if I'm about to collide with this 'map'.

Where am I? Gradually it dawns on me that the forms I am seeing and I'm trying to make sense of are the spaces between the rosemary bush stems. The mystery deepens I 'come to' poised trance like in a squat position, trowel in hand gazing at the twists and turns of rosemary fronds mentally struggling to assert my identity. For a while my awareness is limited to these immediate surroundings and I pulse from within to the earth underfoot. Eventually I articulate thoughts that make conscious sense. My legs are aching and my eyes are stinging. I move slowly testing every centimetre of movement. Space and time begin to fit together. Worldly thoughts are returning and I start to feel very self conscious and out of place. The sound of traffic is baffling and unwelcome. Unsure of balance and feeling alien to my surroundings I totter into the garage and sit down.

People are not welcome. I can feel a rhythmical vibration pulsing inside of me; a kind of winding action. In my minds eye I see the movement of wings. The image and rhythm gradually fades and the noise of everyday life and images of familiar things in my garage become acceptable.

I have healing work later so I wash, change and prepare to drive. I can't think about what has happened –it doesn't make sense. Later that day I sit down to write what I can of the event. Objectively remembering, my visions begin to make some kind of sense –slowly it comes together. I'm thinking I've somehow tapped into the consciousness of buzzards. It's an alien experience yet strangely acceptable to me. The couplet that came into my mind before this experience tantalisingly returns as I walk the dog at midnight. Back in the house I bash away on the keyboard after midnight and produce this:

Lords of the Sky

High above the hillside two buzzards' soar,
Momentary beings: lords of the sky.
Their wings in silhouette
On a thermal chimney write
Poems higher than the tree spires
Unsigned, unexplained.

Know me if you can –they say.

Watching movements I cannot see
They search for food that moves
Always ready to bank and dive
Soundlessly, claws outstretched.
These are natures' patient hunters.
Guided by ever present cosmic maps

A Cyclops Tormented

Over field and copse they fly

Eyeing warily the treads of men.
Their quest to survive never ends
Because end and beginning
Are the same broad wings
Closing, opening, sky dancing
Feathered warm hearts gliding
Moon bathed and sun kissed.

These buzzards have no I to care
They are momentary beings
Expressions of ancient harmony
In a world governed by men;
Manifestations of Right Order
Unconscious lords of the sky.

It's you and me who need a name.

Financial worries are never wanted at the best of times, yet the need to get my conscious world in order is strangely welcome as I'm becoming increasingly aware of a desire to 'let go' and slip into other worlds of consciousness. It's most prevalent when I'm solitary or out walking with Kya. Most times this awareness is no more than feeling, a difference to the outer world inviting me to leave it. The 'door' only needs pushing for me to enter a kind of twilight parallel world where people's actions are ignorant of mine.

I feel like a window peeping Tom in search of intimate experience. The desire to 'journey' is very hard to release; an appetite that won't be satisfied like the gambler knows, when for the umpteenth time he pulls the fruit machine handle expecting three of a kind. I even have this want to detach myself in company –if the conversation doesn't hold my interest some part of me distances itself to some place else. When my conscious responses are challenged I feign deafness and ask for assistance!

Chapter SIXTEEN:
Judgement Day

Physically tired I stretch out my legs in bed but I'm not ready to sleep. My brain is still busy and I love to read thrillers, enjoy the constant anticipation of event as I leaf the page –the unexpected dramatic turn of the screw. Reading is a late night pleasure I selfishly look forward to –even so I sometimes clairvoyantly see people (occasionally more than one person) who are generally complete strangers. It's like that tonight –I'm studiously ignoring the phenomenon, doggedly trying to maintain my understanding of the plot. I want to get to the end of the chapter –

I'm conscious of walking on grass with a group of people, mostly adults; a mix of ages and sex. I feel connected with them but seemingly uninterested to know them individually. The surrounding countryside is very English but nobody is taking much notice of it. There is a general hubbub of polite conversation but nothing in particular is said that I hear. I feel somewhat isolated and different and increasingly aware as we walk that even my closest walking companions don't know that I am there.

It's daytime and the sky is clear and bright. I and the group (around 20 people I estimate) are travelling with purpose –heading somewhere with the same intention. I've hardly begun to assess the situation when the group slows and stops. We are now spreading out over a rise of ground to view a cemetery. Some, mostly the elderly, sit whilst I and others stand behind them. In the hollow before us bordered by hedges, are graves –some new, the heaped earth festooned with flowers, others neat and tidy with headstones. It looks like a typical country church graveyard –yet no church or other buildings conjoin the site. The grass paths that divide the plots are trimmed short and lushly green.

Nobody is surprised or comments on what appears to me an odd sight – a cemetery in the midst of nowhere. I sense anticipation in the people about – something is about to happen.

Subtlety the atmosphere alters –openness changes to intimacy and solemnity, presaging ceremony. From the right a procession of priests appear as from nowhere, walking through an opening to the hedge border, dressed in cassocks, cottas and surplices. Some are bareheaded, some crowned with pill box type headgear, others sporting wide brimmed black hats –many carry incense burners.

At the parade's head strides a bishop, perhaps even an archbishop, richly dressed, gold thread gleaming in the stole about his neck. The mitre atop his white hair is lined gold and red with a cross in rich brocade gleaming bright inset with precious stones. The procession halts on the rise of ground to our left and faces down on the cemetery.

The atmosphere is serene as I watch the lighted incense burners swing I feel moved to kneel and clasp my hands in prayer. I can hear words now that sound like a blessing "O you that sleep in Christ's name arise. Seraphim and Cherubim, angels of light embrace these souls who rest before God's judgement seat. Trumpets proclaim the faithful rise". I look up to see the bishop holding up his arms in supplication, shepherd's crook raised in his right hand.

The atmosphere is electric now; his words though I have not heard them all are clearly invoking sleeping souls to rise as the day of judgement has come. As he concludes base and treble sounds of trumpets can be heard, trilling like hunting horns –they reach crescendo and lapse into silence that feels like the washing rhythm of the sea.

We who stand apart are stilled in attitudes of prayer by the majesty of ritual. The prayer finish is a signal for the assembly of priests to disburse about the graves. Some kneel; others stand obeisant with hands clasped after genuflecting. At some graves more than two assemble joining hand to hand and bowing their heads.

A mist now begins to form over the ground gradually rising to about a metre in depth –it being very dense at ground level. The bishop on the rise alone is deep in silent prayer.

I can feel a tension develop, so much so I'm instinctively projecting myself in an effort to absorb it. Wraith like people can be seen struggling in the mist, attempting to rise from recumbent positions. Gradually they become more solid as the priests invoke them prayerfully, encouraging movement with beckoning hands.

Judgement Day

In the crowd of us assembled I can hear cries of recognition and people begin to move forward toward the graves. A strong surge of emotional energy sweeps up from the cemetery and colours of blue and gold permeate the mist. The wraiths solidifying begin to look like living people emanating a variety of warm colours. Now I can see them dressed variously in Sunday best and white gown like garments –most are elderly but not all and none are children.

Reunions are taking place –some scenes are emotionally charged, the newly risen falling to their knees overcome with joy, others hugging and kissing the loved ones who greet them. Some have awoken clearly conscious of the presence of priests and ask to be blessed.

Small groups are forming, those 'awakened' from their graves the centre of attention. It's apparent as I watch; these groupings are generating their own particular kind of energy. The priests must be aware of this as one by one they leave the groups and gradually fade from view. In turn the groups themselves also lose definition and this once so solid scene vibrant with people itself becomes a wraith; the graves fading as does the definition of the ground and surrounding scenery. Finally I am left with an impression of the Bishop standing alone, his form silver in a dark blue space.

I can no longer feel my body or have any sense of place. I am contemplating the power of mind repeating a phrase –'as you think, so shall you be.'

I'm conscious of my book and a blur of type. Straightening myself I hear Pam remind me that my bedtime drink is getting cold. I'm coming too and for once my thriller doesn't interest me. Obviously some people on passing are so steeped in religious doctrine that supposes sleep until the trumpets herald the dawn of judgement day, they cannot express consciousness in the next life until that event occurs.

I am deeply affected by this remembrance, I know of course that some people live their physical lives in expectation of life hereafter conditioned by judgement day philosophy, but to realise people might remain unconscious because of it clearly shows that our beliefs have a strong bearing on how we live the next life.

I am also struck by the apparent togetherness of people –I say apparent because their actions (and by that I must mean their states of mind) have direct effect upon environment. This journey demonstrates to me that different levels of consciousness can exist in the same 'space' but interaction is limited in direction and purpose by the thought bodies of those present.

I recount a bare boned impression of my journey to Pam amazed at how emotionless I make it sound. As I prepare for sleep promising myself to write it with feeling I can't help wondering why it is that in all my experiences I travel alone; and that question burns uncomfortably in my head as sleep overtakes me.

Chapter SEVENTEEN:
Confessions of a Human Being

The following day I'm unusually chirpy –even I notice it! The religious service I viewed last night is stimulating a long held awareness. Shortly after I had begun psychic development a Yorkshire woman sitting in the same group said she clairvoyantly saw a priest with me. I thanked her of course and remembered the name of Clive and other small details provided. In other groups Biblical type figures are said to be with me –politely I thank for them too. All of a year later and then leading a small group of devotees my trance ability manifested. The first communicator announced himself as Clive. I was a little confused on being told about him after the trance; this Clive was an elderly man and the Clive described by the Yorkshire woman was a young Jesuit Priest.

In subsequent trances Clive made it clear he's a spokesperson for a group of communicators. Sitters see a variety of people when Clive is teaching –and many of them are vicars! To be exact, there is an early church father who wears a mitre shaped helmet, a Greek orthodox dignitary, a cardinal, a young priest and a pope. No one pupil has view of all –years pass before all these various manifestations are independently witnessed. I mustn't forget the chaplain who is also a member of the group –he is mentioned to me a number of times before the penny drops and I recognised him as the Reverend Sims-Williams I knew as a boy on TS Arethusa.

Tales of Bellerophon –On the Banks of the Shalimar

I was far from smitten when Clive first made contact and was told he was a Jesuit priest. Baptised and confirmed in the Church of England I lapsed on joining the Navy and barely gave religion a second thought in my quest for worldly understanding. Only after my 'road to Damascus' type experience with the medium Grace Hickey did I even entertain religious thoughts.

Under the influence of my teacher Len I swiftly became a heretic. Not that Len was anti-church, or consciously taught me to be so –far from it. Len's own background was deeply religious. A Roman Catholic who subsequently became a Christian Spiritualist, Len who was seeing Spirit forms as a boy of necessity developed as an original thinker and studied all kinds of psychic and occult subjects.

Under his influence I became familiar with the works of Blavatsky, Waite, Crowley and others and the view I developed of the Christian Church was jaundiced to say the least. You can't read about the trials of witches and the records of séances and healing events without coming to the conclusion that somewhere along the line the Church had got it badly wrong.

I confess also to going into a Christadelphian church simply to oppose their dogmatic views –and this it must be said during my early days as a trance medium facilitating the Clive communications. Over time it's a different story, I've ceased to be a firebrand and become deeply respectful of Clive's teachings. And to be truthful I can still feel a deep seated sense of longing when I hear a peal of church bells; as a boy their music punctuated the pattern of day and evening. And in later life searching where there is likely nothing left to find for writings that shed some light upon the life of Jesus. To me Jesus is the ultimate demonstrator who with his own life gave proof of our eternal nature. So you can understand why I'm chirpy –I feel connected! And for the first time I'm impatient for more journey revelations, but 'duty dog' will not let my new found ability of the worldly leash. All day shoulder to the wheel I strive and by evening time I have a positive outlook to be envied.

Thanks to my wife's astrological skills I know I have a Gemini ascendant. This is mighty useful on occasions when I need to do two things at once but it also has its downside –I can become an out-and-out chatterbox. I linger after my evening teaching class and then agree to give healing to a pupil of mine who is suffering an IBS problem.

Confessions of a Human Being

By the time I get home it's midnight and after dog walking my eyes began to cross. No way, I say to myself; no book reading –read the emails and then to bed and sleep! Ensconced in my swivel chair I change my specs and lean back –that's better, I think the words are clearer…

I am looking through a pair of binoculars focussing upon the top of a tree, observing a bird's nest. I can clearly see movement in the mushroom of twigs and suppose them to be young birds. I lower the glasses and turn to Don who is sitting beside me.

'They're beautiful' I say.

'They survived the winter'; he says pointing at the wheeling birds above the group of trees we are facing, 'Now the spring quickens new life'.

'Human beings don't seem to live by the seasons Don.'

'Oh, but they do', he retorts. 'What you mean to say is they ain't conscious of it'.

I'm intrigued by his answer –I'm thinking of people whose lifestyle I am familiar with. 'I guess there must be some peoples left on earth who live by the seasons –in some out of the way places'.

'Sure there are', Don rejoins, 'they are conscious of nature as is any man must who attends by his own efforts the needs of food and shelter'; he pauses as if to dismiss this particular. 'All men, conscious or not by need, are governed by the seasons'.

'Governed? Much of what I see suggests that Man does what he likes, he can insulate or expose himself to the changes as he wishes.'

Don thoughtfully scratches his ear, 'You would think so, given how he takes of nature as he will, unconscious of the causes he sets in motion or the long term effects upon himself. No –transition must occur for most to become aware that the seasons of heat, cold, birth and dying is an order within.'

It's on the tip of my tongue to ask him to explain further when he tugs at my sleeve.

'Look', he says, pointing to the tree nest.

Distracted, I raise the binoculars and see a large brown hawk like bird attending the nest. The young bird's heads bob up and down and pick food from its mouth. 'You know your bible a bit –what was it that Jesus said about the ravens?'

It comes to mind directly. 'Consider the ravens, they neither sow nor

109

reap', I say. He cocks his head and looks at me, something like triumph in his eyes.

'And?'

'Consider the lilies?' I say hopefully, realising I'm about to get a lesson on what I should have known.

'How much better are you than fowls', he exclaims, 'and which of you with taking thought can add to his stature one cubit? If you are not able to do this which is least, why do you take thought for the rest?'

I am silent and feeling not a little uncomfortable. As the bird flies away from the nest I recognise it.

'It's a buzzard!'

'It sure is –and you know something about buzzards, now don't you?' I immediately became aware of the recall I had experienced –a strange state of being in which I am alien in a bird's world.

A change begins –my consciousness moves away from Don and the talk of human lives, my thoughts such as they are no longer reason –the desire to know absents itself; my whole being is held in a vice like grip, a prison comprising energies flowing about me like wind. I'm conscious of having many limbs, not the awkwardness of arms and legs, more a many-jointed complex of sinews and flexible bones.

Seeing! Yet not with eyes; knowing without thinking, moving but not by intention. I am moving in a condition I am unable to describe of which I am a part. It's a world of acute sensation, of smell, taste, hearing and feeling –and I'm free of history! I feel complete. And yes I am seeing but not with eyes that figure shape and size, convey meaning and agree what is an external sense of being. I can feel shape and read in their colours a deep yet clear vibration that neither proposes nor disposes of me. The means I have of myself are dependant and part of movements kaleidoscopically unfolding in a borderless world.

It's changing –I am changing. My sense of individuality is returning and I'm beginning to realise objective thoughts. A sense of separateness develops between me and this strange world of colour and shape. Gradually my human perspective deepens until now I am conscious of watching an incredible world of movement, shape and colour miniaturising and contracting as if it's being pulled away from me into a tube.

I can feel something tugging at me, gentle at first then more insistent and physical.

110

I open my eyes and am daunted by the size of everything. I am small and can't make much sense of what I see. I'm looking down at a copse like wood from the vantage of a hill, unsure of what or who I am. Again that insistent tugging –and a voice, but I don't understand it. Then I do hear something I can relate to, the sound of a bird cawing –a call of reassurance.

That voice again, it's a comforting sound now and I turn my head toward it. Moving feels strange and I see a large shape but cannot think –the form is alien. Then it moves and I see with human eyes. It's Lone Wolf.

I open my mouth to speak, I'm in slow time and it takes an age for a word to form and sound.

'Don?'

Lone Wolf smiles knowingly. He leans over his face close to mine and I can smell a kind of sweet herbal freshness mingled with a faint aroma of burnt wood.

'Even Solomon arrayed in all his glory was not like one of these'.

'No', I croak, 'How could he be?'

And with that Lone Wolf grasps me firmly by the wrist and pulls me sharply toward him and I feel suddenly pulled in two and a heaviness like the lead of all the world sends me plummeting down and down into blackness.

When I come to I'm hunched over my desk being watched intently by one of my cats. I can hear Don's voice as he laughingly says, 'And you want to know why we don't have cars!' His laughter is still filling my mind as I stumble out into the kitchen to make a hot drink.

Chapter EIGHTEEN:
A Walk on the Wild Side

Why do I travel alone? In a strange kind of way Don and Lone Wolf unexpectedly provide answer to this question. The manner in which humans interpret the sensory world is directly connected to our ideas of self. We function and develop the idea of self by interacting with other 'like' beings. You and I don't function as 'islands' even if we desire too. Consciously or unconsciously we autonomously function, continually making and breaking our defensive borders in search of self awareness. Identity and purpose is developed by socialising. My unconscious has awareness of 'like' beings that my conscious nature has yet to relate with. My thoughts of aloneness are conscious pleas of understanding that cannot be satisfied by interaction with physical personalities.

My experience in the garden and now this in the astral world has driven 'a coach and horses' directly through my physical world order of consciousness. Liberal that I am I believe my mind to be open and eclectic in view, but these experiences are overturning the basis of that belief and putting my rationality into question.

I'm describing the best I can the experience of irrational events with a rational mind and the only way I can 'square' the difference of being that and being this is to accept my nature is not only dual, in the sense that it's both male and female, but it's also in part non-human. I'm still full of questions but I'm beginning to think that some of them are a waste of time. It's dawning on me that I'm accepting 'inexplicable' astral experience not only because I'm a different self in those states but because I'm also something other than human.

A Walk on the Wild Side

To say I'm humbled by this awareness doesn't adequately describe my state of mind. I'm sort of annoyed as well; irritated by the reminder of reality I somehow instinctively know and in the same breath reason unimportant. Am I to believe Man's reasoning mind is flawed?

I've always understood the biblical wisdom 'judge not lest ye be judged' to be a guide on how best to conduct oneself, not to hold opinion or make decision unnecessarily. I now have sensory experience in which opinion and power of decision did not manifest –period! Have I in my bird like consciousness experienced the root understanding of this age-old adage? To be a momentary being is to be free of history –the need to judge is not present. How is it possible to incorporate that consciousness into the reasonable physical world?

For days I'm tossing this thought around without arriving at any sensible conclusion, thinking vaguely that living closer to nature and the practise of deep meditation will allow this. I am recalling the psychic outward bound courses I used to run in the New Forest area for my pupils.

On their arrival I'd take away watches, phones and ban all media connections for the week to follow. In a relatively short time my pupils would recover a natural awareness and become conscious of rhythms within and without, instinctively knowing how to harmonise. And their time, regulated by sun and moon, faded the urgency of thought –so much so that when the course ended and watches and phones were returned they reacted as some children do when term time begins. Don't want to go back!

I'd get reports of pupils 'freaking out' on the motorway home and having difficulty adjusting to the bustle of a material world, which only goes to show that even after short periods of 'alternative living' our inner nature can make step function type changes.

Is it possible to broaden and deepen our personality consciousness? Maybe we can get closer. I'm not convincing myself with these arguments and settle to accept that consciousness in alien worlds cannot translate directly into this one –and just hope I've made some sense others can relate to in recording these 'Ariel' experiences.

I'm listening to the music of Alan Hovhaness enjoying a brief interlude in a busy weekend, the passing traffic intermittent, the telephones quiet and the daily urgency of communications absent, visually contemplating the form of my cat sitting regally as she often does on my computer; her image framed against the afternoon light streaming through my office window. Maybe it's the matt black of her coat that triggers my consciousness change – the music perhaps? Whatever, I enter into another state.

I'm standing on an open plain overwhelmed by the vastness of space. The landscape is sparse –occasional clumps of small leafed bushes and patches of small headed flower plants are apparent in the immediate surroundings. The grass is patchy, thin and wiry and a fitful breeze billows dust about me. Wherever this is it seldom rains. I sense a dry heat but do not feel my body reacting to it. There are no hills or mountains –the land flat stretches into the distance relieved only by occasional trees. The sky is colourless and merges with the horizon in a featureless haze. I'm only sensibly aware of the immediate place spreading out from beneath my feet, of being at the centre of a circle whose circumference is unknown. The sense I have of height is an odd experience –inwardly I feel small, outwardly tall and I'm asking myself why I am here. I turn as if prompted to do so and there not three metres away is Lone Wolf.

He is squatting on his haunches and looking at me with a quizzical expression. His leather skinned trousers show the creases and cracks of constant wear and are laced black from ankle to thigh. A leather waistcoat protects the back and a red coloured cloth bandolier keeps the long black hair from his eyes. His arms, chest and face are deeply tanned, the cheekbones sunburnt black. A necklace of small white bone adorns the neck.

He motions me come forward to sit, which I do and watch him kneading the earth with his fingers aware he's concentrating on doing something.

He stops pressing and rubs the earth clockwise for a few moments with the palm of his right hand – then draws back and looks me straight in the eyes.

'They come'.

I look about but see nothing bar the distant trees and the scrubland. I return his gaze with a questioning look. He doesn't speak but his eyes are telling me to prepare myself –now I feel vibration in my feet and notice they are bare. Looking again I notice something moving at the edge of my circle of awareness. Forming out of the haze is a man and a large animal –the man appears to be running. They are closing in on us at speed and I can see the man is tall, black and African. Alongside him moving effortlessly over the ground in long loping strides is a large tiger.

I'm not afraid –inwardly I know neither the tiger nor the stranger present a threat. They stop a little way off and Lone Wolf and I walk toward them. The black man is wearing a leopard skin loin cloth, a leather thong like strip about his waist attached to which is a bag made of animal skin. Atop his large head is a yellow and red pill box hat decorated in black zigzag black piping. A necklace of ball shaped white objects interspersed with feathered tufts dangles from his neck onto his bare chest. As we approach I ask Lone Wolf who the stranger is and why the tiger. 'He is Hinetobada, wise in the way of animals and the natural world'.

'Greetings wolf man', Hinetobada calls. 'And to you fox cub I shall call Peter'. He must be all of 6'7" accentuated even more by the pill box hat on his tightly curled black and grey haired head. He appears to be speaking a foreign language but the meaning reveals itself to me simultaneous with speech. Although he emanates physical strength and moves gracefully, a childlike impression of personality is evident as he speaks.

I considered the tiger that now sits on its haunches behind Hinetobada. 'What a beautiful animal.'

Clearly pleased by my appreciation Hinetobada turns his head. 'Ishotea say hello to the cub.'

At the mere mention of her name she rises and moves toward me. Her large bulk is now bearing down on me and I begin to feel nervous.

'Lay down Peter', Lone Wolf directs, 'lay down. Hands by your side open to the sky and breathe confidently.'

I'm doing as he advises and Ishotea looms into view, straddles my body and lowers her huge head and begins licking my face. Beautiful warmth spreads throughout my body –the sandpapery rasp of her tongue lights a fire inside warming every organ and every bone. I feel childlike and giggle helplessly. She grips my tea shirt in her mouth and attempts to pull it up over my head. Deciding that covering my face is enough she licks my stomach and I double up choking with laughter.

Both Lone Wolf and Hinetobada are smiling and slapping their thighs. Ishotea stops much to my relief, steps back and let's out a deep roar of contentment.

I stand up flushed and happy. Ishotea is now pacing around us all. 'Ishotea likes you Peter –she knows you are a cub.'

He is laughing easy as Ishotea stops her pacing and sits beside him. 'What do you wish of us wolf man?'

'We must teach him to walk and talk wise one'

'That is good for one who is two selves and seeks to remember'. Hinetobada replies. 'Come stand by me', he instructs 'and walk in my steps.' I stand next to him as he asks and wonder how I'm going to achieve this as he is so much bigger than I am. With his eyes he tells me to follow him.

I'm walking trying to keep in step. He's obviously shortening his stride

115

for my benefit but even so he glides and I do not. Compared my movement are awkward.

'You are resisting like a dry tree pressed by the wind,' he exclaims, 'let yourself bend and don't try to walk ahead of yourself.'

Doesn't he realise I'm trying to keep up? I'm trying some more but not making much progress.

He is laughing. 'Do not think of it as exercise –do not think!' I'm feeling confused and tell him so.

'Don't try to walk ahead, move inside of yourself!' he exclaims. 'Let your body bend from the source of its power –there', he says pointing to my lower gut. I continue to try but my efforts are clumsy.

'This', he says patting my head, 'is unhappy –first you ask it to walk for you and it does the best it can–now you tell it not to interfere. Let it be. '

'Yes but then I'm only doing what you tell me too'

'True –so be patient, let your mind be here', he says again pointing to my lower gut, 'remember how to do it naturally. You not learn –you remember'.

I'm walking mindlessly now –I'm only thinking when Hinetobada instructs me. I'm learning to breathe with my stomach, store the air to power my legs torso and arms. Pleased he now teaches me how to breathe with chest and stomach alternately which gives me the power to change the rhythm of walking. As this is achieved he tells me how I might allow the body to breathe and generate energy without trying to direct it.

'Breathe', he says, 'by accepting the first breath (by this he means my in breath) as the word of the Mother. Breathe out your creation as a living testimony of her knowledge.'

And so we continue –I banter with him, he cajoles and playfully taps my head encouragingly when I get it right. I'm now beginning to lose the control that assumes mastery over sense and my body is functioning instinctively, automatically tuning into earth and atmospheric energies. I began to flow – yes flow effortlessly over the terrain. My sense of self is detached; my body connected to an inexhaustible supply of power.

My thoughts drain away until all impressions enter and leave without comment. I'm aware of Hinetobada and Ishotea pacing easily alongside but I'm no longer thinking of them as separate beings. We are as one exercising in different forms.

There are moments when my body seems not to breathe at all and I'm conscious of inhabiting space, aware of trees and bushes, not spatially or visually but as part of the energies I am representing. I'm conscious of changing, of internal rhythms responding to the interaction of my movement with the environment. Soon after these extenuating conscious experiences begin, Ishotea walks in front of us and as I tune into her movement my strength is empowered by a geyser like action that draws out of earth and atmosphere a primordial essence, enlivening every muscle and nerve in my body.

My sense of humanness is overshadowed by the enormity of the force I am generating and I begin to lose awareness of the movement my limbs are making –the flow holds me to the ground and I glide over it like water seeking a level.

I hear Hinetobada calling Ishotea. 'Ati!' and again softly 'Ati'

Gradually Ishotea slows her walk and we likewise match her speed. I'm conscious of my limbs again. Hinetobada gently restrains my movement and we stop. Standing still I can feel a rush of energy shooting up my legs like electricity and then it modifies to a warm gentle wave like current pulsating from top to toe.

We sit and I'm conscious of how I feel harmonised with my surroundings. I'm no longer conscious of a separate space. I keep pressing my legs with my hands to reassure myself that the solid body is still there.

'Let us talk'. Hinetobada says.

'Talk?'

Even in the sitting position Hinetobada looks down on me. 'I teach you how to walk and now wolf man would have me teach you how to talk'.

'Ah, yes he did so ask, I remember'. I look at him and his eyes are laughing, Ishotea lays at our side looking out on the tundra entirely disinterested in our conversation. It's hard to formulate thoughts; the experience of walking has overpowered my consciousness and still absorbed to the flow of energy relationships that blend me with the environment. All my senses including the sense of smell and taste are combining to express the flow; even now as I sit on the ground. It's as if the ground itself vibrates in waves beneath and my body has blended into it.

'What is talking wise one?'

'Ah, ha', he exclaims, grasping the top of my head with his huge hand and gyrating it side to side. 'Ah, ha', he exclaims again. 'Now you talk good, young Peter. Now you talk good, very good. Where you think voice come from, eh? From there? He points to the sky. 'From here? He says holding both hands over his heart and assuming expressions of beatitude. I laugh at his comic stance. 'Whatever I say it's going to be wrong I think.'

117

'From here', he says, grasping at the earth with his hands, 'from here'. He ceremoniously brushes the earth from his fingers, motions me to copy the action and crosses his arms over his chest. Expressionless, still as a statue he gives the impression of waiting triumph.

Tentatively I lay my open palms on the earth before me and wait. The flowing energies I feel in my body are expressing through my hands from the earth –the flow is entering me through my right palm, moving around my body like a corkscrew and reconnecting back again through the left palm. Absorbing this experience I become conscious of intelligence that speaks to all my senses and most of all –an order that doesn't bind my mind to a view of what it is but produces a sensation free of the driving and defining powers I normally associate with animated consciousness.

As powerful as this is I am able without tension to lift my hands from the earth and disconnect myself from this 'dialogue.' I am able to call upon those familiar mental urges I recognise as my normal self.

'Is that what you call talking Hinetobada?'

'That is what I call talking young one, which is what wolf man calls talking and what Ishotea calls talking. That is what your body calls talking, what the earth and the sky call talking, what everything and everyone who know the natural world call talking'.

'Tell me more', I urge.

'Ah, I see you want to ask questions about talking!' He laughs and continues laughing until tears course down his cheeks and Ishotea rouses herself and roars.

'Come', he says, rising to his feet in one swift movement. 'I teach you as you walk'. Again we walk, much as before but this time I am spatially aware and sensible of the energies at the same time. The landscape has changed character –there are more bushes and trees. The grass is thicker and we pass areas of standing water, birds are apparent and one species I see look much like flamingo.

'You see more this time eh?' I look up sharply expecting to see his head turned toward me but it isn't –he appears to be physically ignoring my presence as if wrapped in his own world. Again I hear his voice. 'In the world you come from I was once a Bantu and spoke the language of my people. I do not know your earth language but all that can be felt understands all that feels, it is a language given by the Mother Earth and in this my present world the Earth Mother is more beautiful. Her limbs are young and her heart is free of the slow order of decay that characterises the physical world.

A Walk on the Wild Side

How is it that I have form? –I tell you it is the form of the Mother. How is it I have a mind? –I tell you it is the mind of the Mother. How is it that I know Ishotea? –I tell you it is because the Mother named her to me. Ishotea knows me as she also knows the Mother. And I know you and you know me and all the ages of our being because that being is the Mother.'

We continue to walk and as I increase the span of my stride I feel a mounting sense of excitement. I begin to glide. No! I am moving weightless over the surface of earth. I cannot begin to guess the speed as scenes appear and disappear –even the sky moves at great speed; heart like areas of intense colour and brightness in great swathes appear almost to move within and other scenes, dark and brooding like masked cauldrons, swirl and pulsate encompassing me in their differing densities of light. I feel as if I'm sharing view of this with Hinetobada and Ishotea but I'm not speaking or actively thinking. Then I hear the voice of lone Wolf and look to Hinetobada and see Lone Wolf's head and shoulders overshadowing his form. He turns and beams at me, 'Learning to talk eh, Peter?'

'Learning to talk', I say, feeling overwhelmingly confident as if I've been doing this all my life. And then I can feel his shape about me, controlling my energies and a sound like the tapping of sticks, clearly some kind of drumming I think –and then everything changes and I begin to fall like a leaf into blackness and cold air. As I fall I am thinking I cannot break; the Mother holds me. Childlike I reach out with my hands.

Hinetobada

Figure 8

Ishotea
Figure 9

Chapter NINETEEN:
Right Order

It's a while before my brain begins to work normally again. Mindlessly I contemplate my cat sitting on the VDU, looking out of the window. I feel as if I am seeing with her. When she turns and meows I start to think. She noises but once and stares.

Such attention is not uncommon of course –she meows to be let outside or be fed and keeps on until I respond. She's not asking now to be fed or to be let out. I put her on my shoulder and pace up and down my study room. I'm cold but not shivery, inwardly strong and strangely detached. I feel heavy and ponderous despite an apparent smoothness of movement. What am I learning here?

Is this taking place in real time? This question arises because what I've been learning from Hinetobada and Lone Wolf is relate to the mind and body tuning techniques I practise and teach –though nothing comes near to this mind blowing experience.

Early in the trance teaching work my control Clive informed pupils of a method of energy development he called BodyMind Power Meditation. He introduced it as a practise with these words.

'All states of energy are Beings of Mind & Matter and have an interactive 'Blueprint' of Harmonic relationships continually seeking the Foundation Design."

Clive went on to describe this process as Right Order and the meditation techniques taught designed to harmonise the human BodyMind system and expand consciousness. What I now find particularly interesting after my experience of walking is that Clive stated that "the BodyMind accepts Being *without differentiating* between states, orders and relationships, by invoking the universal root of Being outside of Space and Time".

Is this the Earth Mother being that Hinetobada talks about? Clive teaches that breath is intelligent and is in two forms –the in breath being the primal 'discovery' breath and exhalation our conscious reaction to it. By focussing the 'discovery' breath on various body parts and accepting its consciousness without differentiating the experience when breathing out, the brain rhythms alter and function 'instrumental' of the inward breath. This process educates the body being about itself; general health is improved and higher consciousness connections can be achieved.

He teaches as does Hinetobada the brain of the BodyMind being is in the lower body –not in the head. I have used this method successfully for over 30 years and in that time Clive has expanded the method advising further breath control and visualisation techniques. Although the methods can be practised individually to great benefit it's also effective as a group dynamic providing environment as an energy power development tool. A guided approach rests pupil's thinking nature and awakens the BodyMind. Essentially Hinetobada was teaching me BodyMind practise that not only engaged that primal 'Mother' intelligence altering inner consciousness, but practise that changed awareness of form.

Some 15 years ago when the communicator 'Wolf' appeared –who I now realise is Lone Wolf, he taught me BodyMind movements. I later realised from book study the movements taught were very similar to the practise of Qi-Gong. He taught various techniques on how to move and stress the BodyMind that are entirely in harmony with Clive's teachings. I then incorporated them into my teaching programme.

This journey shows me that much of what I've been previously taught is only partially realised in the conscious world. In all my endeavours I have never achieved such oneness of expression as I did in the company of Hinetobada, Ishotea and Lone Wolf. I look at my hands, at my feet, feeling the heat slowly returning and listen to the purring of my cat. I seem to have taken a further step in understanding the non-human side of my nature. Not content to leave it there I am asking myself –just exactly how are we made?

My cat appears happy enough, is she aware of her true identity? If not she appears satisfied with her lot and now my dog appears as if to satisfy herself I'm still present in the house. Why doesn't she exhibit signs of searching for meaning? Maybe she knows, like Ishotea knows and looking in is simply a response to a change in atmosphere; there being nothing to learn –only confirm? I'm moulded I guess just as you are to assume animal consciousness is of a lower order than Man but it doesn't sit happy with what I have experienced with the buzzards, Ishotea and the activities of Hinetobada and Lone Wolf. I am insulting my own intelligence and denying the astral world experience by assuming my cat and dogs' consciousness is a lower order than mine –besides it doesn't answer my questions.

I have to smile –here am I disputing the knowledge of Man and my enquiry is purely selfish. It's *my* creation I want to know about, never mind the world! I'm querying the nature of forces that form my identity and should I not be thinking about the bigger picture?

What are the implications of my awareness upon the consciousness of Man and our planetary being? Man teaches that consciousness is an order arising from physical awareness whereas my experience is telling me that a superior order of consciousness is attained on losing physical identity. The relationship between the physical and non physical worlds can hardly be described as seamless –else why do I feel so completely different in my astral worlds? Yet Hinetobada has me subjugate my form in such harmony I do not incredulously stand apart from myself as the 'outside' and 'inside' join together.

I can't put my finger on it –yet. I have the feeling of unlearning and shedding unworkable knowledge. Are we looking through the wrong end of the telescope I ask myself?

Chapter TWENTY:
The Teacher is taught by Children

My teachers' main guide Joey, who I used to speak with when Len was entranced would say when I was struggling to understand something that the 'answer is under your nose.' By that he meant it was so simple I couldn't see it.

In the days that follow I'm reminded of his guidance as I fail to get clear answers from my own analysis of recent events –then I recall a game I used to play as a child.

This very private game formed in my mind as I watched people pass the front garden gate of the family house. We lived in a rural community and our house was situated in a residential area on the side of a hill. Movements of people and vehicles, unlike town or city, were infrequent and I took notice like most others when a car or cyclist came into view or someone walked down the road. You also got to know who was in and who was out when the curtains parted or the doors opened, and the hidden form behind hedge or wall straightened up to look. And you got to know who to expect, like a neighbour of ours (he owned orchards that backed onto our property), a Mr Perrin who would walk down our road around teatime.

You could set a watch by his appearance because before disappearing from sight at the road bend below my mother would call to have me wash and ready myself for the evening meal and soon my father would be home from work.

The Teacher is taught by Children

Mr Perrin's dress never varied. He wore shapeless trousers that were always dusty, light brown leather boots smeared with mud and a trench coat whatever the weather. And he trailed over his shoulder, a bag I later learnt was a gas mask holder issued to just about everybody during the war.

He would walk a kind of rolling gait that every now and then changed in rhythm as he hitched up the shoulder bag. If he was self conscious of this action, it never showed; his head seemed to be permanently thrust forward as if leading his swaying torso to a premeditated goal. And he chewed, he was always chewing. This I found fascinating. Chewing gum was unknown to me, so as far as I was concerned it must be cheese. I would beg a piece from my mother, perch myself on the garden gate and be chewing it as he came into sight.

Occasionally he would cock an eye at my sitting form and something like a ghost of a smile would alter his masticating jaw –then he would pass the gate leaving me to contemplate his receding form. I was so fascinated by his movements I would watch until he disappeared from sight and the sound of my mothers' repeated calls had faded from my ears; then returning to the house I would walk like him, I would chew like him, I would hitch up an imaginary bag and thrust my head forward. As far as I was concerned I was for that brief period Mr Perrin, an old man worn by life, my limbs distorted by work and the only, only thing that made life tolerable was chewing cheese!

The recollection makes me smile; I have many times since experienced sympathetic rapport. Most memorably in my youth I observed the pitiable sight of a woman suffering from elephantitis. Her difficult walk, feet almost hidden by folds of flesh immediately conveyed a painful shockwave of feeling that shot up my legs and upset my stomach. I wonder –is this sensitivity evidence of the borderless nature of Man? The impression on my mind and body is invariably accurate and represent feelings and the mental character of the sufferer. I've even been aware of animal pain, discomfort and fear. Is this a window in the objectively minded self that points to a metamorphic ability in human kind?

I'm resisting the urge to delve into books in search of view; I'm going to let these questions hang in the hope that my views are confirmed by further astral experience. Ah! Curse of the brain mind. Can we never be still?

I did not have long to wait –but as usual I am completely 'wrong footed' by what takes place. I awake one morning with a heavy sense of foreboding. It doesn't take me long to realise these feelings have nothing to do with conscious world events. Worrier though I am about material matters nothing is outstanding and demanding attention. People relationships are fine –leastways I don't find any problematic. In the afternoon I'm due to conduct a healing session so I dismiss the feeling with a train of positive thought.

It works. The healing work is successful and I feel lighter and clearer as a result. Later after my client leaves I sit in the quiet, relieved and untroubled by the mysterious feelings I awoke with. I should explain to the uninitiated, in the aftermath of a healing session a healer can experience a sense of timelessness –and I don't mean hanging about on cloud nine. You can be directly connected to the conscious world and able to function normally but the normal tensions that arise when effort is conscious of time are absent.

I was enjoying a cup of tea and writing up my appointments diary, slowly and legibly (I scrawl most times) when I heard a voice –the voice of a young girl. I remember reacting by asking myself –is this a mediumistic communication?

'Do you want to play or not?' She sounds plaintive as if I have somehow already promised and now changed my mind. As I listen to the clear and innocent tones of her voice I become aware of being in a horticultural nursery. It is a greenhouse type of building, open walled with a glass paned roof supported by stanchions and heady with the smell of plants. I'm sitting on flagstones that form a square about a patch of churned up earth littered with empty flower pots, bamboo sticks and a small roll of green netting.

Beside me are three children, two girls and a boy. The girls are about five or six years old, both white skinned, their features suggesting east European origin. The boy is a little older, perhaps nine or ten. The stockier of the two girls, dressed in a tracksuit top and bottom is arranging the pots into a square or more accurately is directing the other girl to place them –then when she does, taking a bamboo stick and planting it close by.

'There now it's a castle with a flagpole –see?'

The other girl clearly enjoying the experience laughingly agrees with her companion. The boy looks on with calculated disinterest, though I suspect he is looking for an excuse to criticise their endeavours. Dressed in shorts and singlet he's dark skinned and handsome for his age. I know he originates from Calcutta. Feeling that I'm being ignored I reach out for a bamboo stick and begin to scuff the loose earth into the shape of hills and valleys –then carefully cut roads into the folds. The boy kneels down at my side and observes my creation.

The Teacher is taught by Children

'What are you doing Peter?'

'I'm creating a country, but at the moment', I say reflectively, 'I'm wondering how I can make trees'.

'Oh, I can do that', he says imperiously, stands up and disappears into the greenhouse rows of benches filled with flowers. A little while later he emerges his hands full of leaves and small twigs.

'Ah, that looks good'. I'm feeling carefree and the heat radiating down on my head is making me feel lazy. I'm happy to see him involved but no sooner he dumps his load when the two girls look up and query what we are doing.

'We are making a place', the boy says, clearly not interested in sharing the experience with the two girls.

'Can we join in?'

She is the smaller of the two girls; now standing, smoothing down her dress which is smeared with dirt. It's the voice of the girl who queried my involvement.

'I'm sure you can', I say eagerly looking at the boy.

'Balaaditya, you don't mind do you?'

'It's OK, I guess'

I'm very familiar with these children; I know their names –the girl I've just spoken to is Sasha and the other bossier girl is Natala. They call the boy Bala, clearly considering his name too much of a mouthful to pronounce. Familiar though we are with each other a voice within me says, 'I'm going to test the water'.

'And what is my name?'

Natala looks shocked then burst out laughing. 'Is this a new kind of game Peter', she said gleefully.

'Maybe, maybe', I'm amused by Natala's reply and add mischievously; 'maybe Kings have special names'. Natala hasn't connected to the country theme yet and says seriously; 'Shouldn't you be working with Jim?'

Natala refers to Jimuta and his family who looks after the nursery. 'Jim doesn't need me today. Now if we are going to create a country we had better get started'.

I divide up Bala's heap of leaves and twigs and we all begin to plant trees and bushes, each suggesting to the other how best it can be done, proudly showing off example. This country is clearly going to be a dense forest.

I do as little as I'm able without raising suspicion of not taking part in 'the game', otherwise observing the event and the place about. The children are from different racial backgrounds yet they play together without the slightest indication of difference, Bala is a serious minded boy; for him the game must have a useful outcome and he labours over getting the right effects with his sticks and leaves.

Natala on the other hand is a forceful personality and not overly concerned with getting the right effects; so she plants the most trees and bushes. Sasha repeatedly makes the point she's planting bushes not trees and I can see, suppressing a grin, she's about to change her mind as Natala's and Bala's 'trees' rapidly fill up the spaces.

Now she is saying 'I have some trees too –look, see they are as big as yours.'

I'm observing with pleasure the detail of colour and shade in the nursery –the brightness of the plants in relief to the shadow. The entire nursery has been watered recently and the air is sticky with vapour, but I don't feel any damp sensations on my skin.

I feel a small measure of anxiety –a concern for my playmates that quite naturally are now getting boisterous in their enthusiasm. I intervene pre-emptively a couple of times –and they give me old fashioned looks, as if to say, have you got a problem?

As I carry out my watching brief a gentle breeze starts up and fans the plants and small potted trees in the near vicinity. Every now and then I look back toward a house that adjoins the roofed space in which we sit. It's a familiar sight, an untidy collection of empty pots, hoses and implements. I look as if I'm expecting someone to come out. Then my attention is diverted by a scuffling sound over to our left emanating from behind tables stacked with plants. Here we go again I'm thinking –the pigs are out.

'Do you hear that –that noise?'

Only Sasha turns her head and then gazes back at me. 'That's only the pigs; they've probably got out again'. I get to my feet and gaze over the bench rows to where the plants are shaking and the sound of pots falling and breaking.

'Well they are making a mess'. I glance around at the house again and call, 'Jimuta!' A man dressed in a dhoti and cotton shirt appears and I jerk my thumb. 'They're out.' Looking not a little displeased Jimuta picks out a long stick from a bunch of cane nearby and proceeds down through the benches beating the ground with its tip. 'Out, Out, Out, Pena, Sallie, out – naughty, naughty girls!'

The Teacher is taught by Children

Jimuta is a friend and I've helped him many times in the nursery area – his two pigs are penned to an enclosure on the far side. Several indignant squeals later all is quiet and Jimuta returns.

'What am I to do? –they've eaten through the fence, twice in two days', he says holding up the index and second finger. I grin, 'Then you must wire it up good this time and give them more to eat maybe?'

'More cabbage and carrots', volunteers Bala.

Jimuta shakes his head dolefully, 'they eat too much, not good for them'. He disappears into the house and returns with a reel of wire and carrying snips. As he goes off to repair fences I ponder his problem, aware that his wife, Sahana, doesn't understand why he wants to keep them. We've had conversation before in which I've tried to explain that Jimuta is endeavouring to help the pigs regain their identity. Being near tempting smells helps reawaken their sense of being and over feeding puts them to sleep. Sahana is still struggling with her own sense of identity and doesn't understand the argument.

They both have problems of identity; their earthly life was cut short by drowning and it's still necessary for them to relate back to memories of families still in the flesh. They still sleep and awake aware of communing with the 'sleeping souls' of their loved ones on Earth.

We've had many a talk about that –the conscious expressions of earthly incarnate souls awake in the lower astral worlds is different again to earthly conscious personality. The loved ones they meet in their 'dreams' maybe enlightened in one experience and unaccountably obtuse and obdurate in the next. Jimuta and Sahana understand that physically incarnate souls travel in their sleep state but find it hard to accept they cannot always be influenced to their better good.

They have yet to learn that desires and ambitions of the sleeping loved ones are governed by the souls' physical incarnation. Jimuta is a little more advanced than Sahana in this respect and is accepting and understanding more. In the physical world they were hard working practically minded people and naturally 'gravitated' to this nursery as a place of work and pleasure, instinctively knowing that the consciousness of plants is of a healing nature. People come to this nursery for flowers and plants of all kinds' intent on making gardens, not only for themselves but to prepare places for family and friends expected into their worlds.

The immediacy of consciousness presently experienced is accepted easily enough, but when their earth memories activate they conflict with the momentary sense of being that characterises this astral world. When this happens they withdraw into sleep, else they eat and play with the children. Working the nursery also helps of course –the contact with plants refresh the momentary nature of the present life. Friends also help to take them out of themselves, visiting and going with them to festivals and the like. None of this is uncommon to souls who have left the earth life before their time.

It's getting cooler and I insist my playmates get some warm clothing from the house. Off they go and return almost immediately clutching glasses of fruit juice, Sasha and Natala with shawls and Bala wearing a track suit top. 'What are we going to call our country Peter?' Natala enquires.

'Well, let me see –we have made a place of many trees, roads paths, plains and mountains. And see here where the shadows fall? That could be place where people and other kinds of beings live. They sleep here when the sun goes down and at sunrise go about the business of living and understanding who they are. 'Here', I say drawing my hand across the area between the mounds, 'here there are no shadows. Hot by day and cold by night; whatever lives here is used to living underground to protect their bodies from the heat.'

I can see that my description has them thinking but they remain silent in expectation of me telling them more.

'We could call it the land of the Dodo, how does that sound?'

'What's a Dodo? Bala asks the question but they are all eager to know. 'A Dodo is a bird, a bit like a duck with a curved beak –they were known to live in the physical world but don't anymore. Once upon a time it used to fly but lost the use of its wings because all the food it wanted could be found on the ground'.

'Isn't it better to fly than walk?' Sasha asks. 'I think so Sasha'.

'I fly when I lay down to rest', says Natala

'It's not flying Natala, its gliding using your arms and legs. I've never seen you with wings'. Bala says emphatically. 'I do, I do.' Natala rejoins. 'I can turn somersaults in the air, so there'.

'When you put your arms up, you go up', says Sasha entering into the argument. 'Flapping your arms don't make them wings. It's gliding, that's what it is'. Bala is not going to be moved on the subject so I intervene.

'You are all right –it feels like flying right? It's also like walking but not touching the ground. Let's get back to what we were talking about –a name for this place. I suggested Dodo because it's a new world and the bird had to leave its old world and find a new one'. 'Why did it have to leave the place it was in, you make it sound like it was a good place for the Dodo? Why?' They all chorus.

132

The Teacher is taught by Children

My role with these children is that of a teacher but truth is they don't know much about me. There is a sort of acceptance that I arrive at odd times, join in with what they are doing, answer questions and disappear. I feel responsible not to upset the balance of their consciousness. They are learning the joy of being responsible for themselves and my own view of purpose and being must not overshadow theirs.

'You are all aware of dreams are you not? Dreams of another place that's not so bright and beautiful as here?'

Sasha shudders, 'What like people shouting and hurting each other? I've had dreams like that and don't like them much –they were cold people and I didn't understand what they were saying'.

'Yes and best forgotten –but you've remembered nicer things than that haven't you?' I try not to sound anxious.

'Well, yes', she says doubtfully, 'suppose I have –a lady cuddling me and drinking something, don't know what it was, but I know I kept asking for more'.

'Goats milk, you told us before it was goats milk,' Bala reminds her. Natala makes a face at Bala.

I lean forward and take Natala by the hands and say smilingly, 'yes you are right it was a good experience –an experience of love.'

The lady she refers to is her earth mother. I knew of Sasha's background; born to an environment of internecine strife between Slavonic peoples in Eastern Europe. This present world is infinitely more satisfying than her physical world of life. Thankfully her passing event no longer troubles her. Dream awareness of negative emotional experiences can weaken the astral soul. I wanted her to accept positive loving experiences.

Bala assumes his serious self and says, 'I remember wearing a coat that was silver and had gold threads in it and great plateful's of yellow rice, and all kinds of yummy things to eat. It was a party I think –lots of old people with grey hair and ladies dancing –and lots of clapping', he adds in afterthought.

'Yes you all remember different kinds of dream, some nice and some not so nice. That's the same kind of dream life that the Dodo once had, it wouldn't have any people in it though, maybe other Dodo's, other birds, animals, insects and trees. It was a world with a sun in the sky just like you have here but it was also a world in which animals used to kill and eat other animals, unlike here and now.'

They each showed facial expressions of disgust and I shrug my shoulders to convey understanding but not acceptance.

'What is killing?' Natala questions hesitantly, unlike her usual confident self.

'That is the act of changing life that causes a new body to be grown before it's naturally ready to take over from the old one. Everything changes all the time of course. You see that in plant life don't you? For example; our talk is changing us; we change things when we made our new world here from the earth, the leaves, twigs and sticks. Flowers change when they grow new leaves and shed old ones, when buds appear and then change again into flowers. Killing is an act of taking life energy to satisfy needs. Animals might also do that out of fear to protect themselves. We don't use the word here or invoke its meaning except to remind ourselves of an act that belongs to another world. The world you sometimes experience in your dreams. Sadly human beings in that world also engage in killing one another –for them it's a wonton act to establish power over others.'

'What do you mean when you say 'wanton'?' Bala looks at me intensely. 'Wanton means the act is unnecessary and takes away from the being killed the power to determine change for their self'.

'Was the Dodo killed by man then?'

'Some may have been but it was also killed by other birds and animals'.

'Why would they want to do that?' It's Sasha talking this time.

I sigh heavily. The teaching is proving difficult –how to advise the differences between the worlds they once inhabited and their present world, without sowing the seed of action that is destructive. My young audience is so charming in their innocence it spurs me on to provide the right answer. 'It is a big question Sasha, a very big question and I cannot answer it completely at the moment –what I will say is this. You have seen children born, haven't you?'

They all nod. 'They are lovely!' Sasha exalts.

'Indeed they are', I say, and have you noticed how demanding they are?' I'm suppressing a smile now.

'Grown ups make a lot of fuss about them'. Bala clearly feels they warrant too much attention. 'They can't help themselves, that's why Bala!' says Natala belligerently.

'No they can't Natala, you are right, which is why adults fuss over them so. Sasha is right too –they are lovely because they are innocent and pure. In the human world adults are also very protective of the young life they have conceived, but because they don't understand life is continuous and new life is not new at all but like a flower bud is part of a plant, because they cannot feel other forms of life like you aware of their communication in return, they grow up defensive of what they know and protect it by killing if they feel threatened.'

The children are silent. I know they understood what I have said but they are not happy about it. Somehow I must bring their minds back to the present.

'You find Jimuta's problem with the pigs amusing don't you?'

They laugh. Bala uncharacteristically begins to act out a scene in which as Jimuta he is alternatively scolding and cajoling the pigs to behave. When he's done we all clap and Bala flushes victoriously.

'Very good', I exclaim, 'Jim would laugh at that too!' As if having heard and witnessed the event, Jimuta appears with Sahana.

'Are you succeeding?' Sahana says smiling sweetly. I smile and beckon them to sit down and continue my teaching.

'What the pigs are doing is learning to communicate with Jimuta –and they don't find that easy because they have been born with an understanding that doesn't include talking with other beings unless they are food of some kind. That's why Jimuta is patient with them; it takes effort to accept what you don't understand. Learning to communicate helps break down barriers in ourselves. So remember, we must strive to understand because what we don't understand we ignore and ignorance is the mother of fear'.

'That is true Peter –you put that well. Yes –ignorance is the mother of fear', I like that phrase'. Jimuta nods sagely.

The two girls stand up and crowd around Sahana, Natala with her arm around her ample waist, Sasha embracing her neck. Bala puts something in his mouth he's taken from his pocket.

'Always hungry Balaaditya, come if we are to go to the festival you must first eat'. Sahana's announcement is greeted with cries of affirmation and in the general excited hubbub I enquire of Jimuta, 'What festival?'

'Alagan is playing sitar and he tells me there are new people with some strange new music –so we will go to enjoy and be educated!'

I'm dimly aware of Alagan and I'm about to question myself about him when I become conscious of the children departing –running into the house and as they do I hear a dog barking. Ah! That'll be Ben I'm thinking.

Chapter TWENTYONE:
Answers

I come to gradually, images of the nursery experience flooding into consciousness. When I move I feel heavy and awkward and it's a while before my brain computes and I'm able to make notes of my journey. My sense of foreboding has gone but I feel unhappy for some reason –not the unhappiness one associates with loss or frustration but a sense of being lost.

Clairvoyantly I am aware of people in my 'space' –no one I recognise from memory and vaguely wonder if they have any connection with my present astral experience. I sit at my desk looking out over the street. The people passing by are solid and silent; closed books floating across my vision. It's a familiar world, society appears to be in control of itself but to me the passers-by I view are unaware of who they are and move like autonomic beings. Conscious of this I feel distant from them.

I guess much of what we understand of this life is related to the need we have of belonging. Relationships of whatever kind have to pass this test –we are unhappy when in places and with people we are unable to interact and connect with. My astral experience tells me that time and space consciousness exists in other worlds. The world of Bala, Natala, Sasha, Sahana and Jimuta is not that far removed from Earth and it's ordered, differently perhaps, but ordered by time bound consciousness. Young or old they have a sense of belonging that is different from ours –it is not possessive of place or person.

Happiness is not determined by what one has but by sharing. Belonging is achieved by giving away not by taking. This kind of relationship releases them of earthbound memories. Their consciousness is interactive; even the pigs are happy with their lot as Jimuta is as their tutor and shepherd.

In the grey spheres experience this sense of belonging was not evident – the soldiers I observed were self conscious and insular. I could not connect with them. In my London' visit' with Georgie my vision of events was objective and my sense of curiosity controlled by his directions. Without his guidance I would likely have been in danger. It has to be said the experience is memorable because of a sense of 'belonging' with Georgie –when my ego took command I lost his connection. I was agog at what I saw but he appeared relatively uninterested –and that makes sense when viewed from an awareness of self that shares without the fear of self denial.

In my astral journeys the question of belonging only arises when my earthly mind is evidently present –the mind responsible for asking questions, disputing the 'obvious' and the cause of 'headaches' on recall.

I am struggling to accept and 'square' the relationship of this life with the next, which leads me to suggest the issue of belonging in our world is a different practise to that of my experience of the astral worlds –grey spheres excluded. In our world love and care are possessive expressions that develop from our sense of belonging –in transition we talk of losing and gaining. Loss and gain doesn't figure in the awareness astral beings have of themselves.

The Nursery remembrance is different to my wanderings in the desert witnessing the struggles of the newly dead, different again to my dance hall memory that comes across as a preordained event in which I feel more open and integrated with the environment and the people. I acted like a man with a mission connecting and 'remembering' only as required. In my talks with Omar, Don and Lone Wolf, events appear to come into being for my benefit – I can almost describe them as healing experiences.

In the world of the nursery I am integral to their development –not simply the questioner, not the tourist. Part of my earthly mind was present – it was the anxious mind that cared for the children's safety. Natasha gave me a curious look when I expressed concern over the pigs breaking out of their compound -she could not see it as a problem. The children had already understood in their short astral life that sharing informed and developed their sense of life, whereas I was thinking like a physical man; speaking protectively and masking my fears for their safety.

Now I know why I feel lost –it's the effect of having been conscious in a world in which belonging does not mean possession. Progression for Jimuta, Sahana, Bala, Natasha and Sasha is brought about by releasing their earthly sense of belonging. Here in this life in the aftermath of this journey I am bewildered because I both need and reject understanding that is born of security. And I felt this before I experienced the journey! Once again my sense of time is destroyed –had I already lived it?

During the early years of my psychic development when my questions were less tempered I asked Joey, Len Burden's main guide during a trance session what the future held for me, thinking I could steal a march on events to come. He said I would be alone, unable to share my thoughts with others – I was nonplussed by this answer and not a little disappointed. I'm beginning to think this is what he was alluding to –I don't belong in the astral worlds I am a visitor –yet there I am a person unlike here.

These journeys have me feel I don't belong anywhere. An inherited familiarity in the astral worlds and in this world a sense of belonging resulting from experience –both of which I am contesting. I am living on a bridge between two worlds. The 'balance' when I do experience it is achieved by the action of travel –like a gypsy; comfortable and rested when vistas of the unknown unfurl before me.

The more I attempt to explain my understanding of these journeys, the more I feel my sense of identity breaking up –yet for reason I can't explain I am impelled to relate my experience to the physical world.

'This won't do. I have to get a grip on myself and learn to live with more than one kind of reality'.

As temperature rises and the spring sunshine warms I look forward to spending more time outside. Today is a precursor of what to expect and I stand on my small patio contemplating the jobs I plan to do when paint will dry before sunset and building jobs can be started and left overnight without fear of frost. And my poor lawn; patched yellow and green –that too can be repaired. High on the trellis I view the brown stalks of grape vines. I think of Omar and wonder when next I will remember a talk with him.

Perhaps it was the warming sun, who knows? I loosen my hold on time and find myself looking at the bending figure of Edward turning a key in the lock of a door we have just passed through.

'I think you will find this room pleasant. I used to write sermons and speeches here, found the atmosphere most helpful'.

I'm aware of us having just left the library and meaning to ask whose place it is. He straightens up. 'The library room is Ben's, Benjamin Franklin; or rather I should say it was. Ownership is unnecessary in this world. In any event others have added to it.'

Answers

He looks at me curiously, 'You don't remember me telling you this, do you?' I look at him blankly –I seem to have missed that. More to the point I'm suddenly conscious of myself as Tony.

'Over here Peter', Edward motions with his hand as he leads the way to a sofa and armchair situated by French style windows. 'The view of the lawn is restful on the eyes'.

The walls are panelled in dark wood, which give the view added emphasis. I sit on a sofa modelled in the classic Greek fashion, the armchair is the same style, dark wood slatted back and arm rests, the cushioned seats of both couch and chair are striped in a red and blue pattern. The floor is also dark wood and a red rug lies between the couch and chair. I particularly notice the absence of pictures, either standing on the small cabinet or hanging from the walls.

I note that Edward is dressed exactly as in our previous conversation; a dark coat buttoned double-breasted style, grey blue trousers, a high white collar and a blue cravat. His hair slightly wavy and iron grey, the facial mould serious but the eyes are very expressive and lighten his countenance.

'A drop of wine perhaps?'

He takes from the cabinet a decanter a small silver tray and two small stemmed flat-bottomed glasses.

The offer surprises me. He smiles and pours two half glasses. 'Just as there are people in the physical world who would frown on such pleasure, so also do some people in my world'.

The wine is very pleasant, being full bodied and fruity tasting. Edward sits himself down in the chair, sips the wine and smiles disarmingly.

'The talk we are about to have concerns the nature of your identity. I have a relationship with you as Peter that is different to that which I have with the man Tony. At this moment you are more the man Tony even though in form and expression you are Peter. I will address you as the man Tony but be aware we cannot repeat this experience –else it will put you into danger.'

I am feeling myself thinking as Tony but don't understand what the issue is that Edward alludes to. 'I know you have been agonising over your writing; your nature hard pressed to believe in what you are producing. You generate more questions than answers and feel the whole process lacks order and theme'.

He looks directly at me for a response.

'My sense of time is virtually destroyed when I recall events of this world, an effect that carries over long after I have ceased a session of recording. As I speak with you I have no such fears or concerns; though I must confess that some experiences have conflicted with my earthly nature. Both concern and excitement is felt in my earthly world on recall –yet here I am aware of the answers I seek –and right now my questions seem foolish and unnecessary.'

Edward studies me for a moment, rises and places his glass back on the cabinet and begins to pace up and down in front of the windows.

'Other people have written of this world but they have been orchestrated pieces, supported by interested minds on this side of life. The mediumistic instruments in your world have received such communications in a limited state of consciousness. Earthly consciousness actively limits its scope in order to focus –needs that vary from the hunt for foods to pursuance of ideas are all advantaged by this ability. Communications from this world are made possible by the functional limitations of humanity –but in turn it also means the nature of what you can understand is also limited.

A second birth for the earthly mind is realisation of inner being, of knowledge that cannot be contained and expressed, which invariably reshapes the conscious nature of the soul being. Rarely is a soul twice born capable of access and awareness of this world and able to interpret such experience to the worlds of limited consciousness.

He stops speaking and again looks hard at me before turning to stand facing the windows. I am being overpowered by a strange yet familiar feeling of pre knowledge, conscious I am acting out what I already know. I am also aware of myself as Peter and a sense I can't define of being a third self. I don't feel a conflict between these 'selves' –it's as if I'm as I should be.

'How long has this been in preparation?' I ask.

'Since as the man Tony you were eight years old.'

I can feel an acceptance but the measure of time is prompting a question. 'Is this event in real time?'

Edward doesn't answer and resumes his pacing, every now and then looking sideways at me with a quizzical expression. 'We could have a long conversation about that,' he says eventually, 'but for now it's not the wisest course of action.

He stops pacing, smiles reassuringly and walks back to his seat. 'As I understand it, when you refer to real time you mean this event is taking place in the same time period in which you are able to recall it. Is that acceptable?'

'Yes –that's how I mean it Edward'.

'Then let me confirm to you we are conversing in real time'.

I just knew he was going to say *that*, just as I know my question intended more than my words conveyed. 'The trouble is, as well you know, when I'm back in my physical head the reality issue arises no matter what I learn and recall'.

His eyes become serious. 'We are having this conversation because we believe there is a way to progress your work'. Who is 'we' I wonder –me and Edward and who else? In preparation since the age of eight! What is he trying to tell me?

'Yes, of course I believe it possible but my earthly nature is in doubt, it's confused.'

'Stop there!' he commands, 'You are travelling uncharted waters'. He comes over to me, sits at my side on the couch and takes my hands in his.

'You are more than just two –four in your present awareness and each self expresses consciousness differently, but yes you do have an agreement to express the order of this grouping; each self has so agreed. What you must now recognise is the earthly self has limitations expressing different forms of consciousness. Some gaps in your remembrances as an earthly being will be filled, some will not and some states of consciousness recovered from your journeys in this world will have the tenor of fairy tales.

I know he is addressing me as Tony but I feel I'm Peter self as he speaks.

'Am I not Peter?'

'You are –it is Peter's consciousness you share on arising in this world.

'I feel unsure of my earth nature, being here in a present world takes away my sense of action.'

'Your earth self intelligence is governed by the space time continuum and that consciousness is necessarily fragmented as it becomes aware of this world. The personality beings physical and mental order of sense has developed self coherence in a linear form –this is particularly true when the earthly self communicates to other earthly selves; harmonic understanding is short lived because the objective world is perceived differently by every soul. Another way of saying this is that conventions of expression are established. They may appear language based but I assure you they are not. It is the intellect, the output of sense recognition that determines the form of earthly consciousness. The earthly self cannot know reality –it is selective of what it perceives.

'I can accept that Peter and I think differently but are you telling me we are unlike as soul beings?'

'No I am not; the soul is not confined to one form. In this world human consciousness evolves differently –it accepts the higher order of self determines how the senses express. We are not governed by the space-time continuum and evolve between events rather than within them. When connecting with time formed realities Peter knows them to be illusions – reflections of a higher reality. The link between yourself and Peter is expressed as an instrumental form of consciousness –in such manner you can accept Peter totally unaware of Self difference.'

I nod emphatically. 'Yes that is how it works.'

'True and it will continue but now a change has occurred in the patterns of consciousness causing you to experience the phenomenon of astral awareness and be aware of Peter objectively. Peter is now experiencing a restriction in consciousness as he is focuses on the arising of human nature to this world. Both your selves are bound together in a search for common identity. In the present state Peter is the providential instrument and you are the pupil.'

'Can there be harmony between us in this new pattern of consciousness?'

'The harmony between you both is unquestioned when ascending in the order of known being and you channel the revelations of astral consciousness. The opposite is true when you are aware of this world as well as your own. Questions abound and identity threatens to fragment. What is happening now is a sharing of differences as your consciousness seeks to be reconciled with the higher order of its Being.'

'I sense awareness of beginnings but I don't properly understand why the pattern of consciousness that has worked harmoniously for many years in my earthly life has changed. I can point to some events that have been an influence but not to the cause.'

'Recall as a young man still serving in the Royal Navy you were introduced to the delights of Shakespeare and how then you started to write –first poems then becoming interested in dramatic dialogues?'

'Yes I can but I never actually wrote any dialogue –I felt unsure about my inner voice.'

'Unsure?'

'The dialogue was Shakespearean in character and I couldn't bring myself to write it; I thought I might be ridiculed.'

Edward raises his eyebrows and looks at me questioningly, 'and?' For some reason I feel embarrassed by his questioning tone, 'and what?'

'For a while thereafter you became confused about your sexuality – remember?' I nod.

'That occurred because your astral self and personality self harmonised in that connection –you wasn't channelling instrumentally, you was actively, albeit unconsciously, changing the order of the conscious path.'

I have this strange feeling that Edward is going to connect the changes that have allowed this form of astral communication with that event –yet this is over 40 years ago! 'What are you telling me –what am I to understand?'

'You were born to the flesh as a man of two paths –how that manifested depended upon a number of different experiences but that event in which the personality mind and the astral mind harmonised had a direct bearing on the outcome we are discussing now.'

'In what way?'

'Peter was conceived.' So that's it. I sink back into the sofa. 'But he didn't make it into the physical world -did he?'

'No –had it been so this conversation would never have materialised.'

'And what would have happened –had he been born into a physical body?'

Edward puts his hands up in a gesture of helplessness. 'How can I answer that? The possibilities are endless.'

'Why have I not known this before?'

'You have –but it hasn't meant anything to your earthly mind –now that this new pattern of consciousness has arisen you are aware of the separation of yourself.'

Edward stops speaking and I am conscious of him studying me. I glance over toward the bookcase and fancy I see the works of Shakespeare beautifully bound spanning a shelf. I am looking back at Edward and he is smiling as he begins to speak. "Who would fardels bear, to grunt and sweat under a weary life, but that the dread of something after death, the undiscovered country, from whose bourn no traveller returns, puzzles the will, and makes us rather bear those ills we have, than fly to others we know not of?"

'You know the soliloquy of course?'

'Yes –and I've always puzzled over the meaning of the phrase 'from whose bourn no traveller returns' –am I not proof of the contrary?'

'You are if it's taken literally –but not so if you accept he was speaking figuratively.'

'Can you explain?'

'Peter cannot enter into the flesh —if he were to incarnate his identity would fragment.'

'Yes —but what of me?'

'You are sharing Peter's world —that is the uniqueness of your experience.'

'Are you saying that in remembering as my physical self I must accept a fragmentary explanation of my travels?'

'No'. He says sharply, 'certainly not.'

Again he stands up, straightens his coat and begins to walk meditatively in slow measured steps in front of the windows. 'Tell me, as your earthly self you have a phrase you are fond of repeating when teaching your pupils, that to you nothing is new; The Wisdom of Solomon, eh?'

'Yes I do'.

'As Peter in this present existence you don't use the phrase, in fact you don't think like that at all'. It's true; as Peter such thinking is completely unnecessary, any enquiry human or otherwise accounts for the awareness I possess.

'Why do you think your earthly self needs to make such statement?'

'I don't know, the human ego perhaps raising it's I function head? Courting mystery?

'It's true the human ego needs little encouragement to assign mystical values to itself —but no, the statement is made because your earthly self and your Astral self share the same being —your present frustration arises from the new relationship now forming between yourself and Peter.'

Edwards's analysis has me feeling I'm a 'square peg in a round hole. 'If I understand you right the struggle I have on remembering astral journey arises because of who I am?'

'In part —in part only', he stops his pacing. 'You are at the crossroads — you cannot go back and to progress you must be prepared to make changes. You are beginning to feel the need to make assumptions in order to understand; that is the cause of your anguish. As Peter you are expressing the relationship as you always have done. Peter's reality is your mystery.

These astral journeys will continue until the physical binds you no longer —the self thus aware of its separation will share experience. Until now Peter has acknowledged the needs of the linear mind only as your own education demanded.'

Answers

'You mean that our relationship is now changing?'

'It has been changing since conception –but radically so since you have become conscious of Peter in the astral world communications you are recording' I understand what Edward is saying but I don't understand what it is I must now do differently. 'What must I do?'

'I can only suggest', he says carefully, 'there are questions, need of knowledge to be satisfied of. There are matters you care about, but don't accord with Peter's need in this world. Your awareness and his will intermingle –on occasions you will feel imprisoned by the influence you cannot express. Where all this will lead you I cannot say'

I sit and watch his still form as he gazes out on the garden and lawns beyond the window. I can feel myself changing; my physical form losing its boyishness and becoming wholly female. I am taller, my hair long and black; I wear a long flowing red dress and my sense of being is aware of many cycles and seasons. Edward is speaking again.

'Nothing remains the same; everything changes. This world is changing, we must all do what we must –the higher orders of our selves determine that'. He turns and looks awhile at me, smiling contentedly.

'Alpha and Omega; that which is first shall be last and that which is last shall be first. You are not alone –you never have been. Truly reality is not knowing –the great awe-sight of ignorance, isn't that how you put it in one of your poems? I rather like that phrasing'.

I feel him most intensely –my entire sense of being is focussed upon his which begins to illuminate from within until gradually his shape fades from my sight. I am suspended above the floor and the room retracts and moves into miniature. I have an overwhelming sense of leaving something behind I do not want to be parted from. The last thing I remember is Edwards' voice soberly saying, 'there is yet another obstacle to overcome –yet you will, have faith.'

Chapter TWENTYTWO:
Man of Two Paths

Astonishingly I am still standing on the patio; my lower body feeling as if it's encased in a cast of heavy material. I'm immediately struck by the dullness of colour of all things about me. There is a kind of emptiness in the atmosphere. My body normalises and I walk away from the house down the garden into the garage –I cannot face talking to anyone and need time to readjust.

I'm not doing anything sensible; overwhelmed as I am recalling this astral event and the remembering my reactions at every turn of the conversation with Edward. After a while I mentally calm down and start thinking of tasking myself to write it down. I'm having guilt feelings about walking away from the house –not immediately dashing inside and exulting to Pam about what I had just received. Self discovery is making me sensitive and holds me back from sharing –so I make a determined effort to concentrate on simple things and make myself useful about the house.

Grounding helps and later after lunch my usual self control is back in place. Recording this journey is near to a nightmare as my conscious mind keeps getting in the way when I try dispassionately to make notes. It takes a whole week and many hours before I'm satisfied that the most of what happened is written down. Only then do I allow myself to fully consider the implications of my conversation with Edward.

I'm immediately struck by the connection between the previous journey talking with Edward in the library and this in the 'room next door' –as it appears to be a continuation of the same experience. We leave one room and entered another still talking apparently. Edward locks the door which seems unnecessary –yet as I recall it felt right at the time and assume it was done to have me feel we were talking in private. When I consult my previous journey notes I see over three weeks have elapsed since the library room journey occurred –no wonder I was asking if my experience was in real time! Even more startling is the change in my character –in the first journey with Edward I was clearly Peter, in this I am remembering myself despite the fact I was not in my body but in Peter's. It makes my head reel just thinking about it.

Anyhow I've got some answers –I'm no longer thinking my state of mind has been 'altered' by smoking cannabis and regretting it, but can acknowledge that whilst it was a 'trigger' along with a series of events that have occurred since I was a young boy, the cause itself is my peculiar nature. As Edward puts it 'a man of two paths', Peter in effect is *me* in another self relationship. Many things now begin to make sense.

The reference that Edward makes to being in preparation since the age of eight can only refer to an experience I've always been curious about. During the summer of 1949 I was returning from school with a neighbouring lad of my own age –his father was a major in the army and the class difference was not lost to the neighbours as I vaguely recall my parents having conversations about them. It was expected that Brian my school companion and his older brother and sister would go to grammar school and onward into some glorious career whereas my elder brother and I were destined for something less grand.

In way of underlining his 'class' superiority on the way home that evening Brian said of me after I ventured an opinion about something that I would never amount to anything. I smarted at that –feeling he was trying to put me down. After parting to our respective homes and feeling angry and wronged I wandered into the garden still brooding over the issue.

Looking up in the sky for no particular reason there I saw a cloud shaped like a saintly man looking down at me and in the same instant heard words clear in my head. 'Your time will come', the voice said. The voice rather than the words expressed suddenly calmed me and I sat down on the path as if transfixed. I didn't stay there long as I realised my school trousers might get dirty and mother would have something to say about that I'd rather not hear –so I stood and looked up again. The cloud was no longer there –nothing remotely like it was there. I never did tell anyone, wary even then of speaking my mind.

As for the 'Shakespearean incidents' as a teenager whilst still in the Royal Navy –I remember it well and looking back I regret not having written down those internal dialogues that seemed to flow effortlessly despite being in situations when my mind was also engaged in doing other things. And as I recall they occurred again a few years later when I was attempting to write plays and dismissed as not relevant! And yes Edward is right about my sexuality. For a number of years thereafter I was not sure I was heterosexual. I thought of myself as bisexual but male experiences never satisfied – mentally I felt connected but physically turned off. Eventually I stabilised and had a string of girl friends, finally marrying at 27 happy and contented with the knowledge of myself. My wife and I have three wonderful children.

The sense of being two persons however, has always haunted me –it was particularly strong in the three months prior to my leaving the Royal Navy. I was sent to Haslar hospital to be treated for reoccurring conjunctivitis. Consider my situation; I had prospects to become a special duties officer –all I had to do was press ahead; the road was clearly marked. All I had to do was to stay focussed. Who or what was it that kept prompting my voice as I underwent sight test after sight test that ultimately found me unfit for my branch and specialisation?

I was conscious then of another self that gave 'wrong' answer to the examining doctors –yet I could not argue with my inner voice. I felt compelled. When the final eye examination results were reviewed and I was wearing a pair of John Lennon specs the Queens Consultant surgeon in charge of my case said (with a smile), 'do you want to change branch –be a cook or an administrator –or leave the Royal Navy?'

He gave me 24 hours to think it over. Somehow my promising career meant little to me and I began to justify why I should leave, idealistically arguing that whatever position I eventually attained I would still be responsible for firing the guns and that was unacceptable. Six weeks later after having been discharged I was leaving a pensions board interview – without a pension because, as the examining doctor succinctly put it 'there is nothing wrong with your eyes but there will be if you continue to wear spectacles'.

Standing on the pavement wondering what to do next –I wasn't shattered, upset or thinking I'd done wrong. No. my feelings just said 'OK, now press on', but I was in uncharted territory, I knew no one bar a couple of naval friends. Thereafter I was 'looked after' by influences I later realised were communicators in the astral worlds –and I have been ever since.

I've had no further communications of this kind for over a fortnight. I think it's because I've reached an impasse –understanding but not understanding. Somehow it doesn't matter that my 'mission' is unclear and my questioning mind unsatisfied by events and that they might never be. The desire to remember remains strong and I feel pulled toward this other reality as flotsam is lifted from the shore on a high tide and drawn out to sea by the ebb; the strength of tidal flow governed by that pale orb of a moon. Relentlessly the influence pulls on my psyche. Whither to now I wonder?

Chapter TWENTYTHREE:
Yesterday's Seven Thousand Years

It's raining and my client has cancelled. I'm standing under the eaves of my clinic rooms looking out across a picturesque garden in Petersfield, Hampshire, drinking in the silence. Conscious of pigeons perched on a high tree at the edge of my vision swivelling their heads this way and that. The scene has a timeless feel about it, so much so concerns of every kind dissipate and every building, wall and plant, every impression in sight begins to waver and blur like I am seeing through water. A deep sense of contentment fills my entire being.

I am walking with carefree ease from a grove of trees onto the banks of a lake. Swans and ducks are everywhere –the latter bobbing up and down on the water feeding from the sedge around the lake's edge. I am making my way to a boathouse; it's a ramshackle affair, long since neglected. Much of the planking that formed the roof is missing and the exposed rafters, grey and pitted black, sag with age. Sitting on the planking that forms stage from the boat house to shore bank is an old friend of mine. It's Chan, a communicator I've known for many years. In the bright sunshine his black satin like robe, red rimmed sleeves and collar contrast his lightly tanned face and hands.

'Greetings Chan'

'Greetings young one'

He has before him two decorated porcelain food bowls steaming in the still air. He motions me to join him and we sit awhile looking out over the lake in silence.

'Water, water, everywhere', says Chan smiling. 'And not a drop to drink', I rejoin, 'at least that's what the song says.'

'I don't think the ducks would agree with you, my son'

'No. Perhaps not but we are not in need of it as they are'

'We are, but unlike the ducks we don't understand our needs as well as they do theirs'. Chan strokes his slender goatee beard thoughtfully. The smell from the steaming beverage before us wafts into my nostrils, smelling like a vegetable and herb soup. 'Teach me about it Chan –why do we need the water?'

'Our forms are water –some earth, fire and air but mostly water.'

'And why do we choose to make them so, Chan?' He laughs and wags his head side to side. 'Choose! Choose? We do not choose, it is the manifest order of all things that come out of the earth.'

'We don't come out of the earth. You yourself have taught me that Chan'.

'I have and it's a truth that holds a meaning you now need to understand. The order of our being is conceived in Spirit but the form of life, ours included, arises out of matter and the mind of earthly being. Like the duck we are clothed in water.'

'I see', I say reflectively; not sure what he might be telling me besides the physics of form. 'That which you know is governed by water –water is material of the mind that binds and gives expression'.

'If water binds what else are we made of?'

'Earth, Air, Fire and Aether.' I look at Chan who stares impassively out across the lake. 'Hmmn… yes I see what you mean but this won't satisfy my human mind. Can you explain it further?'

'The consciousness of earth mind being arises from the action of water upon the soul's essence. First, let us understand what we mean by the elements I speak of. Fire is the first element –this is the primal energy created by the Great Unmanifest in order to preserve itself. This act of self preservation creates the manifest order of Being. The manifest Fire has power of defining –to Fire single and many are the same.

Earth is the energy arising from the action of Fire made aware of itself as the first principle of manifest Being. Earth is the material of creation, made single and made separate to be the many by the causal fire seeking to

151

define itself. Individual life is conceived in the Earth element and born thereof in the myriad of forms comprising universal conceptions.

Air is the energy created from the fusion of the fire that defines and the earth that forms –air is the element that gives birth to consciousness and reaches back to the Great Unmanifest. Water is the fourth element brought into being by the reaction of earth and fire to the element of air –water is the cause that seeks to redefine and progress the primordial character of fire, earth and air.

The fifth element is aether, the energy caused by air yet it is governed by water and will continue so to be for as long as Fire gives birth to Earth and they in conflict give birth to Air.'

Chan speaks with quiet authority, his facial and body expression is disarmingly passive, contrasting strongly with the clear and direct expression of speech. I have no idea of his background, his time period in physical life or his present station in the life of this world. Ancient is a word that comes to mind but beyond that I only know him as a communicator who assists me on healing matters where disturbing mind conditions figure strongly as part of the need.

'Chan I thank you, I take to heart what you say. For the benefit of my personality mind are you able teach further how all this affects the souls' development in the earthly world and in this?' He is silent and still for a moment and then reaches forward and picks up one of the bowls. 'Drink with me my young friend.'

Together we sip the beverage. It smells and tastes of vegetable and herbs, the effect calming and mind cleansing (I cannot describe it more accurately). 'Water records everything; by its very nature it assembles –it is caused so to do. Our mind and body being, as we know them are dominated by this element. As I have told you water is the fourth element that seeks to redefine the primordial character of Fire, and harmonise the disparate natures of Earth and Air. It does this by propagating self relationships, and in so doing creates many from the one. You and I are individuals in which all elements are present, it is true of the beverage you drink, of the clothes we wear, the atmosphere, the ground, the water, the sky –these ducks and swans, the wood and stone of this platform and boathouse –all is individual.

Within each individual is the same elemental conflict that brings about eternal change –nothing can remain the same. The wood and stone will powder and dry, forms will change and the power of mind within will change. The element of water will ensure that the nature of everything will maintain existence though it changes continually. Everything your senses are aware of is dominated by water. All this', he paused and waved his free hand dismissively, 'all this is the product of our minds'.

'Do you mean we have invented it, Chan?'

'No. Your question arises from the human mind that develops its intellect in a linear expression; sensing forms of life as separate beings – indeed all forms of life in the physical worlds express the same way though simpler structures limited in sense expression do not restrict, as man does, their form identity.'

'If I understand you correctly Chan, all this here, for example, water, trees, ducks, swans, and fish no doubt and you and I, are all one and the same being?'

'That is correct'.

'How come the ducks move by their own volition, the skies change –and the wood here', I say tapping the stage on which I sit, 'will moulder and decay whether I like it or not?'

'Is that not because of the way that you sense them?'

'Ah!' I'm thinking. Now I understood the relationship between myself and other things. 'You mean that all this is like this because of how I sense it!'

'Yes and no. Yes, it is correct to say that form is as you perceive it. No, because the parts of the whole live as parts by the very nature of their creation. You have experienced perception through the mind of a bird, other forms also –they do not see the universe in the same way as yourself. Yet they like you see and know creation objectively.

The physical world is a world of energy, like this, it is part shaped by natural forces from within and without, by non-human creations and also by humans themselves. When you make things as you must from natural substances and other living forms the character created is indelibly linked to the maker and so long as the maker has need of the creation it will live in that form even though it may be physically destroyed.

This platform on which we sit and the boathouse is an example of what I am explaining to you. This structure was constructed for a certain lord and the use of his family who also owned the lake we now view in the 19th century of the earth world time. It became part of their consciousness – awareness shared by succeeding generations including the local populace. From time to time mind shifting events occurred in which this structure shared experience –some happy, some sad. Gradually as decades grew in number the boathouse ceased to be used and maintenance was discontinued,

153

but those to whom it was part of life continued to imbue its presence with their own spirit.

Here on this side of life the creative impulse has shared the character with many who had no life in the locality in which it is constructed. In this way not only was this structure made before plank and upright were cut for the purpose but continues as a place of being long after the physical foundation mouldered into dust. It is now part of your consciousness and for as long as you need it will be here.'

I reflect for a moment on my experience with the buzzards and then again on my meeting and working with Hinetobada and Ishotea. 'But there must be differences between this world and the physical world –differences that determine how we see and know?'

'Yes Peter, there are differences. To begin this education we must first understand the law of cycles. All laws are governing principles of manifest being except one that also governs the great Unmanifest –that is the law of cycles. To preserve itself the Unmanifest created the manifest world, the act of creation itself is a cycle –so we know that all this we now refer to in our conversation will ultimately return to the Great Unmanifest beyond which we have no understanding. As you can therefore appreciate, understanding whatever form of being expresses, is subject to the law of the circle.

And that law is simply this; the one is also the many and many are defined by the first and last. That which is last shall be first and that which is first shall be last; that which is born must die and that which dies must be reborn.

The difference you seek to understand is like all being, governed by the causal cycle –life in all its forms is seeking birth –birth that separates and birth that unifies. When the cycle of being approaches the nadir the earth element dominates consciousness and the one becomes many. The earth element weakens as the cycle moves to the zenith and the fifth element determines the substance of a new cycle. The water element pervades all forms as they arise from the nadir but aether gathers strength and ultimately dissolves objective realities.'

'But this world is an objective world is it not?'

'It appears to be'. Chan looks sideways at me with a smile on his old face. 'Relax my young friend, drink and be refreshed'. I reach out for the bowl startled to see that it is again full of steaming beverage. 'How did you do that?' I ask.

'Do what?' he says innocently.

'Oh come on Chan –you know I've drunk from the cup and here it is full again!' I accept he has the capability to change things but feel he is now playing a game and should own up and explain.

'But did I fill it up? I think not, maybe you believe you have drunk from the cup –perhaps you have, but when did you drink from it –just now? Or might it be with yourself and yesterdays' seven thousand years?

He was Chan no longer, he was my beloved Omar. I raised my cup and saluted him. 'To yesterdays' seven thousand years'

I drank and I was inwardly peaceful. It no longer mattered what I thought –I cared for nothing and the stillness was absolute.

Chapter TWENTYFOUR:
On The Bridge of Two Worlds

I'm pleased with myself; for once I'm not in contention with anything that's occurred. On arrival of my next patient I still feel very much 'connected' to the impression of peace and tranquillity experienced in the aftermath of my journey with Chan. This patient, a woman in her early thirties suffers from asthma and gut disorders –this is the third time I have treated her. After the session ends Tina remarks to me how evenly balanced she feels; aware of an inward sense of strength and confidence. She eagerly books a further appointment.

Naturally I'm pleased to receive such positive feedback, particularly so as the nervous tension in her upper body has disappeared, but what impresses me more than anything is the attunement I experienced during the session. It was intensely intimate; an expression of knowing the depth of her being. During a healing session I attune myself to a higher state of consciousness and as energies flow will have an awareness of my patient's nature and need. This was different –it was as if in attunement I had joined with Tina's higher nature and *together* we were instrumental of healing energies to alleviate the problems of her conscious nature.

Curious as to her reaction to the healing I ask if she is feeling anything different about this session as compared to the previous appointment. She looks at me oddly for a moment and smiles, 'it wasn't you, was it?'

On the Bridge of Two Worlds

It's on the tip of my tongue to tell her my view –but I choose instead to agree and honour Chan the connection. With a wave goodbye Tina walks out of the courtyard leaving me thinking. The healing bridged two realities –this one and some other in which Tina was a wholly balanced being working with my higher nature to effect healing upon the lower BodyMind system. I've no doubt my journey with Chan made this kind of intercession possible and accept the experience as proof of Chan's teachings. Everything is linked and Soul progresses by harmonising the 'is' of different states. From the many *is* born the One.

I return home in the evening refreshed and more relaxed than ever since the astral journeying began. After recording the experience with Chan I feel able to switch my attention to other matters. The questions that have goaded my consciousness in previous weeks are all but faded to memory and I no longer feel driven by these astral events. It's a bank holiday weekend and with family matters high on the agenda I'm happy to be involved, but notice, almost as an aside, glimpses of astral world activity. In the days and weeks that follow this kind of experience increasingly happens, until one evening understanding of this practise of glimpsing, as I must call it, begins to coalesce in my mind.

Until recently astral journeying events have claimed my attention to the exclusion of everything else –some causing me severe disorientation on return and followed by an indeterminate state of awareness during which my sense of time was confused. I'm now noticing that my mental and physical response to travelling is changing –beginning with my meeting with Edward. I'm able to recover my objective self more quickly and accept more easily what has occurred. This is particularly true of my journey with Chan. I believe the practise of glimpsing is made possible by the inward harmony I now have with Peter.

Changes continue to occur. I awake one morning with a clear remembrance of a vivid dream in which I am flying. The experience is particularly convincing since I am instructing someone else. For the record my instruction took the form of encouraging the innate ability of my pupil: a young woman whose strident personality got in the way of learning. I'm not aware of knowing her in the flesh. With patience (born of Job I would think) and after many mini demonstrations I eventually get her to rise above ground long enough to realise she doesn't need the solid earth to propel and maintain flight.

This is not my first experience of flying but it's been some years since a previous vivid dream of this kind. I awake at my normal time, the experience vividly alive in my mind but with pressing things to do I got out of bed, dress and breakfast in 'autopilot' mode.

My first task is to bank some cheques –I open up the garage to take the car and begin to think better of it –surely I should fly? It occurs to me that other people also have this ability but for reasons best known to them don't use the skill. It would look odd therefore if I were to fly whilst everyone else is walking or driving so I decide after my banking chore I will find an open area away from curious eyes and do the natural thing.

On leaving the bank the brain mind engages and my flying mentality comes down to 'earth' with a thump. I don't feel foolish as you might expect –I'm disappointed. This state of total belief lasts approximately two hours during which time I am conscious of the world around me and able to interact sensibly with other people –yet at one and the same time I am aware of a another reality; a kind of super sensible physical world.

Another recent experience appeared to operate in the 'clairvoyant manner' –something I'm very familiar with. I was talking with my eldest son in his London flat, a heart to heart talk you might call it about concerns in his love life –then without warning the atmosphere behind him became wavy lines of fluid like energy. A communicator connected to my son appeared on the other side of this curtain –the body language of this man indicated he was listening to us. As our talk continued I was conscious of being watched. The communicator showed signs of obvious pleasure as our conversation came to agreement and then, just as quickly as this condition appeared, it vanished. This experience was different to clairvoyant expression I'm used to –I felt as if I was standing on a bridge between two worlds. Even more extraordinary the experience felt familiar, which of course it is not.

Some days after this occurrence I am in Kent with my wife, visiting my mother and younger brother. We are sitting in the living room of the family house discussing possible tree cutting scenarios. The family house is bordered by tall pines my father planted some 50 years ago. Sitting in the living room that overlooks these trees we discuss the pruning actions now needed to thin them out. My mother disappears into the kitchen and the conversation lulls. Suddenly my vision is extended and I see past the trees, past the recreation ground behind them and on and on –unlike any kind of vision I've previously known. I feel as if I'm visually experiencing interconnectedness with everything in sight. Clarity of detail doesn't cause me to think and neither does any form or substance my sight penetrates. It's as if my visual ability has mind that knows about everything it connects with. Then without weakening the condition of 'seeing' stops and my normal sight returns. In real time only seconds elapse and neither my brother nor Pam aware of what has happened to me.

Later that day we all take a drive in the countryside. We motor along a road where I and my older brother David, in the aftermath of World War 2, walked to infant school, Geoff tells me the building is now converted to a private dwelling, then as an aside before the house comes into view says, 'on the left is where the spinney used to be'. As the word 'spinney' is said I can see, hear and smell the old steam train that used to pass behind the junior school nearby. In my vision I stand in the school's spinney garden waving to the steam engine driver as his locomotive puffing black smoke edges round the bordering banks to pass over a bridge into the local station.

What makes this memory return different to the usual recall experience is the intensity of sensorial remembrance whilst simultaneously aware of sitting in the car. The entire event could not have lasted more than a few seconds because we were talking.

Last week during a daily dog walk circuiting the local cemetery I was conscious at one stage of passing through a thick soup like energy. I looked down but couldn't see anything out of the ordinary. At that moment two people passed by talking, their voices easily heard, but strangely I couldn't understand what they were saying. This condition lasted a few minutes only and thereafter until I left the cemetery my feet felt odd as if they didn't belong to me and for a while I lacked the ability to be cognitive of events about me. Kya showed no sign of being aware of a change. On reflection it felt as if I was *physically* bridged between two dimensions of reality.

Today I am working in the garden, a physical therapy I much enjoy and made that much more relaxing because it's the first really warm sun of the year. A buzzing noise, intermittent at first then consistent, manifests; looking around I can't place where it's coming from realising as I scan about the sound holds spatially close to my right ear. As I listen I become conscious of being in another place –standing on a street pavement in a city. A tall building with long slit like windows towers ahead across the road. Looking left and right I notice that other buildings look similar having at their base shop windows and wide doorways. Here and there some buildings are in process of construction others being demolished. People move along the pavements like automatons seemingly unaware of one another in the half-light of evening. There is an overall dullness to everything. Shop windows are barely lit; detail of their fascias lost to silhouettes and the lighted windows of taller buildings merely glow. The only transports I can see moving are cars –no Lorries, vans or buses. And they pass quickly in the street, streaks of light illuminating their darkened shells.

I'm still conscious of standing in my garden –apparently in two places at once. I've been aware of bi-locating many years previous but then only by being told of the other state I was in by a person who witnessed me being there.

The people I observe passing by appear to move unthinkingly –almost mechanical. Facially they are pictures of distraction as if some inner world of thought absorbs their attention. Oblivious of me some are dressed leisurely, others in business style suits and coats and all are adults. Both sexes wear tight fitting glossy looking fabrics, the men have high lapelled coats and cutaway collars and their neckties vary from standard to loose fitting cravats. The older women are mainly dressed in trousers with slimmer and younger women wearing skirts slit just above the knee and plunging false neck lines. Most have necklace jewellery and sport an array of stylish handbags. The sound of conversation behind me changes my focus. I turn to observe a group of young people in their late teens and early twenties. A young man informally dressed in a floral shirt offset by a white cravat like scarf is speaking.

'Come on Tuesday, come on! It's your scene, you've gotta believe it. The place will be fucking packed. Cool music, an all night moving show, believe me. Pills if you want.'

'I'm not going on my own', replies a pretty girl stylishly dressed in calf boots, short black skirt and a shawl like top. At the centre of a female threesome she exchanges glances and whispers with her companions who in turn shrill with private laugher.

The young man in the floral shirt tugs at the sleeve of his male companion. 'Come on, come on', he says anxiously. The body language of the group is overtly sexual –the young men stand self consciously hands in pockets and shoulders hunched, the girls are grouped separately and are making efforts to appear uninterested but their posturing tells a different story.

I can hear other voices now emanating from a shop front behind me – voices on television advertising something. The words are not clear but the invitation to get something free is constantly repeated. A man has now stopped in front of me talking to a woman; they obviously know one another. His voice is low and inaudible but I get the distinct impression he is explaining something. A loud banging sound distracts me; it sounds like a pile driver. It stops and I hear a voice calling my surname, over emphasising the leading vowel –I think I should no longer be here, but the voice persists, repeating my name and my curious nature pays attention. I'm vaguely aware of a man wearing a wide brimmed hat and a long cloak standing in shadows. He addresses me again, this time more intimately.

'All is vanity my dear boy, show me if you can the eyes that have lights that shine from within'.

I look again at the busy scene, the thronging streets and observe the attention that some pay to others, how conversations sensed from my vantage point either defend or demand and those that don't talk in their passage through this scene either determinedly ignore their surroundings or are wrapt up in their own concerns –I'm not sure which. There is urgency in the atmosphere, a sexual imperative seeking resolution pervading even the most platonic of encounters.

I'm curious about the voice –the man is quoting a couplet from one of my poems. 'Are all these people dead?' I query the voice.

'That's a bit strong my boy, let's just say they are searching for their identity –and yes some live on your side of life. Fascinating isn't it, don't you think?' I'm not sure how to answer this, instead I ask about the buildings. 'The architecture looks ultra modern as if it belongs to some future time.'

On answering the voice is firm, definite and not a little musical, 'Masks my dear boy, masks; the perfect companions to these searching souls'.

'It's all just memory and imagination then; this place doesn't feel real. It feels solid but not real'.

'Not real you say? It's real I assure you, the world you are accustomed to often behaves like this, the only difference is that here the thought is naked for everyone to see. Look at those people on the elevator'. I look across the street to a tall building and espy a series of connecting lights up the side facing the street and within the glow make out forms of people passing up and down an elevator.

'Some stand still and let the moving staircase carry them, others press ahead anxious to get ahead of time, some are going and some are coming – business done or yet to be, satisfied, disappointed, frustrated –isn't that familiar?'

I admit that it is.

'And what do these souls gather in their mad pursuit? I fear they exercise only their primal passions and these they mostly do not admit too. It's always someone or something other than their person that progresses consciousness. Causes are with the causer and many you see are living out a

161

rebellion they themselves have not instigated.'

Again I agree, 'but surely you are not saying these are all bad people?'

'Bad? Good? One man's meat is another man's poison –these people are neither bad nor good, they are searching for peace of mind, and that my boy, is not a moral certainty; it's the inevitable reaction to knowing'.

'I don't follow?'

'We are born aware of missing parts and such awareness gives rise to the pursuit of knowledge –the language of search. In the hunt you will build and lay waste that which is built, you will break, terminate and cause to grow new things, ideas and ways of being.'

'You make it sound like learning is achieved only by making mistake and destroying'.

'There you go again', he sighs dramatically, 'talking rights and wrongs, but it's understandable, dear boy –I've been there, and we all grow from the same pain'.

'So we all do grow then', I say doggedly conscious that this conversation is getting away from me and I must pay attention. This man is no mean intellect.

'Yes we do, but some grow slower than others'.

'How would you suggest we improve our rate of growth then?'

'In this world and in yours witness that which is within is found from without. What you find in others is the way of finding yourself; that which you like and love is confirmation of what you have found; the cause of pain and problem yet to be embraced. Man has no governance over the law of attraction. Look to art dear boy; the painter interprets –their art is the joining of that which is without and that which is within. Great art results from an inner acceptance of the subjects' unrealised nature. Great artists whatever their mediums are arbitrary creatures out of step with the norm –difficult to live with, difficult to understand.'

'And?'

'And Man is a great artist!' He laughs as one who enjoys his own jokes. This conversation is becoming so interesting I find I'm working the same patch of garden over and over again. I look about to regain my composure – yes I'm still very much into my world.

'What are you intending to grow dear boy?'

'I'm not sure to be honest –if I can keep alive those plants already rooted I will be well pleased. Perhaps I need to buy some plants for this area'. I say referring to the border by the wall I'm cultivating.

On the Bridge of Two Worlds

'Think of a lily my boy, I would love you to grow a lily or two –soil is not ideal but something can be done in that border.'

My consciousness is changing –I can hear and see this other world and be present in my own at the same time, but now the images and sense of space in that other world so clear and intense a moment ago no longer prompts my inquiry; it is becoming a picture and the meaning of it receding from my consciousness, but the voice still holds my attention.

'Do I know you? I ask sensing that this is not a first meeting. 'Oh, yes I've been taking an interest in you for many years, ever since you discovered the talent of writing. The last time you retained image of my connection you described me as like the man on the label of Sandeman's Port!'

I can hear him laughing, clearly amused by the description.

'You are Oscar, right?'

He doesn't answer but goes on to say this –'we are losing connection; keep this in mind when pondering the question of growth. The greatest sin is I suggest deferred responsibility. We all suffer from it and I suffered needlessly because of it, yet would I have achieved if I had not? I will leave that question with you dear boy; ponder on the necessity of sin! In the meantime Au revoir and remember the lily.'

In the minutes and hours that follow memory of this journey virtually disappears –I even forget about the lily. Now three days later I partially remember the event and begin to write it down –as I write more returns.

My sleeping pattern is being interrupted by the need of loo visits, not once but often twice and occasionally three times in the small hours. Yesterday this stopped and I slept through till late. I'm remembering looking at the face of someone convinced I am looking at myself. It doesn't make sense because the facial features are different to mine. The eyes are markedly inset and folds of flesh line down either side of the nose and above the eyebrows; the mouth has thin lips and is small when compared to the broad span of face. The chin is pointed, the hair short, wiry and blond. The impression is of a person who is not entirely human.

I try to put it out of my mind. Three days have passed and today suddenly by no apparent cause the identity of the face is revealed. It's my teacher Len –dead these last two years.

If ever I needed a steadying influence –Len was the person to give it. We first met some 40 years ago when I had no intention of being connected to such 'quackery'. Needless to say I changed my mind, greatly influenced by his extraordinary ability. Although calling his self a Christian Spiritualist, I learned he was as unorthodox as you could possibly be. He had that rare gift of deep trance and some communications were of alien dimensions and it was not unusually for him to remark of the presence of elemental creatures and of mind shifts occurring as a result of linking with alien beings. Different as chalk is to cheese, not only in temperament and sexual proclivity; our backgrounds and general approach to life were far apart. Perhaps those differences made our psychic relationship that much more intense; we had attunement allowing ESP communication over distance and an inner sense of unity that crystallised in the acts of service we did for others.

This is my teacher attuning himself to me in a form that shows the influence of other beings. And I know I've only to concentrate on this memory to be able to consciously travel. It's a revelation. I can now see looking back over recent events how my travelling modus operandi has been changing; I am now showing signs of an ability to experience consciousness simultaneously in this and other dimensional states.

Chapter TWENTYFIVE:
Where Angels fear to tread

I'm beginning to feel I have control; my awareness of Len is giving me confidence. I am enthusiastic and receptive to the idea of Len helping me attune to other dimensional realities. The days wear on and I become impatient for events to begin afresh. As nothing happens of its own accord I carve out some time and sit meditatively linking to the memory of my astral view of Len. Nothing happens.

OK –so I'm not in the right state of mind –I'll prepare myself before sleeping for connection. Days and nights pass without incident –it's over a week now with no hint of activity. I'm beginning to think that somewhere along the line I've screwed up. This morning I'm feeling particularly sorry for myself when I hear Don's voice clairaudiently. It sounds distant –all I know for certain it's not a greeting. Frantically I clear my desk and prepare myself to record any reception I have direct to the computer.

In computer language WYSIWYG means what you see is what you get but in these events what you see is not necessarily what you understand! I see Peter (instinctively I know it his him) standing in Don's kitchen at the day's end. I am aware of him having been there for some time, of conversation he's had with Don about the spring, the garden and plans to extend it. I also see a woman, a rotund and cheerful lady preparing food and again instinctively I know her to be Don's wife.

Tales of Bellerophon –On the Banks of the Shalimar

For the first time in my travels I view Peter objectively. He looks no more in age than 20. Elvin faced the skin smooth and hairless he has a sensuous appearance. The hair is dark and long to the shoulders, is slim, of average height and moves about with feline grace. I see him wearing a loose green coloured shirt and shiny black tapered trousers. This is definitely not me, not only is he much younger I have to admit he is better looking!!

Don and Peter are talking but I cannot hear anything they say. I see Don take the pot that has been warming off the stove and pour what looks like coffee into two chipped enamel mugs. He is wearing an open neck deep red check woollen shirt, faded blue jeans that are well past their use date. His brown boots are scuffed and muddied. They are in what I believe is the kitchen but it looks more like a conservatory with large windows. Potted plants adorn the sills and curtains of a faded red flower design are tied back at the uprights. Blind cords dangle at every window.

Don ambles over to the wooden table where Peter sits and sets down the mugs, turns, bends down and extracts from underneath a work surface an oil lamp. Peter is talking animatedly waving his arms and pointing his hands – he is very graceful. Don is talking now as he trims the wick and lights the lamp. It's like watching a silent movie. Finally he sits down and takes a long draw on his coffee then leans forward and begins to speak in the way of one who is imparting a secret. Peter leans forward listening then sits back covering his face with his hands but before he covers his mouth I can read his lips saying 'Oh, no!'

Then there is a break and now next I see Ellie move into sight hugging Peter –after that nothing. Try as I will I can't remember anything thereafter.

Initially this doesn't bother me as I accept believing what I don't understand will reveal itself in some manner later. As the day wears on I begin to feel uncomfortable –like I've been eavesdropping and shouldn't have. The following day I sit again to make a link without success. I try again the following day and again the day after. After my third attempt depression sets in and I start to feel that this was it, nothing more will be received –I've reached the end of the process that started in January –it's now the end of May. I look back over my written work and realise it is not complete, but for some reason I'm now incapable of receiving any more.

Two weeks elapse –no glimpses, no dreams, no voices, nothing! I feel somewhat sorry for myself and not a little guilty –somewhere along the line I've fouled up, but how? What exactly have I done?

I'm modelling. I have a model of HMS Victory almost completed. It's really fiddly getting the sails and rigging right and I make mistake after mistake. I give up and go back to my computer and re-read this MS in search of a clue –and on finding none I sit back bemused, abashed and consoling myself with yet another cup of tea when I hear Edward's voice.

'It was going to happen, don't perturb yourself'

Mentally I respond, 'what have I done?'

'Free will can sometimes take a path that leads nowhere –your astral journeying is dependant upon Peter, he and you are joined in my world. In your quest to understand how you are able to travel you have sought to know Peter as a separate person –if you persist journeying in this manner it will cease entirely.'

I didn't have anything to say in response and Edward continues, 'if you are prepared to accept relationship with Peter as it is revealed in your travels, journeying will commence again. You will learn more about him and understand more deeply why you feel it is necessary to know. In part this knowledge will be revealed in your writings. The full awareness must wait until it is your time to enter this world.'

Feeling very emotional I acknowledge. 'Is this how I appear to know how nothing surprises me, how the so called future is to me the present?'

'In part –remember we have the ability, we of human kind, to view the scheme of things, like we may see a clock and observe the connections of wheels, spindles and pendulum action, yet we are in reality a cog in a wheel, or a spindle that holds one or many. Evolution as you will discover is the spiritual path we all tread –to go forward we must go back. Going back is not what your conscious mind believes it to be, a journey into the past. When the parts of self understand themselves for what they are they are no longer separate, divided by space and time, they are present. To unify is 'going back' and realising the One and only spiritual path.

You began this quest in search of answers believing it will help your fellow man understand the 'veil' does not in reality exist –that the barrier is man's ignorance arising from his desire to be king. The reality is that your quest is you in search of yourself. Give no thought for what others might gain. Rest your mind, there is time enough for what you need to do.'

Chapter TWENTYSIX:
In the heart of a mountain

I'm taking Edwards advice to heart –whatever good intentions I can claim, meddling is the result. I've been close to destroying a process that has been in the making many years. So to hell with trying to complete this narrative as soon as, besides I need to assuage my guilty feelings by taking notice of friends and loved ones and most of all spending time with my darling wife who is not demanding but likes to have me around. Not some distracted human being who communicates in grunts and monosyllabic sentences.

One evening late we are happily doing our own 'things' in the same space –namely our living room. Pam is wholly absorbed in an historical film romance (and not for the first time) and I'm patiently putting together a ship model. The painting of some exceedingly small gun carriages with a virtually hairless brush in one hand, tweezers and item in the other, through a magnifying glass demands concentration. I'm deaf to the drama that has Pam glued to the television and completely unaware of losing that present state of consciousness.

In the heart of a mountain

I'm standing on a rocky outcrop at high altitude conscious of low clouds. As far as my eyes can see there are mountains about me their snow caps stark white against a risen sun. Powerful wind gusts tug at my body, moaning about the serrated rocks towering to my right and whistling through the scrub growths at my feet. I'm drawn to observe a ridge track some twenty feet below though it barely warrants the name; it's a cutting through wiry dark green grass littered with stones winding and undulating toward me. I don't know how many thousands of feet I'm above sea level –a thick mist obscures the detailed topography of the lowland valleys.

I've walked some distance to arrive at this spot, presumably with Lone Wolf since he is standing next to me. He wears (as I do) a poncho type garment over leather clothes. A sweatband sleeks back his long dark hair and his forehead is smeared with white chalk, the cheekbones highlighted with a red paste. His attention is focussed on a group of four people some 50 yards below to our left walking the path I've been observing. In view I now see three women and a man. The man is elderly, sparsely built, with long grey hair tied in a pony tail and wearing a wide flat brimmed hat that flaps in the wind. Of the three women, one is powerfully built and native to the area, whilst the other two are westerners from city environments.

All wear poncho garments like us, being made of a worsted wool mix material. None seemed to be suffering fatigue though one of the 'city' women, perhaps the youngest, walks in an absent minded manner. The man who I take to be the leader of this party frequently glances in her direction as they make their way toward us.

'Where are we?' I query Lone Wolf.

'So you are awake eh? The Sierra Nevadas.'

'And these people?' Lone Wolf shrugs, 'we shall see –Paulo will tell us.'

I'm resisting the temptation to ask who Paulo is as I admire the ease of his climb toward us. Approaching he is smiling broadly, hand raised in salute, 'Santee, greetings old friend!'

'Santee –you are Santee?'

Lone Wolf grins sideways as he moves forward to greet the group, 'One of many names.' Lone Wolf embraces Paulo and the native woman in turn, who says 'it is good to be with you again.'

Nodding his head to the other women Lone Wolf beckons them all forward to where I am standing. 'This is Peter.' I bow my head, raise my arms and bring my hands together, 'A blessing on your company. I am delighted to be meeting.'

Tales of Bellerophon –On the Banks of the Shalimar

The native woman's face lights up with a smile and she gives me her name as Elenda. Paulo grins knowingly and inclines his head, the other women nod pleasantly. 'Come, let us rest and refresh ourselves before we walk on.'

At his bidding we follow Lone Wolf along the ridge through a maze of standing stones and overhanging rocks. Paulo takes up a position in the rear, every now and then making encouraging noises to the youngest of the women. Bright as it is and likely cold at this altitude the wind doesn't chill me, neither Lone Wolf, Paulo or Elenda show signs of reacting to cold, however the other two women do, their faces look pinched and the cheekbones red. I hear their uneven breathing as we alternatively climb and descend rocky gullies. Elenda is a strong well built woman; her broad face and tanned skin suggest she's a South American Indian. She wears a long red check skirt and a low crowned hat that caps a dark shoulder drape. Talking casually with Lone Wolf she turns and smiles at me from time to time. Those beautiful laughing eyes have me smile warmly in response.

We are walking a flat stretch now and I turn and ask the women immediately behind, her name. 'Jenny.' She smiles encouragingly. 'It's breathtaking isn't it?' I agree and remark the mountains have seen more lives than any one of us.

'Yes, I suppose you must be right, I wasn't thinking of it like that'. Jenny appears to be in her early forties, light coloured hair cut to her shoulders, a pleasant face with a small birth mark high on the right cheek. From her speech I judge her to be English.

I try to catch the attention of the other woman but she seems not to be aware of anything around her. Paulo notices my attempt and simply says, 'later my friend, she not with us yet.' Jenny looks puzzled and I shrug easily and smile at her reassuringly.

We have now arrived under a massive overhanging rock and pause in its shadow. The wind here barely whispers. Paulo lowers a small rucksack he carries as we all sit down. 'A warming drink eh?

He hands about small handle less cups half filled with milky looking liquid smelling strongly of coconut. It's fiery and a sip alone warms my entire body. I'm not cold but I welcome the warmth. Paulo and Lone Wolf draw apart and squat close together exchanging tobacco, which they then proceed to roll into cigarettes and smoke, talking away to each other in low tones.

I turn to Jenny, 'And what brings you here?'

'I've become very interested to know more about other beings, Now that I'm more contented with myself it seems the right thing to do –Paulo is such a marvellous teacher I've become quite used to the unusual. Mind you, I still feel like pinching myself every now and then, uncertain of my good fortune.'

'Good fortune eh? How long have you been in this state?' I say casually, conscious of not wanting the same question asked of me. 'I'm not sure. Nobody talks of time –I've almost forgotten what it is', she laughs. 'Been with my folks. My uncle Ray introduced me to Paulo and his group and I've sort of drifted apart from them. I see things differently with him and Elenda. It's a different world entirely and I want to learn about it –does that make sense?

'Sure it does', I say, 'there are many worlds of Spirit, needs be we know more than one to know ourselves.' She leans toward me confidentially, 'Paulo says we carry the worlds with us, it's our ignorance that makes division. Do you agree?'

'Wisely put', I say, 'and what was it that the old sages said? Nine steps make nine lives and nine lives make one prayer; numberless are the days of creation.'

'That's interesting, I haven't heard that before.'

'Yang-tse[12] teaches that nine is the ultimate number; the nine steps represent all the changes we need to assimilate, freeing ourselves from the wheel of knowledge; nine lives to know the one need before we can accept the order of creation.'

'And the one prayer?'

'Need –the ultimate need; that's why we are here is it not, expressing need?' Jenny looks at me curiously a smile dancing on her lips. 'I know we represent the self to others as we know ourselves, but you look so young – there's not a line on your face. In earth terms how old would you say you are?'

'I am not earth born yet I have a brother who is. I am not one but many – and my teachers know more of me than I do myself!' Her face is a study in concentration and I chuckle –she's thinking!

---

[12] Having never heard of this Philosopher I researched the name –I found only one, a Yang-tse who lived circa 500 BC and described by contemporary Chinese philosophers as preaching individualism and egoism. He apparently founded no school and none of his writings survive. Is this he referred to by Peter?

Then her eyes brighten. 'It feels right and Paulo says if it feels right it must be right, and Santee –is he your teacher?' I acknowledge, 'Yes –a man of few words but he gets results', I laugh at my own thoughts. 'For example, I'm here without fully realising why!'

'Is that Santee?' The younger of the two women queries leaning her head in Lone Wolf's direction. 'You are with us Sarah!' exclaims Elenda and puts her arm about Sarah's shoulders and hugs her gently. 'Oh, hi Elenda, where are we?'

'Here my daughter, here, in a place out of the wind and sheltered from the sun in the high mountains. You remember asking Paulo to take you to the mountains?'

'I do, but we were somewhere else, a lodge I think.'

'Hotel I call it. That's Santee'. Elenda inclines her head to the squatting figure of Lone Wolf. 'This is Jenny and this is Peter –now you know everyone'. Sarah has a bright intelligent face; the eyes are quite beautiful, blue and childlike. Her hair is long, fair and slightly wavy. She is dressed in faded green jeans, white blouse and close fitting leather jacket; charm bracelets dangle from both wrists and she looks no more than 20.

Just then we become aware of a shadow moving in air above us and watch as a bald eagle appears and alights on the rocks nearby. Paulo and Lone Wolf gaze at the bird as if in meditation, then Lone Wolf unfastens a small cloth bag from his waist and carefully empties its contents on the ground. They are small animal knuckle bones mixed with shiny round stones of various colours. He picks these up working each between his finger and thumb before placing them in some configuration –Paulo watches this exercise, as does the eagle to my way of thinking. Having moved them several times he starts to speak, as if to himself, in a very guttural manner. This unintelligible language is directed to the eagle that in turn appears to be taking notice.

Paulo beats the ground gently with his hands, rapid movements interspersed by stillness then a single tap, tap, followed again by a staccato thumping action using the heel of his hand. The eagle is now in flight hovering above them –Paulo ceases his drumming and Lone Wolf scoops up the stones and bags them. The eagle is flying away, up and out of our sight. After some moments gazing skyward they talk quietly as if making agreement over something. They rise and stand before us under the rock roof. 'We are ready to continue, said Lone Wolf, 'are you rested and awake?' He looks at Sarah, Jenny and then me with a knowing smile. As we nod eager to continue, Paulo speaks.

In the heart of a mountain

'We go into the mountain now, soon the energies change –your sense of being may feel confused from time to time,' his voice is gravely and serious, at the same time soothing. 'We must look out for each other. Jenny you will walk with Elenda, the both of you walk with me. Sarah you will walk with Peter and both of you walk with Santee'.

Lone Wolf (I still can't think of him as Santee) is handing the cups around again and pouring out more of the drink. 'One more drink eh? And then we walk'.

'What can we expect to see?' Sarah enquires.

'See?' said Paulo stroking his grizzled chin. 'I think you do more than see, you know with other senses too: a world different to what you know; beings unknown to you. Santee and I have made this journey before, many times, so have no fear; we are your guides'.

'We go underground, what then has the eagle to do with our journey?' I ask.

Lone Wolf replies, 'the eagle holds a map of this area and reads all movements, she knows its present order and that gives awareness of the place we seek.'

We stand up to leave grouping as Paulo has instructed. I'm excited about the impending events and a change is occurring that lightens and stimulates me. We move off with Lone Wolf leading descending along a passage of rocks that so narrow we have to negotiate it side on in many places. The gully twists and turns, levels out in places and eventually inclines sharply downward encasing us, blotting out the sky. We are now inside the mountain. As we descend deeper light fades and the rock formations take on a phosphorous glow. Descending deeper the white glow gradually colours into a variety of red, amber, gold and blue hues. The emanating light is sufficient to show the shape of the stone chimney we move within.

We climb downward in silence but as we progress I detect vibrations of sound that change in pitch and tone, it's as if the rock itself speaks to us. On reaching a level area which has now widened and heightened I turn to Sarah. She smiles nervously and grabs my hand.

'Can you hear the music?' She queries.

I had to think for a moment –music? Then I realise she is listening like I am to the vibrations which are now more intense in the cavernous space we travel through. I nod.

'It sounds like thousands of tiny creatures living in harmony', she whispers.

Paulo begins to make hoarse whistling sounds; short sharp expressions that echo about the cavern shape before fading. The sounds both Sarah and I experience disappear as Paulo's whistling grows louder and changes tone, taking on a life of its own as it bounces around the stone. Eventually his whistling stops and the rock sounds return stronger and more definite that before.

Jenny and Elenda also remark on the phenomenon as we press on. The cavern now opens into an even larger space, made it appears by a giant hand that has softened the rock and pulled it apart so the floor on which we walk has a centre where the rock is smooth and fused together. Above (I estimate some 30 feet) the ceiling is a patchwork of interlocking slabs of gigantic proportion. The rock sounds, stronger still, emanate from beneath our feet.

We traverse this cavern still lit by the rock light emanations and enter another chamber through a portal of ringed stones –stones that appear to have been shaped to fit and make the opening. Lone Wolf motions us all to stop as we pass through and we draw close about him. 'The light is much weaker here', he points into the chamber beyond the portal. 'Stay close and you will find your footing without difficulty'.

The change I felt on beginning this descent is still present and getting stronger. My body feels wider, my limbs thicker and my face broader. Sarah has grasped hold of my hand and I squeeze it reassuringly but I can't turn to face her less she see what I feel and is afraid.

The rock underneath our feet is very uneven, at first sloping quite sharply before levelling out. We are all joined now hand to hand and as Lone Wolf advised we move without stumbling with sureness of foot, albeit progress is slow. Then suddenly without warning of change the floor becomes smooth and featureless. A defused reddish glow shines upward from the stone flooring rock and we can see our own forms once again.

The chamber has narrowed and the roof is lower. We enter into a floored area that curves like a concave mirror, the rock surface alight from within. The centre area is deep red and here the ceiling rock is no more than 10 feet above us. Lone Wolf turns, 'we need go no further' and pointing to the cavern perimeter he says, 'the flat surface makes a good seat.'

The vibrating sounds are still evident but muted compared to the experience of the journey here. I take up a sitting position as does Sarah and Elenda.

Paulo speaks, 'look about to one another and share your thoughts.'

In the heart of a mountain

For the first time since entering the chimney I feel able to communicate freely with my companions. I am both surprised and relieved at what I see – Sarah's skin is olive green and tiny lights of white energy spot her face like freckles and she is noticeably shorter by some six inches. Jenny is slimmer, her eyes slant and the skin bluish green -her hair thick the colour of straw. Elenda has grown in stature and though her facial features have not noticeably changed her eyes are bright fluorescent green, the pupils dark and small.

I look across to Paulo who is younger in appearance, his body more angular and thinner. The skin tight, the bones of his face pronounced, he looks reptilian. Lone Wolfs' form is unchanged but his body emanates a red glow. The white chalk paint on his forehead is almost transparent, the red spots on his cheeks appear to vibrate and give view inside his face. I am changed, being thick of body and I note my hands are no longer slender but short and muscular. For what seems an eternity we say nothing but look at each other, silenced by our transformations.

Breaking the silence Lone Wolf speaks. 'We have entered into the elemental world that has evolved from the physical order of planetary being, the creatures you sense all aware are no longer dependant upon the need for individual body but live in community. They have no need to protect their identity and are therefore quite unlike us –they understand our need for a sense of identity. You need not fear them.'

'And we are all different', Paulo says, 'in each of you there are connections to different elemental beings –as you respond to their influence your inner nature will directly relate to the elemental powers present.'

I am the first to find my voice. 'I am aware of a difference of being, I feel as if I have grown from the earth in some form and my nature is knowledgeable of stone, the root of trees, plants and all earthly things'.

'You are in tune with the Barrow Wight's, earth spirit beings who are born between the astral and physical worlds, but they no longer physically manifest –their earth time was many aeons ago', Paulo says.

Jenny speaks next in a halting voice, but not the voice of fear. 'I am some kind of plant. I know that sounds impossible but it's as if I'm aware of every internal movement and feeling and sensing every present living thing.' Again, Paulo explains. 'The spirit of woodland takes many forms as it is also doing with Sarah. The strangeness you feel is awareness of living in more than one form simultaneously.'

Sarah appears inebriated as she speaks, swaying from side to side. 'I haven't a care in the world, nothing and yet everything interests me.'

'That is because you have elfin character and they are free spirits beyond our imagining —they love to enter the currents of earth formed energies and congregate to centres that have the power of altering consciousness.'

'Elenda', says Lone Wolf, you have been here before, how say you?'

'I think I have this time found the crystal energies, they give great clarity of mind and I am able to extend my self being in a healing manner.'

'This is good', Lone Wolf responds, 'it will help to keep our company together as we invoke the worlds that this mountain holds key to reveal. Speak openly whenever you feel you must. By sharing thoughts we maintain our unity. What you are about to witness is living in the present and part of the worlds we inhabit —to you and many their influence is unknown. Paulo and I make this communion to increase your understanding of the great Manitou.'

Chapter TWENTYSEVEN:
Alien Worlds

Paulo and Lone Wolf move to sit opposite each other at the centre of the sloping bowl of stone; the reddish glow enshrouding their forms. As they sit, much to my surprise they begin making cigarettes and after lighting blow smoke into the centre of the red glow where it is noticeably more intense. Sarah is fidgeting but in my altered state of mind it doesn't concern me. Elenda appears to be in a kind of trance, her whole body shimmers with light; Jenny looks like she is made of wood, her eyes fixed open. The atmosphere is now alternating between warm and cool currents of air, the rock beneath us vibrating as by a quake deep below our mountain cave.

Smoking over, Paulo sits shoulders hunched, his reptilian looks even more pronounced. Lone Wolf appears to pulsate and by the moment less and less solid. Paulo speaks distinctly in words I don't understand but sound like an invocation and a greeting.

'Hiaee, Hiaee, Ostara.'

Lone Wolf is looking less a man and more a body mass of vibrating swirling colours –and is growing to more than twice his size. No longer recognisable his energy mass changes shape to stretch horizontally over the cave floor. The shape of an animal is materialising –a huge tiger, some 14 feet from head to tail, large fangs extruding from its mouth. Suddenly it roars and the entire cavern shakes. I shake –I think everyone else does too.

Only Paulo appears unaffected as he repeats the greeting over and over again. The animal is moving now —it's solidified and paces about the stone bowl looking at our forms. The tiger is close and I can smell its thick carnivorous breath. The eyes are green and dark grey, the haunches matted in mud.

He growls a greeting and deep from within me my voice sounds out slow and guttural —I am responding, how and with what meaning I cannot say. My companions also make sounds, Sarahs' is high pitched like a wind sound, Jenny makes a fluttering sound and Elenda purrs like a cat. The animal goes over to Elenda and begins to lick her head. It's mesmerising, the tigers' head is much larger than Elenda yet he appears to be treating her as it might a cub, with great tenderness.

As we watch, a change in our sense of place becomes apparent; it feels and smells like a world of dense vegetation, of tall grasses and plants, smooth dark ebony trees and rich soil. I am communicating with the sabre toothed tiger, aware that over aeons of time it has learnt to understand its place in the order of things; to harmonise the essence of its nature with the worlds of other creations.

The animal draws back from Elenda and turns toward the centre; Elenda appears to be asleep. It pads silently to the centre of the bowl completely obscuring Paulo from my vision —it then enters into the red glow and disappears below the level of cavern floor. Anxiety floods into my consciousness.

'Lone Wolf!' I call, my voice strangely broken and distorted.

'Fear not little one',

The words hiss out of Paulo's mouth and I feel energy being drawn out of me. The temperature in the cavern is dropping and the red glow intensifies into a coloured mist swirling in light and dark shades. Gradually it forms into the shape of a person. I breathe a sigh of relief; Lone Wolf is returning.

As the form begins to solidify Paulo makes sounds not unlike a whistle; undulating sounds making me giddy and distorting my vision, but still I keep my eyes focussed on the emerging form. This is a person taller than Lone Wolf —is it female, is it male? I cannot tell. It is slim like a stylised African basalt figure but the skin is bluish and scaly. The eyes look large and slanted and as the form takes firmer shape I notice a facial make up, powder blue and ochre yellow.

There are fine blue lines on the forehead vertically reaching for the hair line. On the head is a close fitting tall flat topped hat shaped to fit the skull

178

about the ears. Hair is not visible; perhaps it is curled up inside the hat. The cheekbones are high, the mouth small, and the nose long thin and flattened. Some kind of garment enfolds the shoulders having a tall blue collar –not unlike velvet. The chest and stomach is bare but there is such a softness of skin I think this must be a woman. From the waist is worn a pleated tunic the same colour as the shoulder garment. The tunic is banded at the hip by a golden belt studded with white stones. Brown (possibly leather) shiny material clothes the calves and the feet are shod with simple thong sandals.

The being steps out of the centre and I estimate height to be some seven and a half feet to the crown of the hat. A sense of peace that is totally indescribable overcomes us all –I cannot breathe; the need to breathe has gone away. With sublime natural grace the visitor moves a few steps toward us. The eyes are all knowing; they focus on each of us with great intelligence and I feel my form changing and becoming feminine, my mind assuming the power to listen and know.

I am so absorbed with changes that are occurring within me it is only as the figure stands before Jenny, do I realise that the stiff and wooden form of my companion is now held in the visitors' arms as if she were a doll. Then the being speaks in a strange language, a lilting sound not unlike the whistling sounds Paulo makes –expressing in a continuous manner that takes no pause to breathe. It's as if the communication is addressed to the elemental spirit possessing Jenny –not Jenny herself. Slowly Jenny's form begins to unbend, her limbs appearing as interwoven dark and light green strands about brown bone like shapes; the torso likewise appears as a honeycomb of stranded wood, plant stalk and fine grass, her face is almost unrecognisable.

I watch as if suspended in space aware that this being communicates more than sound, and emanates a life force able to change both form and identity. To my side Sarah trembles with repressed excitement and then unexpectedly jumps up from her sitting position and moves toward Jenny and the visitor. Immediately the figure moves back out of reach toward the centre still holding Jenny. Intervening Paulo quickly motions Sarah to sit.

'Little one wait –let her come to you!' His voice falsetto and pierces the air jolting me out of my trance. I stand, the woman in me totally commanding, with a sense of purpose I stride forward to hold Sarah gently by the shoulders and whisper in her ear. 'She is unused to an approach like this –she is not harming Jenny, she is healing her. Come sit with me,'

Sarah's laughing eyes embrace my own. 'Oh, but I only want to speak with her.'

'I know –let her come to you, as she will –be assured. Come with me'. Sarah embraces me, but I feel it's not me she holds –she embraces another person; a woman of great wisdom and awareness. The visitor has retreated to stand in the red mist emanating from the centre still effortlessly holding the form of Jenny who is now a mass of tubular formations pulsating and changing colour. I am possessed by my feminine character and have no concern for what appears to be Jenny's metamorphous, instead I switch my attention to Elenda who rises to her feet and slowly steps toward the being, her body seemingly naked, her skin configured in the primary shapes of diamonds, rhomboids, triangles, circles and more and shining in rose light. To all appearance she is a body of quartz crystal and a myriad of glittering shapes. Sarah is calmly taking strength from me her arms enfolded to my waist, watching the event develop.

Paulo is encouraging Elenda to step closer and they all begin to exchange energies; all four are connected. The being extends Jenny's form toward Elenda and once again that strange language sounds about the cavern. As Elenda and Paulo receive the still form it begins to solidify and the human characteristics of Jenny appear; at first in the form of a naked child, but rapidly it matures to the Jenny we know. The smile on her face is beatific and the atmospheric coldness is replaced by warmth. Elenda is now returning to something like her normal self, though she still glows in rose light. Paulo's form is becoming darker, the head jutting out from his shoulders like that of a vulture. If Jenny is conscious of her situation she gives no indication of it but stands now on the edge of the red mist, hand in hand with Elenda as the visitor continues communicating her strange sounding language.

Somehow I know this being is a member of the third root race to inhabit earth and the first incarnate of our present animal based form. The aura of energy about the figure is intelligent and knowledgeable of the evolutionary history of man. Over epochs of time this being has absorbed all the so called sub cultures that together give character to our present mind. The communication is assuring us of our identity, reminding us of the different sources from which we have evolved.

Speech ceases and the being (I now think more feminine) raises her arms, smiles and as the hands meet above the head slowly dissolves before our eyes. Paulo is beating the stone with his hands again, gently the rhythm sounds a welcoming note and the mist begins to swirl and fold itself inward, becoming smaller. The prostrate form of Lone Wolf begins to take shape floating upon a carpet of mist. Paulo's beating rhythms slow and become hauntingly peaceful.

Jenny now sits close with Elenda, Sarah has eased her grip on my waist and we too now sit. Lone Wolf lies still and uncommunicative. Paulo ceases to drum and time and space cease to have any real meaning; it is as if we are present in eternity where all is self sufficient and the memory of need is absent.

Small lights appear in the red mist carpet beneath Lone Wolf's prostrate body moving about him in irregular patterns. They increase and grow in size, a moving mass of different shapes that expands above and beyond Lone Wolf's body.

I glance quickly at my companions who themselves now look toward the centre with interest having woken like myself from a momentary bliss. We become aware of a noise, a clamouring sound, as if a thousand voices compete to speak. I sense a light hearted energy and as I respond the 'woman of wisdom' weakens and I feel more like myself.

Sarah is becoming excited and leaps to her feet dancing about the centre –the lights grow in strength and number quickly and include her to their sphere of movement. Paulo rocks side to side unconcerned for Sarah, or of her proximity to Lone Wolf lying still like one dead. The lights are now taking recognisable shape, appearing as miniature persons with short legs and arms, their bodies of varying size and thickness –some thin and wedge shaped, others round and tub like and all transparent like holograph images. Facially some have old looks, others young and childlike. There are moon faces with heavy hooded eyes, long small featured faces, some bearded in a square cut fashion their eyes sunk beneath prominent brows.

Sarah continues to dance laughing continuously in acknowledgement of the presence of these light borne creatures. Even Paulo, looking more like his familiar self, is smiling and encouraging Sarah and the host of beings present –for beings they are, each with a distinct character. Yet they move without conflict. It would seem they should collide with each other; instead they pass through the others form and instantly regain their previous character shape.

And the noise that is first heard like a clamour of voices is musical and vibrant. The sounds are triumphal, wide and sweeping choral like sounds that excite my senses. I can no longer sit still but sway from side to side and bob my head. It's impossible to count the number of beings present as they swoop and dive around the cavern. One comes very close to me and repeatedly shows itself –a large head and short body yet the entire form is no larger than my hand.

The details of feature are exquisitely clear and a fine network of lines can be seen within its amoebic looking body. The overall impression they give

181

is of a complete lack of care and concern –they simply live for the present moment and their influence is irresistible.

They obliterate my sense of history and I become child like, accepting everything –I am not aware of myself and I'm sure my companions feel the same; even our difference no longer matters. This host of dancing beings come together and form a stream of sparkling light, zooming and diving about the cavern and passing through our bodies as they do so. Then without warning they leave –the stream of dancing light enters into the red mist about Lone Wolf's body and disappears. Silence falls like a heavy mantle. The 'I' of our natures cannot be felt; we are merely forms without internal workings. It's as if we have all been externalised by the influence of these creatures. A sense of sadness born of experiencing indescribable joy envelops me.

Eventually Lone Wolf moves, at first tremors shake his form, and then his joints respond to nervous stimuli, finally facial changes show his personality regaining control. Paulo sits close and proffers him a drink. As I watch I gradually become aware of my personality self –the others also are regaining their composure. Lone Wolf opens his eyes and assumes a sitting position. The sense of relief in us is all but audible. After a while he stands, awkwardly at first, then visibly taking control he looks at each of us in turn and speaks –his voice uncharacteristically soft but steady.

'We cannot yet be whole, yet we may know the parts. To be joined is to know less. Birth arises from innocence –each of you according to your need has begun the journey that ends in new birth.'

These simple words hold deep meaning and are much in mind as we wend our way back across cavern and passage to emerge into the bright air and bare landscape. This mountainous world now has a different meaning – outwardly nothing is different to how we first knew it, but inwardly our understanding is changed by our experience in the heart of this mountain. As we look across the jutting peaks and view horizon we know that what we now witness is a passing impression of reality.

I gradually become conscious of the model before me and am struck by the fact that my power of concentration is such that I can't hear anything. I look away from the table toward the television and think of Pam. Sound returns and with it an anxious feeling that perhaps I've been painting badly and have spoilt the model. I look at my work through the magnifier and am relieved to see that the ships cannons are beautifully painted.

How many did I paint during that journey? None I suspect. I'd not been following the film before this 'journey' took over, so can't say what time elapsed. Pam calls out from the sofa hidden from my view, 'How are you getting on?'

'Fine', I say, 'but it's fiddly'.

I sit there smiling to myself as yet unable to take in the meaning of everything I have witnessed. I smile because there are times when the words we exchange that pass for conversation is a world away from expressing our present consciousness.

Thought and language is not simply inadequate on occasions but farcical in the extreme.

Chapter TWENTYEIGHT:
Dwarfs and Scholars

Strange as it might seem I don't rush into my study and write as fast as my fingers can type. I sit there and continue modelling! My journey into the mountain leaves me in a state of detachment that cares not to speak nor hastens to relive those astonishing moments. It's not until later the following day I make my first attempt at recording. As I write I'm reminded of Edward saying that some remembrance would have the tenor of fairy tales –and I guess some will think this is.

But I know differently. I have experienced a state of being totally unlike anything I have previously enjoyed. My words inadequately describe the event or convey my inner realisation. Changes have occurred in the manner of my journeying –I am slipping out into other dimensions of reality whilst fully conscious and able to recall the events in a state of detachment. I have moments when I feel disbelief at what is happened to me – but mostly I do not. And why not amazed?

I am not amazed because somewhere deep in my psyche this is knowledge I have. Somehow, somewhere –perhaps in another life and even then not necessarily in this world my soul has connection. I'm reminded of something I tell my pupils when teaching psychic and spiritual development. As a teacher they might expect from me a knowledge they don't possess –but I tell them this is not so. I guide them to open doors – nothing more. They already have the knowledge. What they lack is the memory of access.

Now the doors are being opened for me. I have no desire to tell anyone about this at present but for different reasons than before. Now I feel wedded to the silence. Later perhaps, later I will speak about it.

A week on and I'm sitting in the side passenger seat of my car bordering a village pond deep in the Hampshire countryside, debating with myself the possibility of fishing it. I have my laptop computer with me and two hours of free time before I must drive into Petersfield and attend a patient. My sweet tooth is satisfied with a bar of chocolate and I'm feeling drowsy. Mums with kids are feeding the ducks –thank God they are absorbed in their own worlds. I am content with mine and have no wish to leave it.

I am seated on a hard chair hunched over a large leather bound tome that curiously smells of sandalwood. This book has seen more summers I can guess at, yet the scratched and stained binding belies the quality of its printing –the pages are heavy and soft and judging by the wrinkled corners, turned countless times prior to my hand.

I'm reading about dwarves; their remarkable ability to bridge between the slow beating planetary energies constituting the physical and lower astral kingdoms. This book refers population of solar system planets and describes how the forms of dwarves develop in different physical and neo physical planes of existence.

I am particularly interested in their origins that according to the author, a Phineas Broadbent, precede the human evolution; their forms arising from the animal and vegetable kingdoms. Relationship with human races is a relatively recent ancestral development. It would appear that their path of progress is to attain fully functional emotional bodies, hence their interest in connecting with the human cycle. Their procreative instincts are interesting, they are not biased sexually, male or female, but have three elements –male, female and a wholly passive identity born of their higher order self that acts in group union to transform, create and harness energies of different vibratory orders.

Dwarves don't have genitalia or childbearing functions within their forms and therefore cannot procreate as humans do. He writes, 'whereas we humans procreate monogamously, they (the dwarves) combine in groups as many as ten and fuse their energies. By so doing they invite entry to their midst of an higher order self, remaining fused in this manner until the being is clothed in form similar to themselves'. He also states that such acts frequently occur but do not produce offspring but instead imbue strength and reassert identity. Child dwarves appear when separating from the conceiving group much the same size as adults, rarely growing more than a tenth more in height. Dwarves are mostly manifest in astral frequencies but can if the required birthing energies are present, incarnate in physical form. All planets in the solar system excepting the earth however have ceased to physically manifest the energies that give birth to their form.

In the phenomenal worlds they have life spans in excess of three hundred earth years and return into the Overself on completion of their cycle. The largest of dwarves will not be taller than three feet. Most physically manifest dwarves are a good six inches shorter and in the astral worlds they can be tiny –no more than a few inches high. They live in family relationships and can be very defensive of what they term territory. In general they live in harmony and tolerance with other dwarf families and other elemental beings, but can 'fall out' if territory is disputed.

This author has clearly worked with others to write this work, he refers to a group of learned colleagues when arguing the case for particular facts and mentions Hermes Trismigestus as the prime source of the groups learning –some contributors have lived in association with dwarf populations not only on earth but also in other planetary worlds.[13]

I am absorbed in this study when interrupted by a voice greeting me. I turn and recognise Michel who walks absently into the room, his mind as always consciously working beyond the space his body occupies. Michel appears as an elderly man dressed in a long robe like coat edged in fur –a flattish looking hat adorns his bearded head to cover a crown of thinning grey hair splayed untidily over narrow shoulders. His eyes protrude, watery and Piscean and the distinctive nose and high cheek bones mark him out as a Jew.

'Hello Michel'

'I see you've been delving into my bookshelves again. Did you find what you wanted?' He looks at me over his specs, his eyes mischievous his mouth working other unsaid words.

'Most interesting, I had no idea that Hermes was the source of authority on dwarves.' Michel peers over my shoulder, 'he is not one to take the word of others –believes in the complete experience; no progress without involvement.'

'But isn't that what we all do?' I query.

'No.' he says sharply, 'come now, Peter, you know better than that.' I smile at him fondly, I love discussions with Michel –they would be endless if he only he allowed!

'There is a difference, wouldn't you agree, between direct and indirect experience?' He faces and looks right through me, 'I see you are not yourself today.'

---

[13] I have tried and failed to find any historical references to a Phineas Broadbent –in point of fact the name itself appears to be unique. Given I'm aware in this experience the work is the product of several minds, it suggests to me the name has been deliberately invented by writers who have no need to promote their personalities.

I laugh, 'that's right Michel –it's the questioning me!' Michel draws up a stool to the table, rests his elbows; makes a chin supporting cleft out of thumbs and forefingers, and looks dreamily into my eyes. 'All experience is evolutionary –nothing, not even these seemingly unnecessary questions, are without merit. Human earth consciousness is orientated by time and space and judged to evolve if it overcomes issues that divide it against itself, whereas human astral consciousness is not governed by time and space; is self evaluating and necessarily divides itself in the quest for harmony. The physical incarnate direct experience is self evaluating up to a point, but in achieving this it causes division in others –arrests the self's evolutionary development in our astral worlds until they are effectively neutralised by harmonisation.'

'And the indirect physical incarnate experience?' I say eagerly.

'I'm coming to that', he says firmly, extending a hand to playfully slap mine. 'Indirect experience is of greater influence than direct; individuals change not by their own volition but as a result of impersonal action, and we mustn't forget', he adds with emphasis, 'the direct effect upon individuals from the natural world they inhabit. In the astral worlds indirect experience is progressively the lesser influence as beings evolve the higher ordered self –but then, you know that.'

He pauses, a smile playing on his lips.

'So,' I say carefully, 'direct experience is the complete experience Hermes refers too?'

'No it isn't', he says triumphantly.

'It can only be direct, surely?' I say weakly, knowing that Michel is enjoying my confusion. 'As you will recall I said that human astral consciousness necessarily divides itself in the quest for harmony. The higher ordered self is not a conglomerate of experience; it is being without the need of it –so the complete experience is the action of a soul prepared to sacrifice everything in their quest for oneness: and that my young friend is total involvement; true progress.'

'Now let me see if I've got that right. Direct and indirect experience evolves but doesn't free the soul –true progress is total involvement and that can only be achieved by self sacrifice?'

'That's right', says Michel. 'True progress is as you call it, is freedom from the rebirth cycle.'

'Hermes Trismigestus has now moved on, I take it –he is no longer in the astral worlds?'

'Indeed he has, what we speak of is our remembrance of him'

I'm aware of the place I sit in –it's a large T shaped room made from three rooms joined together by square arches of dark wood forming upright and lintel. The flat plaster ceilings are ribbed with timbers as are the faded brick walls that can be seen between shelves crammed with books. Overshadowed by books, sideboards and bureau's the floor space is made smaller still by an untidy array of occasional tables and round backed chairs.

Cluttered with papers and a variety of instruments and receptacles that defy detailed description the place looks a shambles. I know better of course –Michel knows where everything is. You have to mind your head too –the ceiling is festooned with oil lamps of various designs and pinned to uprights at the junction of this T shaped room are strings of garlic.

'Rebirth', I muse aloud, 'many different views are there not Michel?'

'Many', asserts Michel, 'to progress we must all come to terms with this cyclic manifestation of life. You must accept there are as many views as there are selves in search.'

'Since change is inevitable what would you advise as a best approach?'

'There is no best approach', he says dismissively, 'besides we don't embark upon the change, as you describe it; the change is wrought in us as and activates when the balance of being is disturbed.'

Michel chuckles away at his words, repeating the word 'disturbed' several times. 'I don't understand –how is it disturbed?'

Michel didn't answer directly and rose from the table and began to search for something –removing books from a disorderly pile; a slow process as he fingered and patted each removal. 'Are you finding me another book to read?'

'No. I'm expecting a visitor and something here will help focus my mind. Ah! This will do well, I think.' It is not a book he selects but a crumpled vellum scroll.

I'm curious but know better than to press him on subject he's not ready to converse about, instead I reiterate my question.

'We have had discussion about the laws of attraction; how the substance of your body being changes by environment, how the internal and external nature conflict –but I can see you don't remember, do you?'

I think about this and am aware of something –sitting before him viewing a large globe and remembering he talked about races, moving the globe to show areas, emphasising with a finger migration patterns marked on its surface joining mass to mass. I shook my head. 'No, I can't remember, not much anyhow –but I have come to see you for a purpose. Of that I am sure.'

And at that moment I become aware of a figure forming within the arched room before me. It is a man dressed in a long cloak like garment and a helmet like hat. He remains still translucent in blue, gold and green hues of colour. 'It's Murk!' I exclaim.

'It is', Michel agrees, 'our mutual friend. He is the visitor I am expecting –we must give him a few moments to orientate himself.'

Murk is a very mysterious person –I'm aware of knowing of him but cannot presently account for what I do know. 'So this is why I have come to see you' I say. Michel seems almost asleep on his feet; he is communing with Murk who still stands half visible in the room beyond. After a short while he returns to the present consciousness and smiles at me. 'I have to say yes and no, Peter. Yes because, as you know, there is no such thing as an accident and no because the visitor you are *expecting* is standing behind you'

I spin round in my chair to be greeted by Georgie Barker.

'Watcha Guv'

'Georgie!'

I am suddenly aware of unfinished business and this has something to do with my discussion with Michel –rebirth, dwarves? I wasn't sure but Georgie's appearance could only mean one thing –him not a bookish fellow; we were off somewhere!

I look back at the form of Murk whose strange presence was even now pervading the atmosphere; the room and all within becoming fixed, definition blurring like the image of a grainy photograph.

Michel speaks, 'not yet Peter, not yet –your journeying is of another kind –discover what the questioning self must know. When he is more satisfied you may once again know your teacher.'

With that Georgie presses a hand on my shoulder. 'OK Guv? Let's be tripping the light fantastic then.'

*

---

* Fantastic as it may sound Michel is none other than Nostradamus the 16th century apothecary and mystic. Slimmer and more untidy in appearance than his official portrait I was first made aware of him in the 1960's as a communicator speaking through my teacher Len Burden in trance.

Chapter TWENTYNINE:
Arthur & Et & Fish 'n Chips

Georgie is really amazing, if anyone has set in their mind the view that 'gor blimey' characters are low in the pecking order of soul progression and cannot be influential on the other side of life should think again!

I am conscious of walking with him through an avenue of trees –though I should say 'walking' does not properly describe it, since we appear to be moving at more miles per hour than it would take to run. This is not 'speed walking' –our limbs are moving leisurely in an energy space that vibrates slower than the space the scenery occupies. It's as if I'm simultaneously present in two objective realities.

Every so often there are breaks in the trees, grassy areas sporting park seats, a table or two and flower beds –in these layby areas I see the occasional person sitting relaxed and unaware of our speedy passage. The end of avenue is coming into view and I can see buildings in the background behind trees.

'Where are we Georgie?'

'It's a town I reckon Guv, not yer big city and it's bigger'n a village.'

'Does it have a name?'

'Depends who you talk too –some say this some say that, names don't matter much anyway.' For a moment I think it's an evasive answer but a quick glance assures me that Georgie is telling me how it is.

The road is opening out with large flower beds both sides leading to a square, the centre piece of which is a fountain. Backing the square are houses, 1920's style I would say with latticed windows, porches and bays. Some of these are interspersed with garages –but no vehicles are in evidence. Here and there a shop, a restaurant. I look closely –all the dwellings as well as the shops are named.

We are slowing down and I'm aware of my feet crunching gravel and a light wind tugging at my hair. There are people walking about, mostly in groups of two's and three's but also persons on their own. Nobody is taking any notice of us. 'Georgie, can they see us?'

'Look over there –on the other side of the fountain Guv.'

I look and see an old man apparently asleep sitting on a stone seat, head cradled to his arms; then I become aware of a sea of vague forms moving beyond him. 'Now look over here', he turns my shoulder and points me in the opposite direction to a road leading away from the square –again I perceive this background of moving forms on the pavements and in the gardens.

'Now take your time Guv, and look around.' Georgie says patiently. I see people in every direction. Some seem to merge into buildings and others occupy open spaces. And now I realise that this world in view; this town of brick, mortar and road, is interconnected to another similar environment – our walk is beginning to make a sort of sense; I'm in between places or maybe I should call them states of existence.

'Are we going to be seen by anyone Georgie?'

'You betcha we are –com'on lets get some shish and fips!' And Georgie strides off round the square heading for some shops, me tailing behind shaking my head in disbelief. As we close up to the pavement we slow down again and I can feel a solidity of ground underfoot. We are in front of a Fish & Chips shop. Stencilled across the glass is the phrase 'Arthur's Fish & Chips'. There is no number on the door or any other information. I can see a man and woman in overall coats busy at the fryers and my nostrils twitch to the smell.

'Luv'ly fish and chips Guv, fancy some?'

I do, all of a sudden I do –but I have no money. I'm wearing jeans I notice. 'I don't have any cash Georgie.'

'Money? You don't need money –com'on I'll introduce you.' He pushes the door open and we stand behind two people being served. Georgie lounges against the wall, hands in pockets and looking every bit the spiv in his check jacket and trousers, narrow horizontally banded tie, pink shirt and winkle picker shoes. He looks at me with an amused expression.

I don't see any money changing hands as the man serving says cheerio –I can't even see a till. As the elderly man and woman leave they acknowledge us with a hello and good morning.

So we are visible!

'Ello Arf, watcha missus. Gotta nice bit o' Dutch eel then?

'Georgie! Where you bin then, ain't seen you in an age. Heh Et, look who's here done up to the nines!' Etta's short rotund form bobs up from behind the fryer. Fair haired and florid faced, her eyes crease into a smile. 'I was just thinking that sounded like Georgie –how are you my dear? I love the shirt.'

'Fine missus, fine –'ere say hello to the Guv', he says, jerking his thumb at me. 'Guv eh? You got something going on then?' says Etta grinning mischievously as she tosses a slice full of chips into serving compartment.

'Nah! Just gettin' aroun', learning a bit, helping out; you know 'ow it is – yer selves? Still fish and chipping then?'

'Yeah, well, we enjoy it, don't we Et? As you know we used to do this in the old life and it didn't take us long to realise we could do the same here without hassle. Get to meet all kinds of people just like the old days, even more interesting, people being more open like –some people think we are God's idea of a good time!'

They both laugh and Etta says, 'you know we had an old fella here this morning, not half an hour ago', she said looking up at a clock on the wall, 'his eyes popping out of his head, saying it was fair mad us giving the stuff away! He was new alright; had his family with him and they were laughing fit to bust'

'New? You mean he'd only just arrived?' Arthur looks at me curiously. Beneath his apron he is stocky with a bit of a paunch. He fingers his ear thoughtfully before answering; Georgie is trying to conceal his amusement at my question.

'I don't rightly know, he could have been half 'ere for some time, on the other hand he may only have just woken up. You see Packa on the seat by the fountain? You should ask him that question –be interesting to see what he says. You new then?'

'No I'm not new', I say quickly, butting Georgie with my knee, 'but new to this' waving my hand vaguely at the shop and pointing outside. Georgie leans over the counter and Arthur inclines his head to share a confidence. 'Ee's a bit of a scholar, you might say.'

'Well, that's good then,' says Arthur straightening up, 'Et and me have got to learning all kinds of stuff –eh, you wouldn't believe it Georgie but we're into horses now just can't believe how intelligent they are. Teach you a thing or two I can tell you.'

'What's it going to be then duck?' says Etta addressing me.

'I'll have the same as Georgie. Tell me (I'm trying to be casual) where do you get your supplies from?'

'From the pantry in Whitwell Street,' she says it in a matter of fact manner. 'Les Chase's. Old man Purvis gave it up. Did you known him then?'

'No. No. Just curious. '

'Jes likes to know where things come from Et', says Georgie reassuringly.

All of a sudden I feel very insecure and impelled to talk with them about horses. 'I'm glad to hear of your interest in horses. Equine history is most interesting and as you may be aware horses pre date man's development by thousands of years. The ancestor of the horses you know is the four-toed Eohippus, a much smaller animal; some no bigger than a small dog –this evolved into the Mesohippus about the size of a large dog. Their idea of family is in the hundreds and their group mind developed and continued to evolve long after man harnessed their energies. The modern western horse is mixture of the Akhal-Teke type from the ancient classical world; an animal of tremendous stamina and great speed. Akhal-Teke was the forerunner of the Arabian horse and of the Caspian who originated in the Urals characterised by its flattish face and small ears. The Caspian is small and very agile. Equus caballus is the modern horse you know and love.'[14]

They have both stopped what they are doing and look at me with open mouths. I suddenly know nothing about horses and mentally cross my fingers they don't ask any questions.

'Did you know you lit up when talking then?' Etta says still looking a bit startled. 'No', I say, not a little embarrassed. Arthur is slowly wrapping up the order. 'What did you say was the horse we know now?'

'Equus caballus.' The name tumbles out.

'Now that's what you call learning', says Arthur slapping down two wraps of fish and chips on the counter. They smell of vinegar.

---

[14] In this conscious life what I know about horses can be written on the back of a business card!

'What did I tell yer? Ee's a scholar.' Georgie says triumphantly.

'What about unicorns then?' Etta is warming to the theme, 'I've seen one but Arthur says it's not real.'

'Oh, they are real I assure you.' I'm talking again –but I'm not in control of my thoughts.

'They are closely allied to the elemental spirits whose realm is between this state and the lower earth. The horses we have been speaking about are related. There is more than one type of unicorn, though they all have the one horn. In ancient times when they materialised in the flesh, man used to hunt them as they prized the horn, believing it to have magical properties.'

Etta has stopped attending the fryer and stands talking to me across the counter wiping her hands on a cloth. 'Why in God's name would they want to do that? The unicorn I saw was as white as snow and seemed to glow from within. I got such a lovely feeling I wanted to go up to him and put my arms around his neck –but as I moved he upped and disappeared.' Etta sounds the disappointment she must have felt at that moment.

'The emanations they produce are essentially pure of thought –they are like other elemental beings of a tripartite sex, quite different to you and me. We feel harmonised in their presence –hence the wonderful feelings you experienced. All human beings remark upon it; they feel as if their soul is being cleansed.'

'Well I be –can't say I know what this tripartite sex is you talk about. I thought male and female was the limit', says Arthur, who is now listening to me with great interest. 'I take it you've had experience of them. Et comes out with all kinds of stuff –some of it is a bit hard to take in, still, I'm getting to acknowledge more now than ever I used too. Seeing is believing, that's what I reckon.'

'We still have our different ways –but we like it like that don't we Arthur?'

Etta and Arthur exchange smiles expressing their comfortable feelings. 'We're out later', says Arthur, having dinner with Bill and Ada. Like us they were separated for a while. Quite a laugh ain't it Et? Ada's a bit like me, likes to think things through and Bill is more like Et and gets quite carried away –so we gang up against each other, gets quite interesting, I can tell you.'

'So you end up having quite deep conversations then?' I ask, hopeful that it would shed some light on how they were evolving.

'Deep? Wouldn't call it deep, would you Et?' Et laughs, 'Don't think the Guv knows what you're talking about dear.' She wipes her hands again and leans across the counter and grasps hold of mine. 'We play cards dearie.'

'Oh, I see –or rather I should say I don't because I'm not a card player – but I understand it can get quite intense.'

'You must come round and play a hand or two –and you to Georgie.'

'Another time Et –it's only a quick visit –the Guv's on a bit of a tour, educational like.'

'I've heard you mention the Guv before, now come to think of it', says Arthur.

'Yea, that's right Arf, he's a teacher.'

'Right', says Arthur, looking at me as if he is now aware of a memory in which I figured. Whilst we've been talking another couple has come into the shop. They are young, in their twenties –they seemed very much in love. Etta calls over to them.

'What will it be then dearies?'

'Bit of plaice, got a bit of plaice?' Says the young man timidly. At this point Georgie grabs my arm and starts to steer me out of the shop. 'Be seeing yer both. Gotta be shifting.' We exchange goodbyes.

'Come back soon', says Arthur. As we leave the shop I can hear Etta saying, 'Now you look as if you could do with a bit of building up dear. Who told you about us then?'

We pass the man asleep on the bench beside the fountain and walk into a road opposite the shop. Although the houses are physically close I feel distant from them. People pass by on the pavement seemingly wrapt up in their own personal worlds. I see some out and about in their gardens tending plants etc.

I try greeting some individuals. Responses are mixed; some appear unaware of us and those that do respond absentmindedly. Every now and then Georgie says, 'leave it Guv; they ain't on your wavelength.'

We come to a village green –or so it seems to be, where a cricket match is in progress. As we eat our fish and chips and watch the game, I venture a question to Georgie. 'How is it you know where to go and who to connect? I sort of half know the answer but I'm finding it confusing. This world', I jerk my head toward the cricket match in progress, 'is visible to us but we are not visible to everyone we see –yet Arthur and Etta were aware of us; it was a two way communication. Can you put me straight Georgie?'

Georgie squints at me, rubs his jaw and shakes his head. 'Don't rightly know Guv –I can try. To start with you're odd, you're a bit o' this and a bit o' that, not that it's wrong like but 'cos your mind is presently conscious of it's physical incarnation it's gonna have a view of this world that am different from mine. Michel asked me to help out and take you places, said it would help you write.'

'I'm fine Georgie, absolutely fine when I'm in one place at one time –but it seems to me we are neither here nor there, that's what confusing me.'

'That's 'cos your experience is being governed by the physical mind. See, it's like this, in the physical world you 'ave the impression that only one thing is taking place at a time –right?

'Well, no Georgie, there are many things taking place but they are all at the same level.'

'You mean like this cricket match, eh? Like them birds singing in the trees over there', he points to trees on our left and I realise there are birds in the branches and they are singing.

'Seems to me Guv that the physical mind doesn't account for much; see that batsman running now he's hit the ball; see that fielder running to stop it? See what the bowler's doing –an' the ref; are you watching him too?'

'Well, OK you're right –focussing on one thing means I don't see other things clearly.'

'And some things you don't see at all!' Georgie is beginning to warm to his theme as I admit he is right. 'And when you say they are all on the same level –it just ain't true, they only look as if they are to you.'

'I can see what you are getting at and I don't disagree but what I'm trying to understand is what I would call the vibrational level of existence. Human beings think of the physical world as one plane of consciousness. Of course there are lots of things we don't understand; connections we don't make because our senses work differently than say the birds or animals –but it's all one level. Am I making sense?'

'Sort of Guv, sort of –see, when you come into this form of life you bring your energies with you, an' yer memories, wishes and intentions. The difference is in you as thought becomes physical so to speak –the background becomes the foreground, if you see what I mean? See what I mean?

'Thought becomes reality?' I suggest.

'If that's what you want to call it –yes it does.'

'OK. This place for example –my earthly mind doesn't recognise it, so how does that fit in?

'Gawd luv us Guv! You ain't the only being in this world. And I don't mean all your thoughts are physical –just as you have an inner level of consciousness in the physical world, so you have one here. There are many different levels here just as there are in the physical world. In this world there's a bit more give an' take.'

'So this is a shared consciousness?'

'That's it Guv –you got it in one!' Georgie is delighted with me and slaps me on the shoulder –then he grabs my arm and in mock astonishment says, 'an' what 'ave you done with your fish and chips?' I didn't have them. No paper, no smell, and neither did Georgie –it's as if they never existed. Yet I ate them, I'm sure of that. 'Now call to mind our meeting with Arf and Et.' He looks at me closely urging me to arrive at the right conclusion. 'You know, imagine it again.' I did as he suggested and watch my hands, half expecting the wrap of fish and chips to materialise, but they don't.

'Can you smell the vinegar and the fat?'

'I can, yes I can', I say hesitantly. 'Them are thoughts you've had see, and this,' he said thumping the park seat we sat on. 'Is a now thought.' I groan. 'I must be thick Georgie –what's the difference then between then and now?'

'Shared consciousness Guv –right now you are part of this', he waves his hand to the field and the trees, thumps the seat again and mockingly places his hand over his heart. 'We ain't part of Arf's world at the moment –we are part of another world.' A massive thwack of the bat sends a ball spinning out toward us, way past the boundary fielders. Georgie jumps up, runs forward, picks up the ball and throws it back into play. The chasing fielder collects the ball and returns it to the bowler. He comes back, sits down and wipes his hands on a large pocket handkerchief.

'I know it's hard for you Guv. It always will be so long as you still have a physical incarnation. Truth is the physical world has many levels of existence but human beings only see it as one. In this world you are more aware of levels –they interact don't yer see?'

'The houses', I say doggedly, 'are they made brick by brick? Is there such a thing as a brick making business?'

'Some people build their own houses, brick by brick as you put it –but most don't cos they are already built as they realise they need them. Folks pass 'em on to one another and then they get altered to suit. They arise from the physical life –mostly being what they wanted rather than what they had; as for brick making business, I ain't seen one in this life.'

'Have you got a place Georgie?'

'Used to when me Ma and Pa came over –but they don't need it anymore and I don't neither. And you don't have one either, do you Peter?' Georgie's right –I don't.

'As Peter you've always lived here. Yer don't stand still –none of us do. You are a partnership, so to speak and there are other parts of self, like Silver Wing and Atlanta. Shared consciousness is what moves us forward, how we evolve so to speak. Some beings got it off so pat they don't 'ave to move around anymore –it's like all they need comes to them. See what I mean Guv?'

I sort of do but realise my 'fractured' consciousness is pulling in different directions and I nod and smile my response. Georgie nods sagely back –I hide nothing from him!

'Come on then Guv, we need to get you back before you turn into a pumpkin!'

Chapter THIRTY:
'Sacrifice' in the Gardens of Versailles

I'm beginning to accept that my identity cannot be satisfactorily explained in terms of conscious awareness –that self understanding is not achieved by analysis and proved positive by reason. In my journey with Michel and Georgie the experience of shared consciousness is giving me pause to think and re-evaluate what I have previously understood. Peter reads a book on dwarfs that he clearly regards as a scholarly work that I would have serious reservations about. Yet in a state of shared consciousness I am able to accept the premise that dwarfs do exist.

In Peter's subsequent conversation with Michel, who is clearly aware of my earthly personality, his educative replies are informing Peter –more so than me. At that moment I was aware of Peter and myself sharing consciousness. I was particularly struck by Michel's summing up, "You must accept there are as many views as there are selves in search." Seen from the perspective of my journeying experiences this statement is significant. Michel uses the word "view" to mean a state of awareness, not 'view' in the particular sense you and I use it in the physical world.

I am also conscious of Peter 'controlling' our shared consciousness state during the journey with Georgie and then finally on the village green standing back and letting me have my head. My analytical mind is sorely tempted in the aftermath of recording to examine the journey experience in detail -but inwardly I know I must not indulge myself. Such action might well 'upset the apple cart' and disable the connections I am now sharing with Peter.

Tales of Bellerophon –On the Banks of the Shalimar

It was Peter's control that 'managed' the conversations with Arthur and Etta. Georgie's timely interventions show that he was working closely with Peter. I can only guess at the outcome had I resisted their influence –likely my journey would have ended abruptly.

How little we know about human consciousness –let alone consciousness of other conceptions!

I look through the papers, now full of post election analysis, and ponder on how blind we are, how little we really know of each other and when we do gain an understanding the polarising action of that knowledge allows immediate 'like' association only. Georgie is clearly comfortable with the practise of sharing consciousness with other people of diverse nature; he is not defensive and can connect in any situation. On the other hand Etta and Arthur's lives are still governed by attachment and necessarily think selectively as a result. However, if our conversation is anything to go by their world 'view', is less judgmental than mine.

As I continue to thumb through the paper glancing at the scandal headlines, at the sport, letters to the editor and so on, I am deeply conscious of how little we truly know of anything –it is no wonder that every dawn brings unexpected, unknown events into our lives. At best we partially share, like for example, with a special person –a loved one. With such people we express our needs and wants –they likewise with us to develop a shared consciousness.

Yet because those needs and wants are stimulated by our inherent requirement for security they become dependants by association and the power of change is limited.

I walk out into the garden and remember for a moment the astral world communion I've had here in this place, of flying with buzzards, of talking to people not here in the flesh. I look at the flowers, at the bricks that make the garden wall –at every see-able thing, and feel small, arbitrary and incomprehensible. Sharing is the least of what I do –even though I make a point of trying to do it. I ponder on this for a while and come to the uncomfortable conclusion that the consciousness we have in the physical world is limited by our inability to truly share. Given my astral awareness I am likening the difference between 'there' and here to the life of a prisoner denied of free society. The prisoners consciousness and that of the 'free society' is mutually exclusive because their 'views' are developed by what divides them. Human beings it would appear are capable of sharing consciousness but the incarnate mindset demands all experience is related to the birth and death cycle, thus causing division –and division limits our capacity to share.

I had a particularly vivid experience the other day –as if someone had unfurled a large cinematic screen in front of me and I was looking down upon an estuary river, its banks shored by timber and steel, the sun bright and the surface water dancing diamonds. A wind blew from my left and below I could see kittiwake's flying across my 'screen'. I watched fascinated by their movements and as they reached the far side of my vision darkness gradually enveloped them. I could not return my focus to the broad expanse of estuary water however hard I tried –a yearning to see the birds again had me stare into darkness as a blinded man might so believe memory of sight invoked would enable his vision. Eventually I returned to normal consciousness with a strange empty feeling –as if I was powerless to influence myself.

The event keeps coming back to mind –I try to relive it but fail miserably. I'm unable to share my consciousness with the event and equally the event is unable to share itself with me; so it remains a picture –at best a still born experience. How many of our so-called waking experiences are merely pictures; still born lives, we believing they are shared?

I lean back in the chair. Today's working drivers fail to impress, instead I choose to reflect upon my journeying experiences; how they have shifted my consciousness and unsettled my mind. My conscious nature has 'bulldozed' its way to the foreground of most events, bringing them and the promise of sharing to a premature close. I'm realising that my inability to share consciousness is at the heart of all my questions and the cause of all my restlessness. Why, I wonder, can I not alter what I am patently aware restricts my consciousness? Are all human beings like this; has it always been so?

I feel as if I'm drifting –going to sleep I guess.

'You are too hard upon yourself Peter, much too hard,' Edward says gently, his arm comfortably about my shoulder as we walk a path through herbaceous borders under tall trees.

These are the gardens of Versailles, or perhaps I should say –the gardens as they are in the world of spirit, a vast colourful panorama of lawns and hedges, objects d'art, fountains, trees and flowers. We are not alone here – some people walk as we do, others tend plants, and some seemingly do nothing –just sit entranced by the atmosphere. Everybody is wearing 19th century clothes. Edward wears a frock coat, leather calf leggings and stout boots and looks the part –whereas I look far from 'roman' wearing a green collarless vee necked gown tapered at the waist. Despite my looking different I don't feel out of place and sense being here out of need. The quiet and orderly nature of these gardens and the atmosphere they generate invites the mind to open unconditionally and encourages contemplation.

I am intent on understanding the issue of shared consciousness and Edward is responding to my questions. 'You are now aware of significant differences between the world of matter and our world of thought. Your earth nature aware of this world feels restricted by the physical world environment. As you now understand the physical mentality functions differently and the ability to share, present though it is in that psyche, is hard to achieve. In this world it is by soul sharing we are able to progress. Your journeys are revealing peoples and other beings at different levels of development; Georgie and your other guides are doing well having you realise this.'

'I feel as if I've come to terms with much since the journeying began, not least being aware of different levels of my own being and yet I'm beginning to think the experiences written about are less revealing than they might had I been prepared to share more of my consciousness at the time.'

We sit down on a bench in a small quadrangle of lawn centred by a stone bordered pond overlooked by trees. It is a scene of utter stillness –not a breath of wind or a ripple on the glass like water surface.

'No. no', Edward says firmly, 'you do well given awareness of yourself – you have progressed to be sure, now you conceive of shared consciousness in a deeper way. All relationships whether they are of human kind, amorphous nature, or beings of other conceptions, are a shared understanding. And it must be said as Peter you have shared in all instances. Progression by experience is another matter –experience is the awareness of earth formed memory and by its very nature limits the revelation of this world.'

'Yes it does', I quickly respond, 'I question experience –asking myself, am I going round in circles, is all this journeying leading me somewhere and if so; where too and for what?'

Edward laughs and affectionately pats my head. 'You are progressing! Just my own reactions after birth in this life; I went hither and thither intent to exercise my new found awareness to expand upon my earth formed memory. It's much the same for all reborn to this life. Gradually it dawned on me that some with whom I developed relationship were different to others –and as such the freedom and openness of their nature inspired me. They were worldly, if I may use that term, of this realm of reality –the mechanisms of their earthly memory had been discarded. To progress myself in this realm of reality a radical change was required.'

'And what was that?' I say eagerly. 'I needed to appreciate Self less the 'I' I knew it by. I had to make sacrifices.'

'Sacrifices, you must explain what you mean –what kind of sacrifices?'

'The surrender of earth world experience, the very basis of what I conceived to be my identity. My new found relationships had learnt to give away the identity by which they had been known.'

I'm suddenly feeling like a fish out of water –self conscious of my attire and mentally resistant to Edwards' views. The corner stone of my philosophy is that all illness and disharmony is caused by the loss of identity and here I am being told that the process of evolving shared consciousness is to lose my sense of identity!'

'I'm having difficulty understanding that Edward.'

'Yes I knew you would, I'm very much aware of your earthly teachings – I have, after all, helped you in these matters.'

'And what you say now is compatible with what I've taught??'

'Yes it is –let me explain it to you. Sharing is like the act of making a cake, cutting a slice for your self and distributing the rest to others. The act of sharing enables the giver to receive. By sacrifice the receiver is enabled to give and the soul nature is made aware of itself. The earth born personality is aware of its fragmentary nature and instinctively reaches out to join with others; however that desire to harmonise is tempered by the instinct of self preservation. It is because of this conflict that man has difficulty in knowing himself.'

I can feel a conflict in myself as I listen to this explanation from Edward. My 'Peter' consciousness is curious as to why men suffer this problem whilst the 'Tony' nature is having difficulty understanding how identity can progress if it gives away its right of experience. 'Do you mean that the act of sacrifice causes you to lose your sense of identity?'

'You might think so –but no. some part of you is forever withheld. What happens is that as you receive 'view' self need is revealed by the difference achieved in the act of sharing.

That which you give away comes back albeit in the form as understood by, say, the other person. The result is that the destiny and nature of that other person or being is shared with you and self knowing develops further. Now multiply what I have said of an instance many times and you will realise that this is a radically different way of living than that enjoyed by the incarnate soul.'

'Is no one incarnate able to follow this path of development?'

Edward laughed. 'There you go invoking your black and white earthly mind. Let us for the moment take a view of your own cycle and put it to the sharing test. As Peter you are not destined to be born in the flesh and instead develop as a human being in this astral world. Tony who is also part of Peter's cycle is already born incarnate and aware of being something other than what he appears to be but does not know what. Both coincide in an act of sharing that neither is fully aware of –'

'Hold it there Edward please', I say anxiously, 'what act are you referring too?'

'For Tony the act was meeting his teacher that unlocked inner awareness of himself –now that also included awareness of Peter but not as a personality. Peter had progressed by the sharing of consciousness to higher astral levels of being, and there established a relationship with Tony's teacher cycle that in turn drew him closer to the man Tony, albeit unconsciously.

Peter then became the facilitator of the cycle of the soul known as Atlanta, birthing an element of it into the incarnate world of the man Tony. Tony became aware of Atlanta but not of Peter –his teacher however was aware of both.'

'So my present state of awareness is a result of shared consciousness?'

'Indeed it is –it is the process by which we are all aware. You ask if the incarnate is able to follow this path –you can now appreciate they all do. To be fair, your question is asking how is it possible for the incarnate mind to be an evolutionary practitioner of this fundamental precept of consciousness – and for that my dear Peter there is not a simple answer.'

'Ah ha!' I say jumping up and laughing with childish glee, 'my question has stumped you!' Edward regards by antics with paternal affection and then raises an admonishing finger. 'Back to the wall I admit but not entirely out for the count', he exclaims.

'Many incarnate minds are simply not aware of their inner selves and cannot therefore conceive of the sharing experience we have been discussing. Some of course, are aware but in a world which puts great store by sensory realities the realisation of inner self being is a life sapping struggle and most compromise to maintain their inner convictions.'

My childish feelings subside and I feel a great sense of love for him as he patiently provides answer to the problem I am trying to solve. I sit back down and lean against him –for a while neither of us speaks but instead we both look out upon the gardens of Versailles. I feel comforted by the ease by which people move about, having conversation or simply enjoying the presence of place. I don't feel like questioning and neither do I feel a need to accept or reject as one does by consciously absorbing differences; instead I feel an awareness of agreement; of knowledge that needs no justification or explanation. Eventually I turn to Edward and ask:

'The best the incarnate mind can expect is partially to share –is that it?'

'Yes', a note of sadness sounds in his voice and I comment on it.

'The most advanced of incarnate beings experience a sadness they cannot explain no matter what their command of language. And remember there are many levels in this world in which sharing is only partial –not only because of earth mind influence of those arising but also minds alien to the evolving human nature. It is only when sharing is absolute that a being escapes the cycle of incarnation and moves on into the great cycle.'

'And the great cycle –can you talk about that?' I say timidly.

'No', says Edward sharply, and then laughs, 'you see how you are anchoring me into the cycle of incarnation! Not now and not by talk shall you know it'

'You know Edward I get definite feelings you will not let me press matters further!'

'There is tension between this world of your being and the earth nature – it is to be expected. This is why we are here; in these gardens men forget their dreams and their pains –it is a place of healing. Let us walk and engage the flowers –all is well, all manner of things are well, for the tongues of fire are infolded into the crowned knot of fire, and the fire and rose are one.'

As he speaks the closing lines of TS Eliot's 'Four Quartets' poem and we walk arm in arm amid this tranquil scene, everything begins to merge so fittingly I am not aware of my change –not aware of returning.

†

---

† At the time of these communications I'd never visited the Gardens at Versailles –the following year I did with my wife on holiday. As beautiful they are, in no way do they compare with the energy I experienced during this event.

Chapter THIRTYONE:
Sharing and Smoking

It's the height of summer and I'm idling in woods having parked my car near Petersfield Lake. Puffs of white cloud move in stately procession across a blue sky. It's hot and the air lazes in every shaded place. I have two hours free before I see patients in the town. I'm half tempted to leave these woods for the lakeside nearby and chat up the fisherman. For more than 8 months now I've not fished –a pastime I find both absorbing and challenging. I am not so much deciding against it as held to the barely discernable path that stretches before my sandaled feet. I am thinking about my meeting with Edward in the gardens of Versailles.

Our conversation has made me more aware of the dual nature of astral experience. I was alternatively conscious of Peter and of myself as the subject of sharing was discussed and my respect for Edward and my other journey communicators deepens as I realise my Jekyll and Hyde nature must be difficult to deal with. I know that I am treading a fine line –what must they feel?

As I think about it here on terra firma the space and time relationship difference between the astral and physical world is keenly felt. In my astral journeys sensorial awareness of space is not overlaid with the sense of time as it is here. Peter seems not to have the mind that measures or notes event as outcomes of past experience –never recollects and doesn't think in terms of futures. As Peter it's like being in a store in which everything you conceivably want is on the shelves –he doesn't need to look for anything nor personalise what he expresses. In short –he lives a present state in which all needs and expectations are met. Or so it seems.

When I as Tony am invoked during the astral experience, self-conscious awareness is immediate. However the sense of looking back is not present and as a consequence I share yesterday and today equally, oblivious of the difference. There I'm quite different to the self here –self conscious yes, but not in the same way. In the astral world as Peter I feel incomparably free and unattached, yet because of it able to express attachment more deeply than is possible here. If that sounds contradictory –there's no better way I can say it. I guess this is evidence of the sharing theme Edward advises me is the medium of creation in the astral worlds.

Here on terra firma I have a problem relating the space time difference experience my other selves have in the astral worlds. During my journeys surroundings are objectively realised albeit restricted by my reception. Nothing is two dimensional, be they objects or the natural world – everything, even the atmosphere, is inviting union. Purpose is paramount. Without Georgie's guidance and Peter's influence would I have made it across the square to Arthur and Etta's Fish and Chip shop? I doubt it. Yet my remembered experience of sharing despite limitations is deeper than anything in this world. As I travel my feet don't sink into the ground and I can feel bodily –the action of energy within and without as I walk. This is a present awareness which doesn't 'age' whether I'm stationary or moving and the activity is changing my consciousness. As a consequence I don't feel the passage of time whether I be stationary or travelling and aware of moving landscapes. In our physical world the kind of space we occupy affects our sense of time. Wide open spaces are synonymous with time, because objectively distance is a measure of time, yet in the astral worlds an intimacy is present to all scenes, distant or close.

As I write remembrance I keep thinking I'm missing something out. Ad nauseam I re-read recorded recollections focussing my mind on the seen and felt experience –occasionally a detail will emerge and I add it. Daft as it sounds I'm aware of experience I can't recall. OK so it's not remembered – where does that leave me? Memory is an accrual of time measured events so

207

the 'missing' part is clearly not space and time related.

A couple walking a dog are coming toward me on the path and I step aside pressing my back against the sapling branches, smile and nod my greeting. They pass talking quietly with one another their eyes only acknowledging my presence –the dog is more interested in me and sniffs me out before walking on. Will they remember me? I doubt it. Will the dog? I doubt that too perhaps for different reasons. I look at my watch –I still have plenty of time before heading into town and decide to make my way back to the car and listen to some music.

I ponder the space and time question as I make my way back. I'm questioning the reality that's what I'm doing because it doesn't stack up the same way as this one. Having reached that conclusion I reflect on meeting the couple and their dog and realise the experience is less informative than any passing astral world impression I've recorded –then suddenly it hits me. The entirety of astral experience is meaningful because it's constant! True, I don't profess to understand the entirety, but when I compare my inner awareness of astral life with the expression of this life, the difference is as stark light and dark. In this life awareness of others, human and otherwise, is triggered only when I bump into something!

I look out onto the car park and observe Mums, Dads and children boarding or leaving their vehicles. It's a familiar scene, like those tall beeches surrounding the lake. If I do share myself in some way I'm unaware of doing it and bar the sense of seeing a pleasing picture I'm also unaware of response. If all this were to be wiped away I would not miss it. I sit in the car and switch on the music –Ah! Great! It's Sibelius. Evidence that we too live in a present world. Must we be the spectator?

How would we do that I wonder?

I settle back in my seat and feel that I'm walking away from myself.

I am standing on a carpet of leaves in a small clearing dwarfed by tall cedar trees, the sweet resinous smell of wood apparent. I am with Lone Wolf who is presently rummaging inside a decorated cloth bag he carries. He looks up smiling at me. 'Here', he says, proffering a small leather bag which I take, 'a gift is always welcome.'

'Am I expected?' I ask anxiously

'Of course', he says smiling broadly, 'with great interest.'

Feeling the bag heavy for its size in my hand I pull open the neck to reveal a green stone –or to be more correct, a brownish translucent stone emanating a pale green hue. 'And what is this stone –it's beautiful I must say.'

'It's a moon meteor fragment. It will cause great interest.'

It has an 'empty' feel about it which makes me curious, but as it's a gift I close the bag. It doesn't seem right of me to focus energy upon it. I look through the trees from the glade in which we stand noting the winding path that descends away to our right and of seeing the tops of tepee's in a clearing beyond the trees stark against a pale blue sky.

As we walk the path in single file my eyes delight in the woodland flowers that grow on hillocks of grass and the scrubland borders. I hear birds close by but don't see their darting forms. Lone Wolf whispers they are finches. 'Up there', he points right from the direction we travel to snow capped distant mountains, 'are ravens.'

I look into the shimmering sky and make out four black shapes flying in the distance. 'You know them?'

He pauses and turns –his dark eyes full of feeling. 'They are most welcoming. The have a highly developed sense of community and read the landscape well. Distant as you think they are, they are aware of us.'

'Fascinating', I say but as interested as I am other thoughts are more pressing. 'What should I do exactly? Should I prepare myself in some way?'

'Just be yourself –enjoy the connection. I will watch over matters, have no fear –these people know you are peculiar and aware of your earth nature connection.' I am encouraged by his vibration. Lone Wolf is a man of few words and his assurance gives me confidence. We leave the path and move up a rise of open ground; on topping it the tepees of an Indian settlement come into view. The sight suggests a community of some 50 souls given the number of tepees. There are horses, mustangs mostly, but they are not corralled and roam freely in the upland grasses beyond the circle of tents. I stop to take all this into account and Lone Wolf who has walked on, turns and beckons me forward.

'Have I been here before?'

'As you now are I think not –but there is one here who knows you. And here he comes.'

Running toward us is a youngish man, long dark hair banded into a pigtail, lightly clad in trousers and leather looking waistcoat, not unlike that worn by Lone Wolf. As he nears us his hand raises in greeting. I recognise him as Hawkeye and memory of being with him in a mountainous chasm seeking out the resting places of birds comes immediately to mind. He has the birds' eye for noting movements at great distance, a skill he has demonstrated time and time again.

'Peter! He cried, come, come we are expecting you.' After embracing us both warmly he stands back and gazes in mock astonishment at me. 'Have you journeyed my friend, you look different since our last meeting, older.' He cocks his head to one side and suppresses a laugh.

'Hawkeye, if I look older it's because I'm nervous.'

'No.' Lone Wolf interjected, 'it's because he is a also a questioner Hawkeye –and you know how that ages a soul.'

'I assure you Peter, it will not be noticed, and besides what difference does it make –are you not still the adventurer I know?'

'That's not a title I give myself but I will gladly accept it.' I feel a little embarrassed by my response as if I have not properly remembered myself. We are now nearing the settlement of tepees and I can hear and see children laughing and playing in the vicinity and women sitting in front of the tents talking between themselves.

The environment feels welcoming and energising. 'The atmosphere is good Hawkeye –the energy is strong here.'

'Yes. It is a good place and there is much to do, as you will see. Do you stay wise one?'

'Now what would you think of me if I left my charge?' Lone Wolf says with a knowing look. 'Come then, you must meet with Thundercloud, soft shoes and Jeremiah.'

Anticipating that introduction Hawkeye leads us into the largest of the tepees and in the half light and smoked wreathed air seated on blankets I see three figures. The tallest I take to be Thundercloud, dressed in traditional Indian costume and wearing headdress. Beside him is a slight looking woman in a smock and shawl and a shorter man naked to the waist, full in the face his hair short and knotted on the top of his head. Hawkeye formally makes introductions and we sit. There are smiles but no words, instead an Indian pipe is passed around and we each draw from the pipe and pass it on again to our neighbour. The smoke is smooth and tastes sweet. The act of doing this seems to bind us together. As once again Thundercloud receives the pipe he speaks; his voice is deep and resonates,

'What news do you bring us my friends –for you are sure to have stories to tell and we have ears eager to listen.'

'The old world is as troubled as it has always been my old friend', said Lone Wolf, and the Iroquois are changed –many have lost the memory of their roots. Yet some make special study of Indian's way of life. The red mans wisdom lives on in other peoples as the Spirit of peace.' He pauses as if to invite comment but instead Thundercloud motions to Hawkeye who rises smiling at me.

'I go now', he says, 'the horses await me. Come later and we will talk horses.' As Hawkeye leaves Lone Wolf comments that he has grown strong since last they communed. The comment is obviously received with pleasure as I note by their expressions but they say nothing and merely incline their heads in agreement.

Lone Wolf speaks again.

'My friend here is born of this world yet is now wedded to an earthly self that seeks awareness. He has become a great questioner and I fear if we speak of that incarnate self his consciousness will drift and our communion will be lost.'

'So be it wise one, we heed your counsel.' Addressing me he says, 'Hawkeye gives us account of your love of Ariel beings –we are much connected in this way ourselves as bird life has much understanding to impart.'

'I cannot explain it better than you know my friends –for me the bird is the spirit that makes of form freedom, an ever present testimony of a change to be, evidence that our endeavours will succeed.' As I speak this I feel imbued with authority.

'You journey as one who has purpose,' said Jeremiah, 'tell us what this purpose is?'

'That I might reach the place of my purpose and journey no more,' I say. Soft Shoes looks up at me with a dazzling smile but it's Thundercloud who speaks.

'We have met with many travellers who seek a place –a heaven of tranquillity.'

'He seeks the way of your people old friend', said Lone Wolf quietly. 'And who is to say of the many ways that which is best, said Jeremiah inviting comment.

'I sense many things in my travels; I listen to people and I try to understand their needs. I think when I know better I will also walk in other ways.' I say. Soft Shoes speaks now her voice clear and warm with invitation. 'But these other ways –they are a mystery to you, are they not?'

I nod. She has put her finger on it, no matter how much interest I have in others, how much I'm prepared to be of help, there is separateness I feel after all my effort –a part of me is excluded from understanding. 'Let us smoke some more', Jeremiah says eagerly, 'young Peter should know us better.'

Soft Shoes prepares the pipe and when it is ready she moves about our small circle shuffling on her knees. She wears traditional Indian dress –a smock and trousers, her hair loose about her shoulders. To me she epitomises beauty.

I take the proffered pipe. Lone Wolf leans across and gently touches her shoulder. 'Remember Soft Shoes he is a strange one –he knows all but himself.' She laughs. 'Then this will be an adventure for all of us wise one – let us begin.'

Chapter THIRTYTWO:
Enter the Green Man

I suddenly remember the gift given me by Lone Wolf and take the leather bag from my pocket and present it to Thundercloud. He thanks me and carefully removes the stone from the pouch. Holding it up so all can see he views it approvingly.

'Good', he says by way of thanks and passes the stone to Soft Shoes and Jeremiah who also examine it in a similar way –they too nod in appreciative agreement. 'A moon stone of great antiquity and good strength', he pronounces receiving it back and placing it on the ground. 'This is ideal for the link we are about to make –we should pass it between us as we smoke.'

Soft Shoes leaves the tepee and returns with a lighted taper, sits at our feet and lights the pipe, tamping down the mixture gently with her fingers until it draws well. I note that the mixture smells different to the first pipe – the sweetness more subtle, its aroma more earthy and vegetable.

I draw first on the pipe unsure of exactly how I should smoke it; my throat constricts and I find myself stifling a cough, eyes smarting. I pass the pipe to Lone Wolf who drawing upon it lets the smoke exhale from his nostrils slowly, he then passes it to Jeremiah who does likewise. Thundercloud then takes up the stone and holds it gently between his thumb and forefinger before pressing it into his lower abdomen. He whispers a prayer before drawing on the pipe. Soft Shoes does this in turn and passes the stone and pipe to me saying;

'We invoke the moon spirit.'

I know these beings as Devas and likewise invoke them as I hold the stone close to my abdomen. That strange empty feeling I first felt on receiving the stone from Lone Wolf is present and stronger. The stone's energy enters into my gut like a cold wind and I feel my body heat cooling – the energy filling my torso and creeping into my limbs. Physically I feel as if I'm losing definition and shrinking –the tepee is looking larger and somewhat out of focus.

Gently Lone Wolf takes the stone and pipe and the practice continues. In my turn by copying the practice I draw better on the pipe. Invoking the stone disorientates and weakens my sense of individuality -I feel part of a mental state arising from us all. The external world of the tepee is becoming increasingly indistinct; the forms of my companions grow in stature and the awareness I feel is panoramic and borderless. That strange empty feeling I first experienced on handling the stone has magnified and overshadowed me. My sense of identity is draining away but I'm not afraid, the sense of being joined gives me security.

The change continues and my connection of time, space and personality increasingly incidental and meaningless. I am changing in ways I don't understand and don't care. I am now aware of myself dressed in moccasins, trousers and smock, my hair long and greased in a pigtail. I calmly recognise the person materialised before me and dressed in a green one piece garment as another me.

We are joined in some way and blanketed by silence –the whole world has ceased to noise. I feel relieved of myself –a life influence foreign to the born being removed. The self opposite, who I will call the green man, rises and beckons with his eyes to follow. I rise to my feet as one commanded. We walk together under a canopy of tall protecting pine trees. Outwardly and inwardly everything is silent –I cannot even hear myself move as I walk. I am not awed or fearful but excited, eager and youthful. I reach for and take hold of the green man's hand. It's long and tapered, strong, claw like and firm. I want to give myself to him, have his transforming essence build me a new self. My whole body is emotionally alive; I feel the air caressing my skin with an intense feeling of pleasure that borders pain.

'Who are you?' I ask dramatically breaking the silence; my voice strong and feminine, quaking with emotion.

He looks directly at me a smile hovering on his lips. His face is more angular than mine framed by long dark tousled hair –the cheekbones higher and his eyes glitter like a newborn child. 'I am whoever you want me to be.'

'Then show me you care', I say simply drawing close.

His arm encircles my shoulders and I lean my head upon his chest. My feeling of care is so complete I am still and all sense of identity disappears.

I'm aware of sitting at a table reading a book, a story of adventure at sea in times past, of sailing ships, dangers of the deep, buccaneers and strange new places. About me I hear voices of young men joking and laughing with one another –and I see that some are engaged in friendly wrestling, others playing board games.

I look about feigning interest and at that moment a voice –the voice of the green man says; 'go mix with them.' Reluctantly I close my book get up from the table and saunter over to a couple of boys engaged in a card game. They each have two cards face down on the table between them.

'Who's winning then? I say embarrassed and awkward for intruding upon their space. The smaller of the two looks up at me without interest.

'What's it to you anyhow?'

'Oh, I don't know the game very well and just wondered that's all.' I'm conscious of talking lazily and looking for reason to be rejected –he doesn't respond, it's as if I'm not there. He draws a card then another and faces them down with the other two cards; his opponent stares at the spread, looks at him as if to say 'and what?'

'It's going to cost you.' He says with an air of finality.

Looking at the cards and a wooden block peppered with holes and seeing two matchsticks upended in them –the match nearer to him ahead of the other, and I imagine he is winning. The other boy, lanky, sporting a crew cut, also completely oblivious of me, shrugs his shoulders and proceeds to draw from the pack turning them face up. On placing three cards he draws back with a triumphant look upon his face. 'Oh shit!' my questioner says.

'Does that mean you are losing?' I say timidly. He looks at me then. 'Straight flush beats two jacks, don't you know?'

I murmur agreement and move away –it all seems pointless to me and talk is such an effort. I wander across the room space to three boys who seem not to be doing anything except idly watch others. I sit down near them saying nothing.

'What's your name?' the nearest boy says. I open my mouth to speak and they dissolve from my sight. I'm looking at water sparkling in the sunlight.

I am gripping the railings on the deck of a sailing ship pitching wildly in rough seas. The wind howls about the deck structures and through the maze of rigging. The sails bellied by the gale are stiff and taut and I can feel their driving power heeling the ship. Two other men beside me also hold on to the stanchion rail. I turn to the nearest and shout, 'Come on then –let's do it.'

I stagger forward, grasping the ladder railing leading down to the waist of the ship and look down to where the deck should be. The mainmast pin rail thick with coiled ropes and all else on deck is submerged in a torrent of water. I descend the ladder only to be hit by an incoming wave which pushes me back against the bulkhead gasping for breath. I steady my self as the ship rises and the deck appears in a cascade of foam and lunge forward to a hatch that spans the deck on which spars are lashed between the mainmast and forward bulkhead. Along the raised lip of the hatch are cleats and tarpaulin ropes bound around them. I grasp one of these, and then another, laying flat to the deck as yet another wave rolls over submerging me and the ship lurches downward. After what seems an age the ship recovers and the water drains away. I take a deep breath and crab my way along the deck holding fast to the tarpaulin ropes –ahead the din of flapping canvas and metal banging metal grows louder.

I glance behind –no one has followed me. I will have to do this on my own. I endure two more waves before reaching the next hatch which has sprung its clips. The hatch cover is flung back by the roll of the ship as she is sucked into a trough. On this unstable surface I am not able to balance for long enough or exert the strength needed to lift the hatch cover back –so I decide to work with the sea. When the next wave comes across the deck it lifts again the hatch cover and slams it back down as the ship rises. The impact of the closing hatch cover sends shock waves through my body as the lip above the deck absorbs the impact.

Again I am under water and hang on grimly –then the downward pressure eases and finally stops. As the ship begins its rise to meet the next long wave I take a deep breath and act. I move to the hatch and frantically spin open the clip nearest to me and jerk it upward to engage the spur on the cover, turning for all I am worth using both hands. It finally tightens as the deck angle becomes steep and the hatch clip becomes my life line. I press my body to the deck and hold on for dear life enduring yet another wave. I silently pray the clip will hold –and it does. As the ship rises once again I perform the same manoeuvre and secure the other three clips. I hold on

216

again feeling strong with a sense of achievement –at the next rise I am getting out of here.

At the appropriate moment I turn and crab myself back along the main hatch to the bulkhead ladder. As I hang on waiting for the next wave to pass I see a white and frightened bearded face stare down at me. 'Silly bastard!' he yells, 'give me your hand.' I take his proffered hand to move from ladder to deck –we then both fight our way back to the cuddy hand over hand via the lifeline, a hand reaching out guides us into the cuddy shelter.

'Have you fixed it? The man who proffered his hand shouts to make himself heard above the wind. 'Silly bastard those studding spars could have carried away', says my bearded companion as he follows me in.

'I didn't stop to look', I say offhandedly, 'give us a fag will yer?'

The inner bulkhead door opens. Swathed in oilskins and dripping water the grey face of the bosun mate appears. He looks at me for a moment eyes startled and angry, then expostulates, 'you silly son of a bitch, you blind or something? The lifelines have carried away down there.'

His eyes bore into me as his bulk overshadows my squatting form but his movements are careful and belie his true feelings –relief and thanks. 'Get down below you silly bugger and get some dry gear on.' I squeeze past him heading down the companionway. 'And you're off watch!' –he continues to speak but his voice lost in the roar of the wind. I turn.

'What's that you said?'

I look up the darkened companion way straining to hear him repeat –I make out his form and a raised arm, hand cupped to his face. Everything stops –sounds still and shadows disappear into blackness. I'm not breathing. It's that voice again, the green man whispering; 'What's in a name my pretty one, what's in a name?'

Now I'm sitting shoulder to shoulder with a group of people about a long table. All are middle aged or older, some careworn and others looking less than well. Peoples' eyes, I notice are pale and watery and a florid face here and there suggest blood pressure problems. Everyone is well dressed. The women's elegant clothes impress and their careful make up gives good effect to the most pleasing facial features. At the head of the table are two men –a hawk-faced man with kindly eyes and an older heavier man whose lined face twitches in concentration as he watches the assembly.

'Does anyone have more comment to make?' says the hawk-faced man.

'Yes', I say pointedly, 'I have. I agree the general consensus to implement the standards as soon as practicable –yet we appear not to have an introduction plan besides promulgating when they will come into effect. Is that only what we mean to do? We all accept some sections of the standards will evoke negative reactions. As expected you might say, it's down to us to manage. I suggest we'll get more cooperation if we introduce them stage by stage.'

'Why do we need a plan to introduce an implementation plan -what's your problem?' A severe faced woman across the table poses this question to me.

'The people who are expected to implement changes in their working practises are not likely to make noises back to us –such noising they make will be to fellow workers and union representatives. If we are not careful we will lose workers from this critical care sector who we know for a variety of reasons feel undervalued. They may choose to vote with their feet.'

I hear some assenting sounds about the table and my questioner looks stonily at me as if prompting me to continue –so I press on. 'We need to put a programme in place concurrent with publication to educate the supervisory staff, and date implementation of standards, post an educational consultative period.'

As I finish speaking I am aware of viewing the assembly from above and behind the heads of my seated colleagues. The hawk-faced man's elderly cohort is speaking –his voice echoes and distorts in my ears yet I understand the sense of what he is saying.

He is explaining to the assembly and to me in particular, provisions that exist in the process of publication to send advance copies to supervisory staff. I can see myself sitting as before, my hands grasping the table edge, dressed in a dark suit and looking out of place as the youngest person at the table.

A grey haired, grey bearded man intervenes –he has a cultured voice and is obviously intent on understanding from our leader what exactly the provisions are. Other's follow with questions before either leader is able to respond. I see myself slapping the table and looking tense, emphasising we don't have a recognisable education programme. I in my doppelganger self take measure of the feelings around the table and I'm surprised by what I experience. Beneath the most unlikely exteriors I detect warm and appealing characters.

The man immediately to my right who I know as a dry and unimaginative colleague, known as a stickler for protocols and 'right and proper' agreements, is passionate about plants and flowers. He is sitting there dreaming of his garden patiently waiting for the hubbub to die down as he feels our demands won't change edicts from on high.

The woman to my left is middle aged; rather ample, wearing fashionable specs to compliment her dress and is a known as a 'hard case.' To my astonishment I detect she is secretly admiring my approach. Her appreciation is not intellectual but sexual. There is a secret sensitivity within that suggests she is living two lives, unable outwardly to express her inner emotional character.

The elderly man at the table head with the heavily lined face is considering my contribution and the subsequent reactions with amusement, but he doesn't show this outwardly. There is a sense of fatalism with him – 'what will be, will be'. He is invoking view of himself as a younger man and looks at me (from inside) with affection.

My questioner with the stony face is apparently on my side –though nothing she says directly agrees. Her questioning is confrontational and persuasive of the view that management must not be made to look silly! As she speaks I become aware she has a sister who is a supervisor and likely to feel victim of the changes. She is very protective of her sister –both of them have had disastrous marriages; a sharing of pain that reignited their childhood friendship. Suddenly I am back at the table –I feel as if there is two 'me's' in the same body. I hear the hawk-faced man say; 'then we are agreed? A strict timetable will be introduced and supervisory staff must come back to us if they encounter problems.'

The hammer comes down ending discussion. I am fuming –when to God will these people realise that anyone in their right mind wants to do better, if for no other reason than self satisfaction!

I hear the green man speaking –soothing this time. 'Man proposes.'

'And God disposes' I retort, but the green man is not there and neither am I as that young man, instead I am an older man looking down at my large and distended stomach heaving away underneath my shirt. I'm sitting in a wicker cane chair on a hotel veranda somewhere in the tropics conscious of being tired, touchy and jaundiced about life in general.

I'm drinking beer and apparently reading a novel but the story I am really following is an event occurring in front and below my position. It's the animated conversation of two very pretty young women who lounge by the side of the hotel pool scantily clad leaving little for my imagination to conjure. They're in some dispute about something but its friendly banter which to me makes them more sexually attractive. I wonder if they are aware of me looking over my shades having lavish thoughts and planning how might I get into conversation with them.

I'll go down to the pool I say to myself. As I heave myself out of the chair my wife appears on the balcony. Oh shit! 'Isn't it beautiful', she says pointing beyond the hotel perimeter to ridge of mountains shimmering in the heat. 'We really must get a postcard of that view.'

She has the annoying knack of appearing at precisely the wrong moment. I feel defensive and grunt approval edging my way past her to the stairs, book in hand.

'You off somewhere? She asks innocently.

'Thought I'd go down to the pool', I say lazily.

'Oh, I'll join you –the sun is just right now.'

Stimulated to positive action rather than resigned by her governing presence I set up our chairs by the side of the pool and order drinks. The young ladies are on the opposite side –not a bad view, I think to myself, and reading is ideal cover as I look out over my shades. One of them looks over at me and says something quietly to her companion; she looks in my direction and they exchange glances. I stare back easily under cover of shades feeling really bucked, after all I'm not that old and why shouldn't they be interested in me?

My lovely wife (well, she was when younger) is reading last week's English newspaper –self absorbed I think.

'Have you been speaking with those young girls darling?' I'm startled –is she psychic or something? 'No, how could I have –don't know them from Adam', I reply testily.

I try to concentrate on the book but it doesn't work. I feel trapped and not a little resentful, after all what possible harm can I do? I decide to go for a swim, suddenly getting up, taking off my tea shirt and plunging straight in before my wife can comment.

I'm floating about but it's not in the water. I must be dreaming as I'm looking down on the pool bar. Instinctively I turn round and face the pool. I can just make out that the person thrashing wildly up and down the pool is me. I'm not excited by this and not at all impressed with my shape which looks older than my years. I move toward the other side of the pool where the two girls rest –one reclines on a sunbed with a drink in hand, the other kneeling beside applies tanning lotion to her outstretched legs.

The girl reclining is long and gangly, the other is shorter and more rounded at the hip but looks gorgeous anyhow. If they are paying any attention to me swimming they don't give any indication of interest –and frankly after what I've seen I don't blame them.

What I do find interesting is the feeling I get from looking at them. The long and gangly one being creamed is bored out of her skin and absentmindedly sips at her cocktail. Her thoughts are flying all over the place asking impossible questions like, 'if I drink four of these would I get drunk?' And 'what wouldn't I do to get inside his pants?' I'm pretty sure she's not thinking about mine and look over in the direction of my vacant sun bed to see the bar behind is manned by a young waiter, Latin and good looking.

There's another side of her I'm becoming aware of –an ambitious streak just under the surface and a quick brain to match. She's not above using feminine whiles to achieve her ends either. All in all, I don't find her compelling and physically she doesn't interest me anymore.

I turn my attention to the other girl –she emanates a much softer more feminine energy I find immediately conducive and I draw closer. I feel her sense of care as she applies the tanning lotion. I'm aware that aged ten her mother died and she became a surrogate mum to a brother and a younger sister. There's a deep desire to meet with a strong minded man who will help lift this inherited sense of responsibility.

Having an 'irresponsible' friend goes some way to relieving the family care memory whilst exercising her 'motherly' instinct.

I'm right next to her now and realise she feels unsure and lacks confidence. Naturally shy she gets delight from childish thoughts privately felt. A fear of failure lurks below the surface and I'm delighted to know she writes a confessional diary and paints picture post card scenes she hopes one day to frame and display in a house of her own. Pretty and sexy though she is I feel more like a priest than a poseur and think of presenting her my half read novel to read.

My attention is diverted to my wife –who I have difficulty in recognising, standing at the pool side apparently trying to get my attention; that is of me in the pool. I am now floating face up arms akimbo. Something akin to panic grips my mind but it passes quickly. I breathe a sigh of relief and settle myself to sleep.

As I come to I realise I'm not in the pool, I am not in the hotel. Where in God's name am I?

I'm gradually focussing on my surroundings as one does awakening from deep sleep. I'm sitting in a cleft of branches that splay from the bole of a tree, looking out upon a wide expanse of grass and scrub land. At the extremity of my vision in a haze of heat, purple coloured hills form horizon; in the foreground below me goats are grazing. I wear cotton trousers and jacket top, my feet are bare, my skin is brown. I'm very conscious of being 15 and female.

The goats are my father's who today is at market in the nearby town with my mother in the hope of selling some fabrics she makes and if all goes well will return with something interesting to eat and possibly a picture magazine –because they know I like them. I am listening to the wind that whines in the tree and am imagining it's the sound of a spaceship entering the atmosphere of an alien planet. I am the captain of course and my crew are at their stations awaiting my orders. Will we be attacked? Yes! I look at the monitor screen and see alien craft speeding toward us. My navigator makes report but I already know what action to take and issue orders for our invisible protective screen to be switched on. Here they come –four proton torpedoes any one able to smash us to bits. I order evasive action and our spacecraft dives out of the way.

Open up a channel I command –and with the help of our universal speech translator I talk to the alien ground station telling them we are a federation ship engaged on a peaceful mission to explore unknown planets. Please identify yourself!

'Binta is you asleep?'

'No I am not. I am watching the goats.' I reply crossly to my little brother Chichi who now stands at the foot of the tree with his hands in his pockets.

'What do you want?' Thinking to myself –he is small like the aliens I'm about to do battle with.

'I called you and you didn't answer –anyhow you were not looking at the goats.'

'I was looking for lions', I say lying easily, 'you know we have to be on the lookout all the time,' He is looking bored so I suggest he goes back to the dwelling and gets my Captain Kirk comic and I will read to him. He looks at me awhile as if he's trying to remember something –then off he scurries.

I try to reconnect with my spaceship adventure but seem to have lost the point of it, so instead take a careful look around to ensure there are no unwelcome wild animals in the vicinity and ease myself out of the tree. Considering I am lame and can only stand properly with a crutch to support I do this quite well. I fall over as expected reaching for my crutch under the tree and feel a numbing pain spread across my chest.

Now I'm on my feet and running –this is great, I am running! Both my legs are well. I don't know how it's happened but I'm running with two good legs. I don't have a problem anymore!

That was quick –I'm peering in the hut and Chichi is going through my box, looking at all my things. I spy my comic on the bed –that's where I left it. Angrily I call out 'Chichi I have not given permission –stop that!

He's ignoring me –he doesn't even turn round. I call again and this time I really shout because I'm mad at him. He scratches his shoulder but goes on with what he is doing. He acts as if I'm invisible! Wearily I lean against the hut entrance and fall straight through the wall! Dazed I stand up inside the hut with my feet through the bed.

I stare down at my legs. Dear God I must be dead! In unbelief I reach for Chichi's shoulder but my hand goes straight through his body. I am frightened and turn to my elder brother who is lying on his bed smoking. I shout at him; 'Iniko listen to me!'

I look at his eyes –he is smoking happy weed and looks at me a smile creasing his face. I call again and he opens his arms and his eyes roll upward and his lips are moving, I think he is calling my name, but I hear no sound.

I rush out of the hut and run back to the tree. I must be here I say to myself, I must be here. I arrive at the tree and there at its base is my body all crumpled up with my pricking stick pierced straight through my body. I stare at my face I am so peaceful, I look happy –then I hear that wind sound again. I must go I say, I must go –they wait for me I must go. I can feel unseen hands pulling me off the ground and the soothing soft sounds of caring voices. This is fantastic –I'm flying!

Chapter THIRTYTHREE:
Disassembled

'Peter, Peter, it is I, Soft Shoes.' I hear the words but cannot see or feel anything. Again Soft Shoes calls and I hear myself replying but not from my mouth –from somewhere outside of me. I feel a sense of place though I cannot identify with it –then I feel warmth, a hand in my hand. Now something is being pressed against my lips and a warm liquid inside my mouth. I hear her voice again –it's instructing me to swallow. I obey –it feels like liquid fire. Gradually I am becoming conscious and see the forms of Jeremiah, Thundercloud, Soft Shoes and Lone Wolf. Vaguely I remember coming here with Lone Wolf –then I remember the smoke and the prayers.

Soft Shoes is squeezing my hand. 'Peter do you recognise us –yes?' I nod then speak. 'I am with you and yet I am not if you understand.'

They incline their heads in respect and I continue, 'I am other people', I say hearing my words quaver, 'I feel like a stranger to myself.' Again they incline their heads but I see a twinkle in Lone Wolf's eyes and laughter lines in Soft Shoes face. They remain silent in anticipation I will speak further.

'I have as a young soul witnessed my dying; as a girl, lame yet proud in poverty with dreams of adventure giving hope to her state. It makes me aware of how little can mean much, how fortune smiles on the brave. In dying I do not know what comes next –a power carries me to the next world.

But before that I am other people.

Disassembled

I felt the pointlessness of life as a man materially bound and reactive to the forces of desire, dissatisfied and unknowing of himself in a world of half expressed truths, seeking a way forward –a way that will again encircle and imprison him. And close to a young woman, unobserved, I became aware of both ordinariness and the kind of love that's born from sacrifice and care. As that man apart from his body I made measure of the good and rejected the superficial. I knew that my eyes were deceiving me but I didn't think it important that they did –my senses were not determining what I understood. Only when I realised I was dead did my senses control –for a moment I felt panic. Then it was over and I entered into the kingdom of sleep and didn't care anymore.

As a boy I knew myself innocent of the world, unaware of unseen presence guiding my footsteps as timidly I tried to enter the world of other men. I am overcome with my ignorance and feel a great wall between me and the truth.'

I am speaking slowly aware that each word has to be found again –as I narrate my thoughts I am attempting to rebuild a sense of identity. 'I experienced single mindedness, the compulsion of action; the clarity of being present and a feeling of oneness in an alien environment, experiencing the issue that men call courage –knowing that my risk was a desire to be wedded with the undine spirit.

I was a young man ambitious striving for place in a competitive world –a world of personalities, seeking to be noticed, anxious not to be out witted. And then finding the inner nature bore little resemblance to the outward self, remaining separate, mutually exclusive, unable to share. For a moment I'm aware of the duplicity of everything –then I lose it and become assertive and one-sided again.

In all these experiences I am conscious of sharing, amazed and unsure, as if the meaning of being has dawned but cannot yet be named or described.' I am again offered and take a refreshing water drink from Jeremiah; it smells of meadows.

'Your reactions are most interesting', says Jeremiah. 'These are the visions of one whose feet are earthbound and different from ours.'

'Yet I say the lessons are not so different', Thundercloud rejoins. 'We all benefit from this sharing of experience.' They all assent quietly one to the other but I am feeling unsettled and confused. 'Is all illusion; being not as it appears? How am I to know what must be held and what must be let go?'

They all look at Lone Wolf who after moments of contemplation responds. 'What is it you know that doesn't move? What is it you know that's not born under sun and created in light?'

He pauses here to have me consider his words. Everything I can think of relates to sun and light. All eyes are upon me. 'I confess I cannot think of anything that does not move or does not live under sun', I reply.

'Such is the nature of your travels, Peter. And such is ours that our meeting is under sun and in movement with you. Yes it is illusion –it is the shadow cast by light, yet in its own way it's also a reality. All worlds have physical realities, some slow like the stuff of earth, others ethereal that may only be truthfully explored when the physical order of self no longer determines the nature of enquiry. The truth you seek is unspeakable, immoveable and unknown to the senses –yet the essential soul causes and prompts your journey.'

'Then what might I learn, what progress might I make within the nature I have?'

It's Jeremiah that continues. 'You may learn how to disassemble –learn from the parts.'

I am puzzled and ask him to explain further.

'You seek to make your experiences connect, find common understanding to prove them part of the whole.'

'Yes, I admit. 'How might they make sense on their own?'

'By the smoke you experienced the inside of people and now you try to make sense of it looking from the outside. Given what you remember proposes the inward being wiser than the outer nature, can you be satisfied? What is –is. Experience, memory, dream, call it what you will is the soul seeking itself. When a soul no longer seeks it discovers stillness, the present state, the state of is. The soul seeks that it might be still. The lives you are conscious of are part of the soul –even so that which you don't know –the birds of the air, animals, fish, trees and flowers. All manner of life seen and unseen is part of you. Seek to unify and you have a puzzle that can never be complete.'

Jeremiah pauses and I try to assimilate what he has said. I want to say yes to this understanding but can't understand why I should. Thundercloud places his hand firmly on my shoulder.

'When we first enter this world of Spirit unencumbered by the physical body we are intent on searching out new experience, as you would say, to find fulfilment. The path is stony and hard on the feet and when all is rock and flint and the way is no longer clear we learn it is not the true way,'

Disassembled

'But surely it is natural to strive and learn by experience, the very spirit within makes us do so', I say in response.

'Is this natural? Soft Shoes says, leaning over and kissing me on the cheek, the warm air of her breath and youthful femininity suddenly has me change my mood and I became immediately response to her. 'Yes, of course it is', I stammer, feeling not a little embarrassed with myself.

'It is the expression of self governed by the desire nature', she says, 'the same nature that must endure birth and death, the same nature that in extreme defines itself.' I look at her admiringly. 'Am I young?' she says smilingly.

'Yes and no', I say cautiously,' it is obvious to me you speak with deep understanding –youth is not able alone to know this.' This causes a humorous response; Jeremiah slaps his thigh and Soft Shoes sparkles with laughter.

'You have stated it young Peter, said Thundercloud, 'youth is not able alone. Consider the awareness you have of your own being –some part is truly young yet other parts are not. You have not spoken of the Green Man as yet.'

'Indeed you haven't', Soft Shoes eyes are captivating me, 'we are curious –what brings you here?'

'Have care Princess', Lone Wolf counsels, 'Peter is between identities, neither of us nor of the dark world and it is the slowness of the virgin earth that compels him.'

'I will be gentle with our brother Lone Wolf, I will be gentle.' There is laughter again with Lone Wolf smiling and nodding sagely. Soft Shoes takes my arm and places her hand in mine and looks directly into my eyes. 'Tell me Peter –talk to me of the Green Man.'

I find her compelling –her dark eyes are warm and draw from me deep feelings of love; her beauty so powerful I swear I will say whatever she wishes so long as he holds me like this.

'The Green Man', I begin-

Chapter THIRTYFOUR:
Motorbike Accident(s)

I've never thought a voice could actually *grate* in one's consciousness. I'm familiar with the words' use in thrillers I read describing character emotion, but of course it doesn't sound in your ear. This woman's' voice calling her kids not only irritates with its rough use of words evoking in me a negative emotional reaction, it physically feels uncomfortable. I cannot even begin to make a contrast between her vibration and that of Soft Shoes.

I am feeling out of place with these sounds and others about. I'm disorientated; I keep thinking the tree before the car is moving toward me. It's a full ten minutes before I'm satisfied everything about me is in its place. I look at my watch and realise I have an hour before seeing my first patient. I switch on the engine -let's get the hell out of here for a start.

I've pulled up in a deserted layby and begin to make notes of my journey –by the time I restart the engine and head off for my healing appointment I've made little progress. I am feeling mentally shaky and redouble my concentration driving, switching up the volume on my car radio until passers by turn their heads as I pass. On arriving at my healing rooms I'm much more 'with it' and am able to focus on the work at hand. I'm drinking water like there's no tomorrow.

The following day I carve out some time to recall the experience but before I do I have a chat with Pam, bringing her up to date with my latest 'astral adventures'. Interested as always I sit down conscious of not having explained to her what has happened to me. As I write my notes on the consciousness shift that occurred after smoking and holding that stone (I'd love to know what that potion was!) the events in which I appear as 'other people' strike me as having parallels in my own life.

Motorbike Accident(s)

I have done dangerous work on deck of a ship in stormy seas, though not a sailing ship and nothing quite so scary. I love the sailing ships of the past but it's a romance tempered by some experience, of working sailing vessels and experience of the merciless power of nature. Given a choice I'd stick with a large ship, having plenty of freeboard and powered by an engine. The sailing life experienced in my astral journey was hard, unforgiving and dangerous. I can relate to the boy trying to connect with those around him –can't say I would be that ignorant of the card game which appeared to be poker.

The other boys don't figure in my memory and the place doesn't ring any bells –but the more I think about it the more I feel sympathy with the boy. I too remember a voice telling me to 'go and mix with them'.

The girl experience is strange. Nothing consciously connects unless I assume a general awareness of place vaguely similar, visited years ago in my Navy travels –a tenuous link to say the least. I'm not disabled and can hardly count breaking my leg as a boy and being plastered for some months thereafter as lameness –as I remember I rather enjoyed the fuss and attention I got and was not a little unhappy to see the plaster cast go. But I do feel related to her mentally –living an inner world I couldn't (or wouldn't) share with others.

The man in the pool is all but a complete stranger. To start with my wife and I are much closer in understanding and mentality. We all have egotistical adventures and rarely without the opposite sex playing some part in fulfilment but this a picture of a man lost to himself –it is only when he appreciates the inner nature of the girl he is attracted to, does he and I truly relate.

As the young manager –I can see some parallels in behaviour though he is fierier. I was two people in my younger days –a problem solving suit and tie by day, a medium and healer in tea shirt and jeans by night. It has me realise had that division not existed in me and my sensitive nature extended as a doppelganger to those around me my professional career would not only have been different –it would likely have been much less successful.

It's only after finishing writing this part I consider the time relationships. As nobody I see in these events come from a past before my life, dresses or acts in such a way to suggest events yet to be, I am forced to accept these are present life experiences. So they can't be me! Is it possible I am somehow connected with the lives of these people now? Given all that has happened to me I can't assume past is forgotten when someone dies –so is my destiny interrelated with these people? And who else I might ask?

I find it impossible to let things be as advised. And try as I might I cannot recall what happened after Soft Shoes asks me about the Green Man. I have a sneaky feeling they knew I wouldn't remember and their laughter meant more than I realised. I guess it has something to do with the feelings Soft Shoes aroused in Peter –but then it wasn't a sensuous appreciation and nor can it be described as platonic. I've got to be honest about this; I'm completely at loss as to how I can describe the feelings between Peter and Soft Shoes, other than to say they were powerful and liberating.

I try meditating to achieve a clearer understanding of the 'dissembling' theme I recall and think I'm making progress when the lights go out – literary! As the lights fuse in the house so does the last hope I have of recovering further memory of this journey. I wait patiently to reconnect but nothing will induce the link –after a week of trying I give up.

I'm taking the short walk up the road to the newsagents. Pam is an avid reader of newspapers –I normally get one on returning from walking my dog but today she is up to date and would like one whilst she has breakfast! The preceding night was somewhat disturbed. Pam got up to go to the bathroom and in her efforts not to wake me collided with the furniture and knocked over an ornament –which woke me. Attempting to pick up the ornament in the gloom she hit her head on the cabinet. Apparently I was not in the best of tempers and insisted on putting on the bedside light. On her return to bed one of our cats kept scratching at the door and meowing, so that eventually in a state of ill grace I got up and fed her, which did the trick.

I get to hear about this first thing and try as I can I don't remember anything much to her chagrin. Ensuring she has a paper to read at breakfast will go some way toward showing her I'm still a sweet and reasonable being. I mention this because I've learnt to understand over the years interruptions to sleep that involve astral journeying invariably cause ill tempered reactions, which (I like to think) are uncharacteristic of me.

I am therefore thinking of nothing in particular on my walk to the paper shop until I am suddenly aware of feeling much shorter (I'm 5'9") and walking oddly. I glance at my feet and they are splaying out as I step. Being something of a Qi-Gong practitioner I immediately correct this action, pointing my feet and altering the balance point. A few more steps and I'm at it again and despite my correcting actions this penguin style walk persists for some 20 metres. I pause outside the paper shop to compose myself. I glance at my shadowy form in the window for reassurance. It looks like me but I feel like T.E. Laurence.

I should say here that in my earlier years I'd read about his life after reading 'Seven Pillars of Wisdom' and seeing David Lean's film starring Peter O'Toole. I've also had communications, albeit visual awareness of him only and felt sufficiently tuned to his vibration to thereafter refer to him as Ned, which is the name his family used when speaking with him. I visited his home in Clouds Hill, Dorset and stood at his grave in the village of Moreton where I took a photograph that on developing showed a couple of extras —one of whom I am sure is Laurence. All this is many years ago and in recent times thoughts of his life and exploits have not been in mind —neither have I received any psychic communications either directly or from others.

I put it out of my mind but later that morning whilst sitting in my study/healing room I suddenly became aware of riding a motorcycle, wearing leather gauntlets, conscious of wide handlebars and driving at speed. I'm inwardly satisfied by a feeling of cleanliness that grows stronger as my speed increases. I've eyes only for the road, the narrow road to Clouds Hill from Bovington camp in Dorset. The road is familiar and to some extent I am on 'auto pilot'. My brain mind is blessedly still and I feel timeless.

Suddenly I am aware of a bicycle jigging to my left and crossing my path, instinctively I turn the Brough to avoid and straighten back seeing the shadow of another bike and rider. At this point I am aware that my brain mind is not 'earthed' and I struggle to regain physical concentration. I feel split between the satisfied self exhilarated by mental and emotional freedom and my conscious personality reacting like I'm awakening from deep sleep. In the very next moment I collide with something hard and a loud report like a bomb exploding deafens me.

I'm at Clouds Hill cottage sitting down, absently scratching my head contemplating the gramophone. Mozart comes to mind but I don't feel moved to select a record. I go to my writing desk, my thoughts vaguely concerned with sending a telegram. I can't think who I should send it too, which irritates me. I'm scratching my head again and I'm disturbed by the thought that perhaps I've already sent it.

Feeling rather strange and light headed and thinking I'm brewing another attack of malaria, I get into my bunk, lie down and try to sleep. Eyes closed I'm reliving a particularly stormy day at sea on the SS Rajputana confined to my cabin to avoid prying eyes, feeling sick and not a little depressed.

In an effort to banish this memory I am next at the wheel of P100 driving her as fast as she will go on sea trials in the Solent, the hull smacking down with great thumps as she rides crests and falls into troughs —movements that are sending shock waves up and down my body.

I stay with this for some time as I find the distraction comforting. I feel half in and half out of things now, one moment caring for respite the next not. Now I'm playing with children —it must be Plymouth. Changing again I'm remembering a visit to TH and his wife —two of the few people I know who ignore my past. TH is an excellent observer, very perceptive of character and doesn't rush to judgement. He talks away quite unconscious of the impression he is creating. I get the desire to write again when we talk.

I'm not very comfortable with my next impressions (very lifelike; I seem to be there), meeting with Feisal at the Peace conference. He feels betrayed by the British —he's very gentle about it all, but persistent in his views and draws dark pictures of Arabia, internecine quarrels destroying the alliance he has forged over the war. He gets very angry in private —rants almost. There's talk of oil and trading benefits within his entourage and a belief that France and Britain will invoke the Sykes-Picot agreement to carve up the territory liberated from the Turks.

I'm terribly torn; my inborn belief in natural justice keeps finding cause to promote their claims and political awareness knows to tone it down as the forces arrayed against them are unstoppable. I'm treading the middle line —it goes against my better feelings. Can I do differently? I will try but I'm in a cleft stick.

The desert; I'm in the wastelands of Arabia. I love the desert, it's so clean —thoughts are like crystal out here. I am comfortable with my companions — cutthroats mostly with a childlike sense of purpose. No vaunting of emotions here. I am sacred space to them; the merchant of gold. It gives me freedom to balance my own internal forces. I can go beyond tiredness and pain here — these endless sweeps of sand and bare rock draw on my sense of lost identity.

All change —and now it's intense pleasure as the rod cuts into my flesh but I feel guilty after climax and let him beat me more until the pain becomes pointless. I get control from this —oh God this is such a merry go round. When will this fever abate?

Ah! Some help at hand I can feel caring hands lifting my body. Where am I now? I'm not sure —it smells like an orchard, it feels like a lazy summer's day. How the weather has changed! I can hear voices but can't make out what they are saying. My head is bandaged —I hurt it somewhere. It's not painful, rather it's numb and what a joy I don't feel impelled to think! I actually feel like sleeping.

Motorbike Accident(s)

Half awake is good enough. This is more like a park; I'm sitting with my back against the bole of a tree. I'm vaguely aware of Boenarges parked nearby, but I look around and can't see it anywhere. How on earth did I get here I wonder –I look carefully at the landscape and confirm to myself it's an English environment. Most likely some Lords' estate –is it Blenheim I ask myself? I'm wearing Arab dress –how did I get into this? Nothing would induce me to dress up again, how come?

'Laurens?' I know that voice! Appearing to my left is Dahoum dressed as a prince of Mecca in brilliant white and gold.

'Is that you Dahoum?' I can't believe my eyes –he looks so solid!

His eyes glitter with pleasure. He's sticking out his chin, pulling back his shoulders and striking a pose. I can't help laughing –he is taking me off!

'Could there be two little dark ones?' he says mocking my accent.

I just stare, I can't believe it. I love this boy –he was my inspiration. Ah! And reason followed. I wanted to make him a gift and here he is in a beautiful dream. 'As dreams go' I say speaking to myself 'this has got to be the most interesting one yet. I can even hear myself thinking. Salim you are resplendently dressed! Stay dream let me stand and get closer.'

I am standing up –feel light as a feather, which is most exhilarating. I take a few steps. Marvellous! I can feel the grass and blown leaves under my feet. I look for Salim –I turn and he is not there –damnable reason you only know sadness! It was so good to see him again. I feel so sensitive, can't control it. Why do I feel so vulnerable?

'I'm quick.'

I spin round to where I had been facing and there he is! An incredible dream I say to myself but Salim answers, 'Not a dream Laurens.'

He is smiling and coming toward me his arms open. Instinctively I reach out my arms and we embrace. Incredible! I can feel him. 'What does all this mean? I say uncertainly.

'You banged your head', he says holding me at arms length.

'Banged my head eh? Well, if this is what you get for banging your head, I must do it again sometime!' My feelings are quite unaccountable and I'm totally commanded by the physical presence of Salim. It is as it used to be in Carchemish.

'I'm still here.' He speaks as one reassuring another. 'You weren't there a moment ago' I say accusingly in an effort to reassert myself. He laughs (it's still like it always was girlish in tone), reaches out and takes my hand, 'come' he says, let us walk for a while, 'someone wants to meet you.'

And so I walk, hand in hand with Dahoum. It is as if the future I have lived doesn't exist! 'I have a fever' I tell him, 'a legacy of my past.'

'No. It's not a fever Laurens. You banged your head –remember?'

Banged my head? I'm thinking –yes I did! Where was it? 'Ah, yes I remember now I was riding Boenarges.'

'You were, but now you are free', and with that statement he yanks at my arms and cavorts me around in a merry dance that I find wonderful and liberating. I am laughing –it's all so wonderfully silly, I feel like a boy again. And is this not the grounds of Blenheim Palace?

We stop and sink down to the ground, I'm not exhausted but I do feel overcome with emotion. 'Someone to meet you', Dahoum says. 'Bring on the cavalry!' I say laughingly. I feel so liberated it's not true! I turn in the direction of his gaze and there standing before me is my brother Will – dressed as I last remembered him in Army uniform.

I gaze open mouthed. I can't take this in. 'Hello Ned. We've been expecting you.'

Then suddenly it dawns upon me. I'm dead! 'Is this, what death is like?' I whisper.

Will rubs his chin and smiles. 'You've but a taste of it Ned –it gets better, I assure you.'

But now as the truth hammers home I feel the contradictions in myself as if the very self is being questioned. Yes –both Will and Salim are still here but I feel unable to face myself as if my identity has been scrambled and the power within is short circuiting itself. Is this the beginning I ask of myself? They both put their arms around me. I feel like a lost child.

'It's a new beginning Ned, a new beginning. Come, rest and recuperate. You will get to be stronger.'

It's a dream I'm saying to myself, over and over again and I only stop repeating the thought as I become conscious of my study/healing room. It's me, isn't it –isn't it? I say this mentally until the physical environment confirms itself.

This experience has been so total and involving I am still not sure I'm myself. Mentally I feel different as if I'm hiding something and a sense of being unclean. It's some while before I recover my equilibrium. Looking back I am surprised at how ordinary I felt living those moments as TEL. As Laurence I'm not aware of myself as history and wasn't thinking as one conscious of adulation from others –I felt distanced and unconcerned from society at large, unconscious of demand that others might have of me. I don't know why this has happened. There is one incident in my twenties that may have a bearing on this experience. After I met my teacher and thereafter devoted much time to psychic development I changed my job and a little more money came my way. With this extra money I bought myself a second hand scooter –until then I'd travelled everywhere by bus.

Shortly after acquiring it and on my way to St Joseph's where Len did his work I lost control –the bike and I parting company. The scooter careered pilot less across the road and ended up under the front of a private car. Shaken and bruised but otherwise unhurt I hobbled over to the bike and gingerly extracted it from underneath the bumper. No one seemed to be around as witness of my accident and fearful of an insurance claim I couldn't afford to pay I slunk out of the road and disappeared from sight.

On hearing of my escapade Len said in forcible terms I should never ride such a machine again. Normally such prohibition would have been like a red rag to a bull and I would have done precisely the opposite but on this occasion I had a queer sense of deja vu as if I had come close to some event that would have been the death of me. So I heeded the advice and to this day have never taken to riding motorcycles. Every now and then the desire to ride a motorbike surfaces and I look in envy at the marriage of machine and their black leathered forms and tempt myself with the thought.

I know that some will say it's an incarnation memory –that I had been Laurence in a previous life, but I'm not convinced. How many selves are there and in what worlds do they NOW reside? My astral communications only serve to show that there is more to life than our philosophies dare to dream about. This shift of consciousness, the first since my smoking stone experience with Lone Wolf, Jeremiah, Thundercloud and Soft Shoes has me wondering what next?

Figure 10

‡

---

‡ I took this picture with an instamatic camera of Laurence's grave in Moreton Dorset in July 1979. The face which appeared in the print above the headstone I take to be TEL in his RAF uniform.

Chapter THIRTYFIVE:
Worlds within Worlds

Pam and I have recently returned from a Nile cruise holiday in Lower Egypt. Exotic scenery, fierce heat and the awe inspiring sights of ancient tombs and temples gave unexpected therapy refocusing my mind to the physical world. I feel refreshed and blessedly normal again! No astral journeying occurred during the holiday and in an odd kind of way I felt the space time issue validated by the present evidence of Ancient Egypt. To see the paint that hands applied over 3000 years ago, the smoothness of polished stone and spigots still in the act of cleaving stone from quarry is to realise how close ancient history is to the present day. Stunned into silence by towering majestic edifice and breathless in respect at the detail of their work one has to reflect upon humanities progress as we are pleased to call it. Different as we are to the ancient Egyptians; better is not an assumption I'm prepared to make.

The break has made me conscious of how much of my time has been involved in writing down my astral experiences and I agree with Pam it would be good to have some days out in sunny England whilst the summer lasts. I'm afraid these good intentions haven't lasted more than a couple of weeks –I talk about going away to friends in Somerset and needing to have a 'writing' weekend.

Tales of Bellerophon –On the Banks of the Shalimar

Truth is I am feeling the need to be on my own again –an inner pressure to allow astral experiences the light of day. Charity work intervenes and I beaver away getting work prepared for review at a critically important meeting in September. It is during this period of frenetic activity I am reading in bed until I fall asleep over my book. My wife takes it away, I shudder awake and mutter good night.

I'm aware of being with Don but the environment is totally different to the North American habitat he and I have shared before. Don himself looks younger, he glows from within and a silvery hued sheath surrounds, making him appear larger. We are viewing a large dome shaped structure. I'm aware of myself inwardly but not so objectively as to view my own body state. I am stationary as if suspended in space.

Are we moving? The dome like structure is appearing to get closer. Don and I exchange glances –we are going inside –passing through glass it would seem and standing now on what feels like a smooth marble floor. I have sandals on my feet and notice that Don wears moccasins. The place is a huge conservatory filled with plants and trees rising up in banks above and beyond our vantage point.

I feel incredibly light and move without effort in the direction of my interest –which at this moment is a large creeper like plant growing over the bole of a tree. The creeper arms vary in size from thin tendrils to thick branch like living organisms. The bark is pale green and from the numerous offshoots grow sword shaped dark green leaves crowned in many places by clusters of small white and yellow flowers. This plant and tree is one of many that grow beyond the parapet edge of the marble floor which rises and winds amid a forest of greenery. The atmosphere is warm and a haze softens image and obscures the distant scene. This place is huge.

'This plant is moving Don, look at those creepers on the branch there', I say pointing to the stems of shoots that are pulsing on the creeper like plant.

Don bends down and fingers the leaves, 'yes you can feel the pulsing and when you touch it reacts –see for yourself.' I follow his example and sure enough the pulsing changes rhythm moments after contact.

'We should stand back now', Don advises, 'its working us out', he continues laughing 'and will draw on our energies if we let it.' I'm conscious of someone else with us who I sense is the Green Man. I can't see a form and unconsciously accept that he is present, albeit invisibly.

'I've not seen this species before', says Don intently, 'it seems very intelligent. What say you?'

'Cretaceous period, I believe, a kind of mangrove plant. As you will notice it is not feeding from the tree, in fact the tree is more than normally healthy as it ingests fluids from the creepers that are rooted deep in earth and water. You would expect the opposite now wouldn't you?

Look there', I say pointing to an area of creepers attached to the dark bark of the tree, 'see how the creepers are glistening? Tiny spores within its skin are excreting a milk-like substance that the tree ingests. This is why the tree bark is so dark; the fluid is changing the colour pigment of the wood.'

'And how did this evolve', says Don half to himself as he continues to gaze at the creeper plant and tree that towers above us.

'We are looking here at the crowning glory of its physical evolution – millions of earth years that came to a sudden end as debris from ancient Aster collided with the planet. As you quite rightly point out it's a very intelligent plant and its form continues to manifest in the astral worlds as an expression of the earth Devas mind cycle.'

'Truly, I've never seen this plant before –indeed there are likely many here I am not familiar with.' Don is clearly fascinated by the creeper growth and stands there head arched back searching the trees before us like an incredulous boy.

'As you are aware the elemental kingdom evolves, as we do, in the astral worlds. This park is one of the few focal areas in the form worlds where the seeded earth mind still manifests –and it's not a little to do with human kind being part of a chain in which our own identity can be traced. Over aeons the ascended masters have communed with earth Devas and that connection has given cause to maintain this heredity link.'

We move on from the area to view ancient club moss plants as tall as trees, their bark skins peculiarly configured in primal geometric shapes. Palms with curious ball shaped fruits black as the ace of spades abound. Every now and then Don notices a particular plant or tree and exclaims excitedly that here is species he is familiar with.

I am Peter –yet aware of being more and of Don knowing and accepting it. I feel as one who knows and can instruct and as we walk through this natural forest growing beneath a vast stretched dome like structure of interlocking windows on a base of marble like floors, nothing surprises me.

Holding my attention above all else are the wraith like forms that move about the forest. Some have elongated heads and trailing bodies not unlike octopuses, others long jointed bodies that flex in a variety of angular forms on becoming still. They move at incredible speeds, dematerialise and appear in such bewildering arrays it is not possible to track any individual being.

They become a multitude of silvery grey indistinct shapes with occasional flashes of primary colours lighting up their internal organs and bones.

I am conscious of connecting with these beings and responding to Don's queries monosyllabically –to such an extent Don comments that my conversational responses are in the character of an absent minded professor!

Having ascended the marble paved path between the forest of trees, plants and flowers we now stand upon a ring of paving centred by a large pool of bluish water edged by a white marble surround. Other human beings are here in a plethora of guises; some in robes, clearly eastern in character, others in a mixture of western dress ranging from ancient to modern. Harmony of feeling and being is total –the sense of difference in shape size, sex and custom of history is merely pictorial. The normal earthly reaction of curiosity, comparison and self protection, is entirely absent in me; I feel knowing of the people there.

As we move to the edge of the pool it became apparent that the blue water is an atmosphere of translucent appearance, in which denser and darker blue swathes of colour move about in a seemingly random fashion. As we look into the 'pool' it has the effect of enhancing an inward sense of harmony and producing togetherness between ourselves and the assembly of others.

As I continue to gaze into the 'pool' I think I am looking through a giant portal from inside a spaceship; the indistinct dark blue atmosphere becomes a plethora of planetary bodies that endlessly manifest in breathtaking fusions of colour. This panorama has the powerful effect of making one feel small – and it doesn't stop there, the feeling of miniaturisation continues and I feel as if my own form is disappearing. This process is suddenly arrested by a voice speaking firmly to me.

'No. You are not ready for this –Come follow me'

The voice sounds familiar, very familiar and I suddenly become aware of myself as Tony, inexplicably lonely and conscious of something having been taken from me. I awake abruptly from sleep and stumble into the bathroom. I feel so empty I'm scared –back in bed I'm comforted by Pam's sleeping presence. I try to recall the event but it keeps going away from me. I remember thinking before I fall asleep. This one won't be remembered.

The following day I keep having the impression that Edward is going to speak with me –a view that is reinforced by something Pam told me the previous day. She had in that evening given a talk and demonstration of psychic art to a group in Hampshire and was interested by a clairvoyant observation from someone in the group she had never met before. This man described Edward as he sometimes appears wearing a top hat (whenever I see him like this I think of him being formal) and carrying a walking cane.

What I am about to record to you is the journey that occurred later that day in the evening when I was trying (unsuccessfully) to edit some previous journey pieces and all of a sudden giving up overwhelmed by tiredness. It is only as a result of this communication that what I have just recorded came to be remembered.

'Worlds within worlds –don't you see?' Edward is talking conversationally as we walk through an orchard; blossom carpeting the ground and swirling from the trees in wild profusion wafted about by a breeze. He is dressed in a blue frock coat, trousers and top hat, pacing gently forward with his silver banded walking cane. I am only partially aware of myself but know that my dress is informal of a soft shapeless material that fits closely –the top is open necked. We are making for a garden seat –an old wooden bench with no back sitting midst a shrubbery behind which towers an azalea bush all of three metres high and a mass of red flower.

As we sit down on the seat he leans across and picks a flower from the azalea bush and removes his top hat, then places the hat on the ground and the bloom on the crown.

'There –it does not look so formal now', he said smiling at me, his silvery grey hair shining in the light of the day. 'Well, you must admit it does look official', I say pointedly.

He looks at me quizzically. 'Hmm, I would have thought the word 'authoritative' is better suited to you thinking.'

'Oh, alright', I laugh, 'yes that's how I bring your across most times when teaching. I can't help it you know, it's my earthly personality; somewhat saturnine isn't it?'

'You have been making progress Peter, my fears for difficulties arising between you and the man Tony are not realised I'm pleased to say, however' –He pauses here and I look into his face expectantly. I can see the shadow of concern arising.

'What is it?' I asked.

'There are limitations', he said evenly.

'Yes –you've spoken about that', I say slowly, 'and I accept we have separate pathways as long as he remains in the physical world.' For a moment or so he says nothing in response but twirls his cane between his thumb and forefinger pressing the tip into the mossy ground.

241

'There is a saying, I think that's still current in the physical world; "What's good for the goose is good for the gander". Are you aware?'

'Male and female geese are they not?' I venture.

'Indeed they are, it's a modern rendering of "What's sauce for the goose is sauce for the gander". It means simply what's good for man is also good for women. You are more female than male and the man Tony is more male than female. The key to understanding the proverb is what is meant by good. It has often been quoted to justify the action of one to another but if we are to understand it correctly we must realise that what is good is not necessarily right in respect of a partner.'

He looks across at me to determine if I understand him correctly. I'm not sure what he is getting at but I think I understand what he is saying. 'I guess so', I say. He gives a short quick laugh, 'you are sounding like Don', he exclaims.

'I can't seem to get him out of my mind –I feel as if he was walking with us just now.'

'I'm not surprised', he said mildly, and continues. 'You and the man Tony are karmically bound and your actions that have him writing in response have bonded you closer. You are aware of this world in more ways than he can imagine. For example the relationship you have with Don is only partially realised by the man Tony. Your actions can influence him and likewise his action influences you. Because this bond has become closer he can be drawn into your own enquiries, the effect of which can be to endanger his physical well being.'

'I wouldn't want to do that', I say quickly, 'you must advise me Edward if something is amiss.' With that he picks up the azalea bloom and holds it between us.

'Worlds within worlds, would you not agree?' As I gaze at the flower I am conscious of my journey with Don and aware that it came into being from interests linking my studies with Michel. The journey was at my instigation.

'You are recalling my visit to the Dome with Don –this flower is mutated from the Heath family of flowers that first appeared in Pliocene epoch', I say eagerly recalling the connection. 'And why are you pursuing this line of enquiry? It is because you are interested in forming closer links with the communicator Murk.'

'That's true', I confess, 'but I don't understand why that should be a problem to my earthly self.' Edward lifts his cane and beats the air with it.

'Murk links the man Tonys' earthly teacher who travels in parallel worlds – the man Tony is not yet ready or able to make such journeys.'

Edward is smiling but there is some reproof in his look. 'He will remember this communication and also recover some part of the dome visit. It's not your enquiry of the evolution of plants and trees that are giving problem –it's your experience of parallel worlds that you entered into with Don thereafter.'

At this point in conversation I am aware of another world of consciousness within, of the voice that spoke warningly in the dome. It was the Green Man. I recall the words. 'No. You are not ready for this –Come follow me'. Edward is looking at me, raising his eyebrows, shaking his head slightly.

'Michel?'

Chapter THIRTYSIX:
Healing Experiences

In the aftermath of Peter's conversation with Edward and the recovery of the Dome event I'm conscious of an increasing sense of acceptance, of not arguing and questioning experience so much. Something is changing within me; I'm beginning to regard Peter as a brother. He's different for sure –but then aren't all brothers?

The only thing that 'bugs' me is the voice of the Green Man. Is this Peter's name for him? 'I am what you want me to be' he says –a statement that encourages my conscious mind to query he is more than the name suggests –a person in harmony with nature. And in the last moment of my recall of Peter's conversation with Edward there's another tantalising statement –the naming of Michel.

I am aware of who Michel is –he manifested many times through the trance mediumship of my teacher Len. He would speak on many subjects, most of which were about inter-dimensional travel. Michel never elaborated on his identity and most that had the good fortune to hear him were unaware of his surname, Nostradamus. Is it possible Len's present consciousness is interrelated with Michel? It sticks in my mind that Peter was asking a question of Edward when my recall abruptly ended. Is it that Peter is in communication with Len?

Healing Experiences

Edward is making it clear that there are 'barriers' Peter should not cross when I am aware of him –it would appear a 'plan' of some kind guides the people who I meet in my travels. I reflect on the fact that not only Len but also other key communicators whose expression I have enjoyed in trance and through clairvoyant communication have not appeared in my astral journeys. I have blinkers on –driven as I move by a driver I cannot see.

If I had come to this realisation early on in my astral journeys I feel sure my reactions would have put a stop to them –now an acceptance is present; a kind of submissiveness that accepts it's dangerous to delve. I think about it. Hasn't it been dangerous enough? There have been times when I've questioned my own sanity.

Many days pass and I'm unaware of any astral communications. Uncharacteristically I feel very relaxed about it –I even try to worry about it and yet the feeling of relaxed well being continues. It was simply clairvoyant curiosity that has me focus upon a vibratory pattern of environmental energies that appear one morning as I am, as is usual, walking my dog in the local cemetery, my thoughts concerned with the day's events. I become aware of a pattern of dots and dashes about me of a density not unlike rain, not streaming vertically but around me in the horizontal plane –a swirling effect that causes my consciousness to withdraw from the immediate physical world. I reassert my conscious mind and the condition fades leaving me feeling unsettled and unsure. For the remainder of my walk I guardedly view everything in my path.

Later that same morning unexpectedly I have time on my hands as some insensitive soul has parked their car outside my garage preventing me from driving out to manage the healing clinic as is normal on a Monday. I sit in my study/healing room awaiting the arrival of the police and recall the connection I had experienced earlier and much to my surprise a buzzing sound develops in my right ear on recalling the memory –the kind of sound a bee makes. It is so close to my ear I instinctively look to see if such a creature is present.

I slip out into another dimension of reality and become conscious of a person standing close and aware at the same time of myself in listening mode. We both stand in a space the perimeter of which is indistinct and hazy. The person is male and middle aged, dressed in a hospital gown. There are some structural forms behind him but I can't make out what they are. He looks preoccupied with his own thoughts, though every now and then he looks to the side at something attracting his attention. This focus last a few moments only, then a smile plays about his face and again he appears to think within himself; his body reactions reflecting indecision and confusion.

I feel as if I'm myself, albeit more liberated than usual –my hair is longer, I am taller and I'm not given to question why. I call out to him but my vocal chords don't sound –can he hear my thoughts I wonder? I feel self possessed and entirely confident of my ability to help this man who is lost in some way.

I know he is aware of me as he stands facing about three metres in front, but is either choosing to ignore me or is not able to put his own mind in order to respond. I begin to send healing energies to this man and notice a glow of energy developing about his body –the upper body changes from silver dove grey to shades of violet and blue that interact. His head becomes brighter than the torso and a silvery light begins to emanate from within him.

He responds positively by saying, 'Don't tell me –let me guess? You are an angel come to show me the way.' He sounds jocular as if he's enjoying a joke and tries to move toward me –his body sways but his legs remain rooted to the ground. I notice a stream of smoky substance curled about his lower form and recognise he is still attached to the physical world.

'Not exactly', I say, 'but I can help provided you will let me.'

'This is one hell of a dream', he says, again much to himself. 'Tell me about it', I offer as I realise he is half in and half out of his physical body.

He hesitates as if thinking over the offer. 'I can't do my work like this', he said, plucking nervously at his gown. Anxiety clouds his form –he is frowning as he speaks. 'The doc's won't give me a straight answer.'

'And what does your wife say?'

'Oh, she's in my dream too. I keep seeing her face and she asking me all the time, 'how do you feel and what did they say?'

'Is it Sunday?' He suddenly enquires.

'No. it's Monday.' I notice a discolouration in the lower left hand side of his body. 'What are the docs doing for you then?'

'Bowels not working can't pass anything.'

Throughout this exchange I'm getting information about him. He's forty four years old, a Cancerian, married with two children and a factory worker. Likes football, still thinks of himself as a bit of a lad and has ideas working for himself –though he's not sure what that should be. Name is Dennis.

'They've done your op Dennis and now you are recovering. Don't try to come any closer.' He's trying to close the gap between us again.

Healing Experiences

'You must relax your mind –it won't take long. The anaesthetic is having a weird effect on you. When you wake up you won't remember much. Don't worry about time –there's time enough.'

He seems calmer on receiving my thoughts and I tell him I will continue healing and his post operative recovery will be successful. His form is getting fuzzy and I continue the healing concentration –but I can't help thinking midst all of this I should have told him to revise his diet. He's overweight and his system labours to make changes.

Suddenly, this vision disappears to be replaced by the consciousness of this world. For a moment I'm not sure where I am –then I realise I'm still in my healing room. Minutes only have passed.

I am thinking this is evidence of my being able to project myself at will and set about focusing my mind on a patient I have who is in need of help right now. I find I am able to make the contact finding myself in the same space as that person –a man who is said to have broken his coccyx bone. As I approach his form to put my hands around the area he moves as if to get into a comfortable position. As I apply healing I can sense a heat being applied to the area and the bone and flesh at the base of his body showing a pinkish red colour with small irregular shapes of black in the middle.

He says something complimentary but I can't make out the words. The image of him laying down on a sofa or some piece of soft furniture receiving the healing is glassy and I get the impression this effect is caused by my emotional mind interacting with his physical nervous system. I'm aware of a pair of hands –not my own, moving in close proximity to the coccyx bone.

I snap back into normal consciousness. It's different to my interaction with the man Dennis –in this I feel as if I'm remotely viewing and directing healing from afar. The patient shows some action that is independent of my thought which I take as evidence he is aware of my healing influence.

I try this with another patient but get nowhere –is it because they don't need the healing or is it because I can't make the connection? I feel the reason is at my own door. Human beings may have many bodies that interconnect but the 'seamless' connection results from harmonies we cannot always generate –and they often don't because we have an inherent desire to 'earth' everything we experience.

The police arrive and a short while after my car is 'released' from its garage and I'm on my way to the healing clinic. As I drive I reflect upon

247

on how I ventured over the years to express my psychic abilities. At one time I was demonstrating at psychic and holistic fayres reading people's BodyMind systems. I developed this form of reading as confidence to channel my healing communicators grew. One particular communicator, Heinrich Schroeder, who had been the first of many to en-trance me in my early development days, was adept at identifying health problems.

With his help I made a number of body diagrams and would sit with clients to provide them a picture of their strengths and weaknesses. On most occasions when my analysis could be verified the outcomes were 100% accurate –leaving me feeling decidedly vulnerable, as (a) I found it difficult to believe I was that accurate, and (b) because I feared the next reading would be poor and inaccurate. Gradually I became more confident and would brush aside feedback less my ego began to think it was the capable mind.

Now I channel this form of communication during healing sessions and most often my patient is unaware of the link I am making as it would appear to them I am merely being intelligent in response to their health concerns. Positive analysis that identifies strengths is not expected when we seek health advice from our local GP yet this is invariably part of the advice Heinrich provides. As a healer I find that invaluable as it guides my mind to adopt healing techniques appropriate for that patient.

A couple of weeks ago I was in full flow with Heinrich advising a class who were about to begin a distant healing development course. Yet again for the umpteenth time I was shaken by the accuracy of Heinrich's knowledge of the prospective patients who had only been identified to me by their name and complaint.

As I drive I'm dimly aware of some event in which Heinrich is present and vow to myself I will find some quiet time later to allow that recall. As life (so often it appears) has me busier than I can predict it's not until two days later I am able to sit down and attempt a recall. It works!

Throughout this event I feel a sense of separation from Heinrich –it is as if an evolved Peter stands between Heinrich and my conscious self.

We are walking on a grass path in a grove of carefully trimmed evergreen bushes, some of which rise upward of three metres. Neatly spaced and carefully tended flower beds intersperse. The day is bright and I am aware of a small fountain somewhere to the left. Heinrich dressed in suit and waistcoat is bare headed –his grey bearded full set, bald pate and fine features, make him look like Edward the Seventh.

With us is a small group of people and I have the clear impression they are doctors or healers of some speciality. There is a middle aged oriental man dressed casually in trousers and white shirt loose at the waist –he has a bony face and his hair is short. A western man, likely European dressed in a dark blue tunic top and trousers –it looks like a uniform. Another man dressed in collar, tie and trousers and somewhat shorter than other men present, sports a closely trimmed white beard and moustache. There are three women, one who is Caucasian, elderly and clearly dressed as a nun. The other two are dark skinned, a buxom lady dressed colourfully in a West Indian style and a slim middle aged woman dressed in a trouser suit of plain light brown material.

Heinrich is speaking, his voice is gentle and soft in tone, 'it's all done by atmosphere, as you can't help but notice', he says with short laugh. 'Tune in and you will witness others directly assisting my efforts'.

'Will you use instruments?' says the oriental man.

'Yes and no –depending upon the patients' state of mind and body. Instruments can reassure and give patients confidence. Not in all cases however.'

Heinrich quickens his step and I sense he is already tuning in to the work ahead. 'We have eight patients in this session –all of them victims of war.'

'Is the number significant?' asks the colourfully dressed West Indian woman.

'Significant insofar there's a common background of suffering. They have arisen from the same atmosphere of destruction. The team is looking after them and attending immediate needs.'

We are no longer in the grove but on a field like clearing between trees. A number of people of various nationalities sit crossed legged on the ground in meditative postures. Beyond them is a large walled tent. At an entrance facing us a man and woman look over toward our approaching figures. 'Hello Hannah', Heinrich says acknowledging the tall woman who smiles in greeting.

She is dark skinned, wears a simple one piece dress, a turban type headdress and is bare footed. The man who greets us with Hannah is small in stature and dressed as a Muslim. I notice that despite his long outer garment he is bandy legged. As he holds open the tent door flap to let us enter he looks me in the eyes and says, 'The energies are different in here.'

How right he is. We enter the tent and I'm immediately aware of a change in atmosphere. It is close and warm and smells of antiseptic but it's also calming.

Lightly touching my arm Heinrich says, 'come.' I feel surrounded by energy, so much so I am now only aware of Heinrich's presence and a form lying on a mattress before us. It's a boy around 14 years of age.

Heinrich kneels down and bends over the boy and appears to speak with him. The boy's eyes are open and registering something but I get the impression he is not fully conscious of Heinrich and completely unaware of me.

Someone is placing a tray of surgical instruments beside the boy and Heinrich beckons me closer and points to the boy's bare chest that's a mass of angry red and dark brown colour. I place my left hand at the base of the sternum bone and am immediately conscious of broken ribs and torn tissue. Blood is not apparent but a thick dark energy swirls and pulsates around the rib cage. My index finger enters a short way into the boy's body and begins to swell. I can feel the boy reacting to a pain that repeats itself over and over again like the sound of a record stuck in a groove.

My whole hand now feels as if it's swelling and promoting energy into the boy's torso. Heinrich is talking to him in low tones and now holding a surgical clamp in one hand. He places this below my hand and to the left, is handed another which he places to the right. I am dimly aware of his hands entering into the boy's abdomen and moving something about. The energy feeling is intense and the boy has closed his eyes and appears to be dreaming about something pleasant. Heinrich directs my other hand to make slow passes over his upper body and head and in so doing a silvery light manifests cloaking the skin.

Standing up I see the boy looks peaceful, his entire body cloaked in a silvery grey energy. Heinrich is in conversation with a short swarthy faced woman wearing a nurse's uniform, he pats her on the shoulder and they both smile knowingly.

Almost immediately I am aware of being with another patient. A girl who can't be more than twelve yet she wears the remnants of a combat uniform. Large dark stains of dried blood, pink and red jagged gashes are everywhere, save her feet and head. The left hip and upper thigh are sunken beneath a mass of tattered clothing –the left leg lies on its side. Instinctively I know these are injuries from a bomb blast. Her eyes are open but she looks neither left or right as Heinrich, kneeling, quietly talks with her.

250

Healing Experiences

Two Muslim women in attendance are gently cutting away her clothing. Heinrich directs me to work on her legs. As I focus my mind to harmonise with the healing energies the legs appear translucent. Tendrils of silvery white light bunch and disperse in ever changing patterns following invisible lines up and down the legs. At the base of the torso this activity is so dense only pulsations can be seen –colours come and go.

I begin work in the left thigh and left knee where the inner body activity is most intense. Once again I can feel my hands entering into the body mass – I feel resistance and instinctively know that this is bone. My fingers feel like geysers jetting energy -slowly I trace along the lines of resistance, my hands seemingly controlled in their speed. I am aware of someone else working to my right and being directed by Heinrich.

After a short while change is apparent in the area of my working –light blue and silvery grey colours give body to the limbs and I change my focus and work more intensely upon the lower torso. I hear singing, from above me I think. It's not Christian –I think it's Arabic. I look at the girls' dark skinned face –she looks peaceful.

I'm somewhere different and can feel myself shoulder to shoulder with others grouped before a bed festooned with tubes, blood and saline drips aware of a patient who is writhing and screaming soundlessly. It's a man of about middle age dressed in a long shirt and nothing else. His head is bandaged, also the right knee –no tubes or instruments are connected to him. Every now and then his body contorts as if a force of electricity is taking command. He appears to be undamaged but the energies about him mask and distort the appearance of his form and are intent on destroying him.

As I observe Heinrich place his hands about the man's bandaged head the atmosphere changes –it's almost as if the air is becoming rarefied. I feel incredibly light and mentally drawn to partner Heinrich's work –whatever that might be. Whilst I remain aware of the patient looking across at the bed at an angle of 45 degrees and conscious of people's tall forms in varying shades of blue, silver, yellow and green my consciousness is in another sphere, connecting with natural energies quite unlike the issue of life I see struggling before me.

I can feel a sound –a phut, phut liquid like sound vibrating at high speed and aware of being in a borderless empty space. This vibration gradually fades until I only hear it mentally. As this happens the space like awareness I have disappears and the previous atmosphere returns. Once again I am shoulder to shoulder with others at ground level. The patient lies motionless on the bed and Heinrich is standing. I have the distinct feeling that the 'fever' of whatever it was has left him.

The act of healing is narrowing my awareness of place and people. Briefly I find myself viewing a hospital record card –not the usual kind; it's rather like a guest register. Names and signatures abound. I am not aware of adding mine. I am conscious of healing a woman's arm –tissue regenerating. A bright light green coloured energy I am transmitting appears to bring about the transformation.

My last impression of this event is being aware of the woman Hannah talking to us healers as a group. I don't have the detail but it appears she was giving report on patient's states of recovery and pointing out what more we might do to assist. I have the impression that this kind of work to her is a mission and in its way this was a pep talk aimed at encouraging participation in this kind of rescue work.

Heinrich Schroeder

Figure 11

Chapter THIRTYSEVEN:
The Realm of Compassionate Being

I am finally on my way to Somerset to a small village on the outskirts of Glastonbury. From previous visits I know this rural area to be conducive to psychic communication work –the elemental energies are powerful and facilitate the instrumental channelling of healing energies. I'm not expecting to astral journey here but anticipate the natural world atmosphere will help tune my mind revisit the written recordings I've made. Assessment of the communications received since January has me think maybe they are sufficient to bundle together and form a book. Unintentionally I leave my mobile phone at home and as I drive reflect on its absence as 'guidance from the Gods'.

The young couple who I will be staying with are pupils of mine and sufficiently 'earthed' and real about life to let me get on with what I need to do. Anyone of my nature can expect to be petitioned for help and whilst it's not in my nature to refuse a need I'm hoping not to be noticed –what I have in mind will be helped by the quiet of the place and their laid back lifestyle.

When I arrive I see immediately that my first task is to help young Adam who has damaged the base of his spine. It was Adam who I had projected myself too some two weeks previous and he now speaks of relief he's had, however its clear to me that further healing work is required –he's not exactly been resting since I made the healing link! As a worker of wood and suchlike this injury is restricting his ability to earn. I get to work and soon he has relief from pain.

My recommendation that he should use his son's play pool rubber ring to relieve pressure on the coccyx is the subject of much amusement –and since it works to make sitting more comfortable and allow my healing energies to work, Adam sees the funny side of looking a little ridiculous perched upon it.

I settle myself down in the caravan they have kindly made available and let the natural atmosphere take over. The pace of life here is slower than in the city and the absence of telephone and TV is immediately noticeable. I begin my review of the growing body of journey recollections by adding a personal perspective. Gradually I'm getting into it and by the following morning I'm acclimatising myself to chicken chatter, the grunt of pigs and the inquisitive visits of their two Jack Russell's. There's a coming and going of people to the small holding but they take no notice, I'm pleased to say.

Brilliant sunshine streams in through the caravan windows and Adam strides about his work all smiles. After a late breakfast and a chat with Lisa I sit back in the caravan and continue working on my laptop computer. I begin to feel sleepy and inexplicably nod off –thinking to myself, 'it doesn't really matter –I can work at night if I need to'.

I am standing in an arched circular colonnade; the floor smooth, shiny and veined like a cut of Stilton cheese flecked blue and light grey, suggesting marble. The arches are also smooth; polished matt cream stone without engraving or relief of any kind and their ribs curve above me forming a roof some 10 metres high. I am aware of block joins (because I look for them), pencil thin and barely discernable. The centre contains huge pillars of similar crafted pieces supporting a ribbed ceiling the colour of light blue –it is large and likely more than 50 metres in diameter. The effect is of lightness and freedom and a sense of great simplicity.

In various places on the floor near to the pillars are long box like benches, not unlike burial caskets; these serve as seats because I see figures standing about or sitting on them. I have the immediate lasting impression that this place is a forum of some kind. The atmosphere is stimulating but not anxious or turbulent in any way.

I see figures of both sexes dressed in a variety of national garbs and from different periods of earth's history. Some dress is identifiably eastern and western whilst other garments are more universal; gown and cloak like apparel, which gives neither notice of past, gender or profession. I'm aware of having a female companion –I can't see her and don't know who she is. We stand together and I'm aware of people coming into the colonnade and struck by the ease of movements –figures appear to glide rather than walk toward the centre of this complex where the majority of people are gathered.

The atmosphere is extraordinarily clear –it is as if the simplicity of the structure brings sharp relief to the forms of people within it. I can see in detail facial characteristics at a distance. There is the sense of people moving about in this environment learning from one another's presence. I am not aware of speech, of the audible sound of thoughts expressed in language, but am conscious of receiving strength by being here. I think these people are evolved and barely need form to clothe them.

A bearded Eastern man richly dressed and turbaned pauses for a moment in front of us and smiles knowingly. His greeting promotes my instant acknowledgement for he gives an effusion of feeling that on earth we would reserve for one dearly loved. I am convinced he knows who and what I am –without a murmur of judgement he passes on into another group of people.

I mentally enquire of my companion, 'what is this place?'

'These are halls of learning', she responds, 'it has many levels. Here new connections are made as beings seek to expand awareness of the self.'

'In what way are these halls able to impart learning?' I ask.

'Individual souls are drawn here by connections in being they already have. Each person you see is a library of knowledge –it is from the intermingling of these states that awareness is drawn from the experience of memories. Relationships are created in this environment that promotes new paths of development.

'What kinds of learning? I sense time but not as a condition imposed upon me –it's as if I am not governed by time and able to choose interest and connection at will.

If only I had the will to do so!' I add conscious of feeling powerless to act. My companions voice is heard within –her tones reassuring and protective.

'This is the realm of Compassionate Being –in which the nature of mind manifests ability to understand the purpose of incarnation. Cycles can be influenced to combine or multiply by the action of the minds present.'

I look out into the hall viewing the people and feel inspired by the harmony they generate –their individual worlds seem to me to be complete. 'Are they really looking to re-incarnate in the physical world? Why would they want too?'

I am finding the thought of this difficult to take in –everyone is so liberated! 'Incarnation is more than you conceive it to be. I will reveal to you what I can.'

We are moving out from under the curving colonnade into the large circular hall. Immediately we enter under its roof the atmosphere intensifies and I feel attuned to an order of energy that seems almost to forbid my thinking. I am conscious of passing into and within the minds of those present —as if the hall is crammed with more people than I see, each open to express their entirety; each interpenetrating the minds of others. As I feel this I am aware of withholding the expression of my self; of wanting but being unable to release my consciousness

Whether directly resulting from my reaction of being in their midst I cannot say, but many a face turns toward us in open greeting and I experience a sense of isolation as I move amongst them, despite the strong feelings of love I am receiving. My companion shepherds me through their midst, conscious no doubt of my difficulties.

I lose my sense of place until I am next aware of standing beneath a roofed and pillared structure, vaguely reminiscent of a Greek styled memorial building —circular and some seven metres in diameter, in the centre of which is a round opening in the white marble like floor. Rings of stone steps descend from its rim some six levels. We glide forward to its edge and sit on the floor, our feet resting on the step below. Beneath at the centre is a clear blue surface I suppose to be still water —there are no shadows, no reflections of any kind anywhere. I have the sense of being drawn into the pool. I look up to the featureless concave ceiling shimmering pale blue to reaffirm my sense of place.

In doing so I become objectively aware of my companion —it is Atlanta. I am not surprised —I am inwardly pleased and immediately strengthened by my acknowledgement. Atlanta's skin is a pale rose red —the facial features show a strong forehead, sensuous mouth and powerful neck. Her head and shoulders are framed by long dark hair and she wears a long gossamer light red textured dress cut deep at the neck. The dress seems lit from within giving a ruby like glow to her outward appearance. No ornaments, footwear or regalia, or other items of clothing adorn her form. Physical age is that of a woman in the blossom of her summer years. She is tall —I would say over six feet.

I am vaguely aware of myself now as wraith like and silvery. Mentally I'm curiously detached from my form and uninterested to enquire why I am like this. I feel a soulful communion —and when she speaks it's as if her voice is inside of me.

The Realm of Compassionate Being

'All beings of human origin are composite souls and those that incarnate in the world of matter are legion in number yet they appear in matter as one body and the acts of their many selves are expressions of their physical personalities. In the world of matter reason is born. The process of reasoning arises from the awareness of the many seeking the ultimate expression of oneness. Bliss is freedom from reason and there are as many ways to Bliss as there are men, moreover Bliss is sought by the essence of soul believing it is one –only in this world, the realm of compassionate Being, can the ascending soul become aware of the entirety of self and know its composite nature.

Human beings ascend from and descend into matter constantly –there is no end to the cycle of their incarnation; as they descend selves multiply and group cycles merge and disperse creating new combinations. Ascension from the world of matter carries with it the relationships formed in that state and they too will multiply or disperse in the astral worlds.'

'But, have not the teachers of old taught the cycle can be ended –by right action freedom from reason attained?' I interject.

'This is what you see here in the halls of learning –the evolution of human beings seeking to finalise the cycle of incarnation; here the many are more knowing of their relationships, yet for every soul that enters the hall of learning more than one shall leave it.'

'I don't understand –have you not said here the many are aware of their individual selves and form relationships that join together?'

'I have and so they do but for every being in this plane there are seven fold relationships descending, ascending and incarnating in matter. In these halls of learning pledges are made, the many are imbued with higher purpose; illuminated by the knowledge that is not born of reason; when non-reason being holds the balance of awareness the group soul cycle of incarnation ends.'

Atlanta

Figure 12

The Realm of Compassionate Being

Chapter THIRTYEIGHT:
Light and Dark Matter Worlds

A s I look into the blue water that gives no sense of depth, I feel an awakening, a need to be educated and a thirst to know arises in my consciousness; a desire to join and be complete.

'How is it you are not free of the cycle? Millenniums pass and you are yet in the world of form.'

'You for one are a reasoning being of purpose that arises in me,' she says lovingly, 'group soul cycles of incarnation are not uniform or follow the sequence of time; the order of past, present and future –they mature according to the balance of reasoned and non-reasoned being. There are other factors in the cycle of incarnation you need to appreciate – individual selves may choose to further the development of the reasoning worlds by incarnating yet again into matter.

Such developments bring about changes to the consciousness of man in the earth and astral kingdoms –it is a process that births many relationships. When this occurs the non-reasoned elements of the cycle can separate and new worlds of consciousness form with non-human existences.

Further forms of separation occur when individual elements of a cycle at different levels of existence seek to embrace the non reasoning worlds; not only are new relationships formed but existing harmonies can be ended as a different balance of soul cycle development is created.'

Light and Dark Matter Worlds

I listen intently to this and become increasingly aware that the permutations might well be endless. Anticipating my question, Atlanta continues.

'The cycle of incarnation is without end in the manifest worlds and will continue thus until the great cycle is fulfilled. The great cycle is a balance of Light and Dark matter worlds and within, a balance of creative and neutralising forces. Man is not alone a reasoning being there are many other conceptions who give birth to reason as there are many conceptions that do not birth their self and live as non reasoned being, and there are yet those whose identity is alternatively known and unknown and live in conflict between reason and non reason of both lower and higher ordered states.'

It is becoming clear to me the ancient teachings that guide Man to understand and release himself from the wheel of life and death are speaking of the relationship of reason and non- reason and though one might evolve to escape the wheel, the order of reason and non reason prevails and will continue to do so for all eternity.

'I want to know more of what you term non-reasoned being. Is there more you may tell me?'

'There are bridges between the reasoned and non-reasoned worlds of being. In the human world of matter and its ascendant astral kingdom there are many connections with other species as there is within Man himself, the animal, vegetable and mineral worlds. And it must be understood that these bridges as I term them are active to and from all species and all kingdoms. The bridges link parallel dimensions of form, space and time; also they cross over into the order of your BodyMind being and influence its identity. There are realms that link the planes of reason and the states of non-reasoned being. All these bridges interact creating ever-new permutations.

The community of Man has diverse, fragmented and conflicting knowledge concerning the reality of non-reasoned states. The earth bound disciples of divine reason define the existence of a non-reasoned hierarchy of evolution to embrace the elemental worlds and all non-human species. In reality there are many expressions of reasoning in all forms of life that have a hierarchical order of evolution. Non-reasoned states are defined by the absence of an hierarchical ladder –it is an order of parallel being, an assembly of now states in which both manifest and non manifest worlds evolve.'

Atlanta pauses conscious that I am finding this teaching hard to assimilate. Continuing she says- 'As a reasoned being with feet in the earth world you have difficulty understanding evolution that is not hierarchical.

Your sensorial nature restricts awareness.

The universal like attract like law unifies need –needs are the components of identity and the establishment of their Right Order is evolution. The reasoned being evolves out of conflict; the many resolving to oneness. Non-reasoned being evolves from oneness that has no expressible identity, to a multiplicity of states both manifest and unmanifest within which identity is communal and in harmony with itself. Reasoned worlds contract to achieve oneness; non-reasoned worlds expand.'

The 'Peter' within me is eager to move on and the earth order of myself, only partially satisfied, reluctantly agrees and poses a new question. 'You speak of bridges and speak of them as integral to creation', I say, 'in what ways might Man enter the non-reasoned world of being?'

'He can choose to move parallel or ascend the ladder of divine reason. You must keep in mind that the individual being may not be expressing their own will and that some are knowingly expressing the will of others' She pauses again before adding; 'some may evolve both in parallel and hierarchical orders of life.' I turn and feel the ruby emanations of light from her being, aware her whole form is translucent; the face and arms the texture of eggshell; the eyes soft as one would feel a fleece, the iris in hues of green and blue. I feel as if I am fixed in time and space and the radiation of light holding me in loving embrace.

'Can you give me example of how these evolutions might develop?'

She smiles. 'What I will describe for you is incomplete as the understanding of cycles cannot be achieved entirely by the order of consciousness you enjoy. Before and after, beyond and below are the expressions your sensory nature allows. Be reminded that all is present being. The sun casts no shadow. The shadow is caused by the form given life by the sun. The form absorbs light and becomes self conscious and in so doing casts a shadow. I say this to you that you might liken Sun to present being and shadow to the memory that arises from self consciousness.

Ends are beginnings –life is cyclical. The physical universes are caused by the creation of non-reasoned being achieving communal harmony. They are both seen and unseen –they have as you would call them invisible counterparts. Ultimately non-reasoned being neutralises the last vestige of form consciousness –all identities, and becomes Pure Intelligence and in the act of its own creation Pure Intelligence rebirths a new order of Light and Dark Matter of varying levels and densities. Light Matter has the ability to propagate and divide itself –Dark Matter or anti-matter provides the 'fuel' as you would understand it that make Light Matter propagation possible. To attain awareness Light Matter must absorb Dark Matter and in so doing it becomes many. It multiplies in order to divide –it divides in order to become singular. To be singular is to be harmonised in the Grand Cycle –the ultimate Right Order.

So it follows that on completion of the Grand Cycle bodies of Light Matter cease to propagate as their own hierarchical cycles achieve oneness and are absorbed by the anti-matter universe. Ultimately the cycle completes and returns into itself causing the change that neutralises its nature of being –the resultant act is separation of pure intelligence that once again causes the first principle –the creation of Pure Intelligence. From this you will understand the teaching, "That which is first shall be last and that which is last shall be first." All lesser cycles that arise within the Grand Cycle begin and end in non-reasoned states. The manifest worlds, seen and unseen are the product of Light Matter cycles and at every level the instrument minds of higher reasoned being that ultimately bring about the fulfilment of creation – the production of non-reasoned being.

I look in askance expecting her to continue. She smiles at me as a mother might to her son. 'If I could describe pure intelligence, neither I nor you would be separate or would we be having this communion.

What I now describe arises from the creation teaching I have given you. Man is a hybrid being whose energetic principles are rooted in the vegetable, mineral and animal worlds –the BodyMind character having origin in primordial fire, earth, air and water. His bodies have evolved over millions of earth years from single cell amoebic water based creations that in turn evolved from the primordial elements of your solar system.

The earth itself is not singular as you suppose; a self contained sphere of Being, its matter separate from other like planets –like you it has hierarchical and parallel systems of Being that have relationships with other worlds. In the course of its evolution the Earth Being has been influenced and affected by other conceptions and many Earth life forms, including Man, have absorbed its evolving intelligence and changed accordingly their conceptual identities.

The Earth itself and all other planets in your solar system are children of Aster –a large planet with many satellite spheres that disassembled billions of your earth years past during the formative phase of Andromeda within the Milky Way galaxy –itself birthed by the Lucifer and Christos galaxy whose Dark Matter state enshrouds the manifest universe. Life forms within Andromeda continue to influence the BodyMind of Earth and Man.

Understanding of non-reasoned being requires you appreciate the difference between the reasoning of Man and the reasoning of other conceptions. Man as you know him accords his consciousness superior status because of his ability to be aware of himself as the order of being different from other life forms. He thinks, recalls and organises his thoughts and is able to articulate awareness of hierarchical ordered intelligence. He is aware of parallel dimensions of being, of non-reasoned states but cannot adequately express or relate them to his sense world. He is a group soul of many contradictions –differences that multiply as the conscious ego dominates the development of his soul. On arising into the Compassionate Order of Being he becomes aware of the Right Order relationships of his many selves and thereafter endeavours to harmonise them to end the cycles of incarnation.

There are other reasoning beings who are similarly balanced with the emphasis of the 'I' consciousness arising from the physical conception, yet there are others in which the 'I' nature is born of the compassionate order of Being –such conceptions influence man on his arising into the Astral worlds.

As I have taught and you have witnessed the realm of Compassionate Being embraces reasoning conceptions. Reasoned Beings born of this world have lower order relationships powerless to choose in the awareness of their forms and instead seek to refine their elemental and sensory natures under the influence of the higher 'I' self. All three bodied Beings manifest to the physical world have this higher reasoning nature. Where the compassionate nature has expression in the incarnate man he will seek to harmonise himself with the world of nature and all three bodied forms of life arising out of it.

'You speak of three bodied beings and I suppose there are those of more or less parts of being –may you tell me more?'

'I shall but first you must be clear in your understanding of reasoned and non-reasoned being. All reasoned and non-reasoned Beings arise from the same cause; of the Self-Harmonious fragmenting in the process of transforming into Pure Intelligence. The Light Matter elements of the Self-Harmonious, what you might term outer shell, disburse as fragments of the one identity to ultimately manifest in the physical order of being without awareness of its origin.

The core of the Self-Harmonious form nature, what you might term the inner shell, also disburses attracted by the outer shell fragments journeying into matter searching for self-awareness. Thus fragmented Light Matter forms the foundation of reasoned being and the inner shell comprising wholly of anti matter becomes the foundation of non-reasoned states. Yet as different as these states are they are mutually dependant –Light Matter's ability to propagate is dependant upon anti-matter and non-reasoned states ability to form their present state identity is enabled by the hierarchical order of Light Matter development.

Atlanta pauses and I feel her considering my understanding of this teaching. 'You will need to reflect upon this after I speak of Man's evolution –for he is many things; a hybrid creation.'

I am finding these explanations illuminating and intriguing. 'Why is it that Man is so full of contradictions?' Atlanta looks at me with a meaningful expression, as if to say –are you not aware of yourself? But she answers nonetheless and I sense sadness in the voice within me. 'Man is full of his own importance and worships the uniqueness of his own being. It was not always so. The seeds of his peculiar form of self-awareness are sown by his marriage to the Sons of Thunder.'

Chapter THIRTYNINE:
The Sons of Thunder

'Sons of Thunder?' I query. 'Are these the beings mentioned in Jewish literature?'

'The name has survived but the meaning is long since lost; disseminated as language multiplied and the all aware sensory nature fragmented. As memories needed to be interpreted by the separated sensory expression of self and committed to written language the seminal influence of the Sons of Thunder upon human evolution was lost to the physical world as the conscious egocentric nature of man evolved. It was intended so by the Sons themselves.

'The Sons of Thunder are so called because their Parent appeared on Earth at a time of great disturbance in the elements, before even the Earth's moon is created and the planet had yet to form an impermeable crust and is subject to many collisions with comet like matter from within and beyond the solar system.

The Parent is a being of inexpressible identity, of the kind I have said to you live in conflict between the parallel and hierarchical orders of life. I am not able to inform you fully who the Parent is in any particular formative sense –it is at once formless and manifestly form without number. In earth language the Parent can only be described as microscopic life that originates from outside the earth. The cosmic highways are forever changing as world's birth and redevelop and the Parent's arrival is facilitated by the changing orders of consciousness within and without the solar system. Originating from a planetary cluster in the Milky Way it entered into the Earth Being and other planets in the solar system. The Parents' arrival stimulated the evolution of individual life forms.'

I realise here that Atlanta is expressing her understanding of Earth creation and I'm in awe of what she says. 'You say the Parent –do you mean by this the God before all other Gods?'

'No. This is the Parent of the sons of light and the sons of darkness – otherwise known as the Sons of Thunder.'

'Then you do you mean the Parent started life on Earth?'

'No –but it did change the order of evolution. You must appreciate that the Parent also inhabited all other planets of your solar system –the Earth is the youngest in this context as the other planets' evolutions have reached their zenith and the sons birthed in these spheres have either entered into the Earths' BodyMind being, remained in their own planetary worlds, or returned to the Parents' constellation.'

At this point I am feeling totally overwhelmed but also strangely desperate to ask questions. 'What then did the Parent do?' I ask weakly. Atlanta aware of my confusion speaks gently.

'The forces that manifested the Parent and changed the evolutionary order of earth life came to Earth in the form of comets, asteroids and cosmic storms. The Parent is a highly evolved intelligence able to express within the elements of Light Matter and create androgynous conceptions in the image of itself.'

'And the Sons?' I ask, still lost and wondrous of what she is telling me. She laughs at the simplicity of my question –that's how I must describe the feelings I have within as she responds; lightness, like a breeze in the trees and the sparkling of light on leaves after rain.

'The parent produced beings of a collective nature, such as you might know as a genus of plant, of fish and mammal –an entirely harmonious creation in which the physical order of manifestation knew not its higher androgynous nature. This process took many millions of earth years culminating in a period called by your scientists the Mesozoic age. The Parent became embedded within its creation and a hierarchical order established itself. The Sons of Thunder are born out of the Parents order that suffered change after a cataclysmic asteroid impact upon the Earth brought about the epoch you know in your history as the last Ice Age. The effect of this collision moved the poles of the earth and many physical forms perished. The astral world order of the Parent was divided by the physical world changes and as a consequence the order and nature of birth was also changed and so conceived three bodied beings. Some male and female orders of physical creation prior to the pole shift that survived developed hybrid characteristics and some conceptions that were able to birth themselves. The change in astral and etheric orders of the Earth world attracted a migration of androgynous beings, more highly evolved of the Parent's order, from the astral world of the planet Venus and their influence accelerated change.'

'I have been told by someone or read, I can't remember which, they arrived in spaceships and records do exist in the world history of their arrival.' For the first time in our conversation I feel as if I am contributing.

'No. The Sons of Thunder came into being long before Atlantis, even before Lemuria and Hyperborea, during the epoch of Adamos when the south pole of Earth was green with vegetation and still part of what you call the Americas, equatorial regions were volcanic and uninhabitable and waters covered much of the surface.'

'Adamos –was that the fabled Garden of Eden?' I say eagerly.

'Yes it was but not that which is written to your history in what is known as the Mediterranean basin before the time of great floods. What is recorded there is the beginning of the human world marking the end of the androgynous era.'

'That would mean their involvement spanned many thousand of years?' 'Many hundreds of thousands of earth years, for Adamos was long gone when the land mass that became the world of Atlantis formed and became habitable.'[15]

She stops speaking for a moment, a smile playing about her lips. 'You are believing they came in space craft, but they did not –these beings were of intelligence that inhabited other forms –they were as you describe in your language a virus, able to multiply and evolve utilising the energetic principles of earth formed life.

They entered into earth life at all levels from the amoebic to the crustacean, to the aquatic vertebras, accelerating growth to form new land-based species. Of the many vertebrate species, some reptilian, quadruped and biped creations eventually became dominant -their system of bodies able to develop self awareness.'

'And then did the ape become more dominant than other species?' I suggest. Atlanta laughs –it is like music.

---

[15] I have not been able to find any historical references to Adamos. 20th century surveys have shown that Antarctica would have been part of a much larger continent as spoken of by Atlanta and would have been ice free millions of years ago and home to a wide variety of mammals, reptiles etc.

'No. Man's dominance only began after the androgynous beings were no longer able to manifest in the physical world. Not all bipeds were able to evolve the physical system that expressed the fourth body. All animals in your present world have three bodies, as do birds, fish, reptile and insect. The vegetable and mineral worlds have two –and yet some creations have three.'

'Then how did man come to have an additional body?' I ask, conscious of my earlier question wanting to know more of what she is describing as 'bodies.

'Where the influence of the Sons of Thunder was strong 'self-aware' earth consciousness dominated and absorbed less able life creations. All this came into being as two bodied beings evolved into the order of three. Of those that evolved the order of three bodies, marriage with the Sons of Thunder developed the fourth body and the seeds of self-awareness. The competitive element within the three and four body systems was so strong they competed with their own like. This was the beginning of the second root race, a conception able to refine the vibratory nature of body being to be expressive at the fourth level.

At this point in her teaching a silence ensues in which I feel a strengthening bond as if my entire consciousness is dependant upon hers. I focus upon the blue water like substance in the well below. It's as if I am suspended in a clear blue world and change non-existent. I would call it the experience of oneness.

When Atlanta continues it's as if she is drawing me out of some kind of sleep.

'The physical planet and all its life forms during the epochs of Adamos and Hyperborea vibrated at a faster rate than they do now in your world. The character of the earth life BodyMind has changed significantly over eons of time –then the physical vibrated across a wider frequency range, both slower and faster than now; as the earth ages the outer crust is losing vitality and the inner core reverting to the character of its parent sun. The frequency range of all life forms have changed accordingly as have the relationships they are able to develop.

In those ancient times when the Parent's influence dominated the development of life on Earth the gender of all species were polarised in the extreme, vibratory rates of change were so diverse they created marked differences between species and male and female orders competed for territory.

When the poles shifted they intermingled their relationships altered the

271

character of the sexes –ultimately producing some species that were hermaphrodite. These creations were the first to become androgynous following the change in the physical, etheric and astral kingdoms and the entry into Earth's atmospheres of the Sons of Thunder.

The androgynous life forms were the first to have power of choice –able to evolve hierarchically as reasoned beings or evolve into non-reasoned states. Those that chose to develop hierarchically caused division of the third body and the fourth body came into being from the conflict. These androgynous vertebrate beings were even more competitive than their Parent's predecessors and fought amongst themselves. The changing earth gave the biped and quadruped beings dominance in the air and on land, whilst the aquatic world evolved a multiplicity of forms. Mutations that occurred during this epoch meant that some vertebras had aquatic characteristics and became reptiles whilst some aquatic species became amphibians.

Further changes ensued as the competitive nature of these androgynous beings fought to multiply. Divisions occurred in the conflict between reptilian and amphibian species; their war raged over many hundreds of millennium, again some mutations moved into parallel worlds and some that retained their hierarchical nature left the waters of your planet and became mammalian and land based reptiles.

The competitive order was now an issue of control in the higher levels of their being –so you might understand how this became an issue and the effects of those changes thereafter, I must explain how the bodies were formed and their ancestral development.

The first body is the unique BodyMind character created from the forming Earth. Initially that body was as vast as the planet itself comprising the primordial elements of earth, water, air, fire and ether. As the Earth solidified each of the primordial elements governed different aspects of development; the atmospheres were governed by *air*, physical solid matter by *earth*, liquid matter by *water*, the planet core by *fire* and the outward manifestation and the higher order of all four elements by *ether*.

As the Earth's identity became established as unique within the solar system and relationships of need were developed between the five elements further divisions of the elemental character created amalgams that in turn generated unique life forms and their divisions multiplied. Ultimately life forms of the primordial amalgam of elements mutated between themselves and beings unique to the planet were created –the balance of primordial element different in every form. Thus the first body came into being; part physical and part invisible –the invisible form being a duplicate of the

272

physical and uniquely related to it. This is the foundation of what you today call the etheric body.

The second body arose from the first when 'self-seeding' or propagation occurred –the nature of the first body was a balance of physical and ethereal states. The self-seeding process was 'triggered' by the first body's cosmic relationship with the anti matter universe. This higher order now influenced the propagation of physical life and the second 'self conscious' body was created within the ethereal nature of the first body

Interaction between the first and second bodies was harmonious and mutually dependant. The order continued to refine relationships of difference in the amalgam of elements. As the planet Earth matured and stabilised the 'self conscious' body dominated the development of the first – so much so it became the primary body of consciousness with emphasis to develop itself hierarchically. The first body became mutually dependant upon the second body and unaware of the 'self-conscious' hierarchical influence found commonality of function with other first body beings moved to develop non-reasoned states of awareness.

Eons passed before the third body established itself. The primary and 'self-conscious' bodies continued to physically evolve and the character of earth's land and sea masses became established with simple cell forms of life. It was the element of ether evolving a higher order of the two-bodied physical order of life altered by interaction with cosmic influences beyond the solar system that brought into being the third body. The intelligence I described to you as the 'the Parent' entered into the Earth's atmosphere.

This self manifesting creation altered the balance of nature by attaching itself to the 'self-conscious' body causing it to become self aware, that is, aware that other forms of life and the planet itself were different from them. This was the birth of objective awareness and the conflict and competitiveness of creation increased significantly. The second or 'self-conscious' body mutated and divided –the 'self-aware' body was created and the 'self-conscious' body found itself mutually dependant upon both the primary and third bodies.

Three bodied beings quickly became the driving force of planetary development as unlike two bodied forms of life they had independence within the earth mass. Simple cell structured life forms changed by absorbing other like forms of life and 'self-aware' developed new and unique conceptions. The quest for exclusive hierarchical identity had begun; vertebrate forms of life developed.

The fourth body arose directly from the competitive relationship of three bodied beings having refined gender relationships that ultimately mutated in the struggle for supremacy and following the birth of Sons of Thunder formed androgynous relationships. The androgynous being was not only self aware and objectively realised, they were able to create other permutations of their own being and alter the life forms of two and three bodied creations. And so Gods were born.'

I responded at this point in Atlanta's narrative. 'Ancient myths such as survive in the present world have been written to suggest that the Gods were continually at war with each other.'

'Yes –a struggle for supremacy, which you must remember is search for identity, but the nature of androgynous beings was such that they could reconstitute themselves. Metamorphosis proved to be the means that focussed their struggle in the fourth body. As earth being continued to mature and its mind and matter state became denser affecting the primordial elements, primary, secondary and three bodied conceptions, the androgynous being ceased to manifest in physical form and increased in fourth body constitution within the etheric order of energies. Eventually the Sons of Thunder rediscovered the cosmic highways that brought their Parent to the Earth and departed the planet.'

Again there was stillness between us and as I contemplated the blue water within the well I sensed its troubled being –an activity that could not cease, as it had not the power to command itself. I recalled the sadness I had detected in Atlanta's voice and became aware for the first time that Man might be struggling with an impossible problem –but I could not say what this was or how it might manifest.

'And how did Man as we know him come into being?' I ask.

'In Adamos and Hyperborea the androgynous beings reigned supreme – the biped was but one of the forms; the God wars raged there and as the constitution of the planet changed the surviving species migrated to the European and Asian land masses and then to Lemuria. As Lemuria and its surrounding waters became the centre of their culture the demise of the androgynous being had already begun –they continued to have physical influence over life form development during the epochs that saw the fall of Lemuria and the early development of Atlantis.

The biped and reptiles were the last surviving physical androgynous beings –the reptiles dominating the seas and the biped the land. Both forms became fewer and fewer and three bodied physical beings again ruled the order of change. The androgynous reptile mated with various three bodied aquatic creations and ultimately lost control of the physical ability to manifest change of being. The biped mated with other biped creations from which Man as you know him was born.'

274

'And the sons of God saw the daughters of men and thought them fair? I suggested quoting from Genesis.

'Yes. The passage alludes to the event –then followed a course of events that you are familiar with. What is not understood by earthly man is that androgynous beings left their imprint within Man's psyche and his evolution is forever linked to the Sons of Thunder.'

'In what way Is Man's psyche affected? I ask, aware that my question expresses the emotion of fear. 'To truly understand the effect the Sons of Thunder have on Mankind, their legacy to the earth as a whole must be understood; without them Earth consciousness would have evolved differently. The fourth body would have evolved harmonically arising from two and three bodied beings –a group soul state would have developed. The vegetable and mineral conceptions would have developed a more intelligent primary body and the spirit of this form interactive with the primary state of three bodied creatures would have given fourth body awareness of a kind to engender compassionate being.

The legacy of the androgynous being is the function of self-conscious renewal in two and three bodied beings and self-awareness in Man. In two and three bodied forms of life it is limited to physical and etheric transformation and only effective in harmonically conducive environments.

Some three-bodied creatures are still created androgynously and the functions of self-renewal, a feature of androgynous being, are present in most forms of sentient life.

The astral world of most two and three bodied forms of life is the amalgamation of their essence; however some aquatic, aerial and mammalian kinds have individual forms in the lower planes of the astral world. The fourth body of Man is aware of its ancestry but has lost the ability to influence the development of its' lower body relationship –this causes the lower bodies of Man myopically to seek identity which puts them at variance with the higher self. The fourth body itself is in many parts.'

Chapter FORTY:
A Thousand Things I do not know

I am now acutely conscious of my many selves –the significance of what Atlanta is saying is having a traumatic effect. My BodyMind being is a thousand things I do not know, my eager questioning voice is gagged and for a moment I experience a sense of grief that surpasses description.

Atlanta envelopes me –I feel as if I'm hanging on to life itself. I hear her voice as if it has become my own. 'Come, Omar is greeting you.'

I am once again at rest amid the trees and whispering grass, lying on my back looking up into an indigo sky illuminated by the moon. Fireflies dart here and there burning white the darkness and the music of moving water fills my ears. My head is resting on Omar's lap –a strong smell of jasmine fills my nostrils.

'Omar –is that you?' I query not that I'm unaware of his presence but for reassurance. 'Now is the time to rest your mind, give no heed for the past or future state. Here on the banks of our beloved Shalimar all beginnings end – here you may sip of the wine and eat of the grape and let the morrow care for itself.'

He places in my hand a delicate fiery red glass goblet encased in a silver filigree mesh. Inside a liquid glows. I drink and feel youth enter into my veins –so much so I soon feel light and carefree. In silent communion, with thoughts themselves unsaid, we laugh and eat of the grapes that darkly filled the silver platter between us. Finally, I find my voice and raising myself up on one elbow turn to Omar and say, 'Why me?'

'Beloved, you drank from the well of life.'

Gazing upward to the moon he continues, 'The moon has cycled many times since in your earthly world, but this moon,' he said lifting my hand and pointing to it's ghostly glow. 'This moon is the same as when you first tasted the grape of heaven.'

'Then the journey is not over?'

'My beloved your journey has only just begun.

'Torchlight the night the Caravan is coming
Bringing to focus the Shah:
The decision of Life, the Merchant of Peace
To the banks of the Shalimar.
Heavy is the cloud of dark shadow
That clings to the canvas of wares,
On guard and torchlight the night
The camels are bending onward
Toward a distant Light!'

I listen to the sounding in my ears, I am back in this dark and slow moving world. Gradually the sounds make sense and when they do I am dismayed by the dull emptiness of everything. Now my eyes take in the light and what I see is flat, coarse and seemingly dead. I look at my hands and feel myself shrunk inside a wrinkled skin. Tears course my cheeks and a great burden of sadness enshrouds me. How long I remain like this I do not know but on moving I am possessed by an irrational fear. Incredulous? Yes. Happy?

I do not know.

Later that day I sit alone in the caravan savouring the twilight and remembering the poem that Omar spoke to me. Many years ago, in my early twenties, I wrote it complete in one sitting to my pocket book. It seems now to be more Omar's than mine. From the outset I liked the sound of its words —and thought I understood what they meant. I'm not sure anymore —a journey yes, but who does the Shah represent? Who is this merchant King and what must he bring to the banks of the Shalimar guided by the beasts of burden?

The more I ponder the less I am sure —perhaps the Shah is the Self and the caravan the burden of experience we ultimately shed.

As night approaches I begin to write of light and dark matter worlds. The pen is mine but the mind that uses of language is not.

The End

Epilogue

Bellerophon was as we say in the psychic world the perfect instrument – he was able to achieve whatever task was asked of him, yet eventually with many heroic deeds accomplished and not in demand he became restless and commanded Pegasus take him to Mount Olympus. Zeus affronted by the audacity if this mortal sent a gadfly to fright the horse. Pegasus reared and Bellerophon fell to Earth. Athena intervened to save him from being dashed to pieces and Pegasus returned to Mount Olympus. According to the myth for the remainder of his earthly life Bellerophon wandered alone in search of Pegasus. There is no record of his eventual fate.

This book is entitled 'Tales of Bellerophon' for three reasons –one; I have endeavoured to be the 'perfect instrument' in the course of my psychic & spiritual life, leading from the front, setting example of ability and achieving for the needs of others –two; the communicator Edward Everett is a significant influence in my services and initially made his appearance to me in symbolic form –that of Pegasus. Three, the experiences recorded have had effect upon me, not as you might suppose, consolidating previous experience of after-life communication and deepening my faith –rather the opposite, having me question what before I did not. Truth is not only stranger than fiction it has disturbing effects.

Since the events reported in this book I find it very easy to tune into 'conversations' and am fearful of doing so, unsure of what will happen to me if I do. These lines from the 'Four Quartets poem by T S Eliot come to mind 'Human kind cannot bear too much reality'. Likely he would not have considered my experiences reality but I like thousands before me have had awareness of life that shows the physical world to be illusionary.

Time they say is a great healer, perhaps what's meant by this is environments cause us to change and re-activate ourselves. I am aware of myself as a personality with the ability to refuse and accept as I will and also as an after-life being who when stimulated to act becomes a reality harmonious to the need that brings it into being. When that occurs I am at peace and when it is not my earthly nature has no answers –only questions.

I have not produced this book to impress you, neither supposing its philosophy and revelations better than or an alternative to your present religious beliefs and personal experience. The narrative simply is what happened and all I urge you to do is to let your intuitional nature comment as it will. If that disturbs, so be it, if that confirms so be it also.

As I conclude my writing of this epilogue I hear Edward speaking; 'Imagine yourself on the peak of a mountain enjoying the panoramic view – to be so absorbed is to be included, unaware of your separateness. Become self conscious and oneness disappears; you become aware of the parts, fearful of the unknown. That's the difference between you in the earthly state and us. It is said the Truth will make you free –it does and for most it cannot be until the enfranchised soul finds liberty.'

Tony A........... June 2008

Appendix

The Poetry of Djinn

Pale is my moonlight river
Incandescence cooling
From the spring, the well of night

In the black beyond
The silhouetted shades of sighing trees
The poetry of Djinn
Commissioner of dancing grass
Echoes to the coarsest wall
Coitus Interruptus

And here, the water close
The greening bank does share
My naked feet
And hers
With the healing river